Napoléon

NAPOLÉON

as seen by
ABEL GANCE

Translated by Moya Hassan

Edited by Bambi Ballard
with an introduction by
Kevin Brownlow

faber and faber
LONDON · BOSTON

Napoléon vu par Abel Gance first published in 1927
by Librairie Plon.

This translation first published in 1990
by Faber and Faber Limited
3 Queen Square London WC1N 3AU

Phototypeset by Input Typesetting Ltd, London
Printed in Great Britain by
Richard Clay Ltd, Bungay, Suffolk

British Library Cataloguing in Publication Data is available
ISBN 0-571-14065-3

En Hommage à une Grande Morte*

ABEL GANCE

I enlarged the frontiers of glory. That at
least was an achievement.

> Napoléon

I wish to underline that in his youth
Napoléon was a man of his times, a
revolutionary, a republican. What better
praise could we give him?

> Alphonse Aulard,
> *The French Revolution*

*Ida Danis, Abel Gance's greatest love, who died at the age of twenty-eight on 9 April 1921,
the day he finished shooting La Roue.

Contents

Introduction

by Kevin Brownlow

The discoveries connected to *Napoléon* seem never-ending – not only in terms of lost footage, but also in terms of related material. Outstanding among these is the script from which the film was made. It is important to realize that it does not match the film. It is not a post-production script, the kind of continuity written when all the elements are in place. Scripts are often altered on the set, and this one, although written by the director, was subject to his genius for improvisation.

The script, completed in 1925, was published in 1927, and as late as the early fifties, when I first became interested in the film, I was still able to buy a copy through the French bookshop Hachette in Regent Street, London. This is, however, its first appearance in English. Lorrimer Publishing planned an edition, for which Moya Hassan did this translation, but that was before the restoration of the film was complete, and Lorrimer never published it. Since then the French edition has become rare.

When I was trying to reconstruct the film the script was extremely helpful, but it refused to answer all my questions. It made no mention, for instance, of the scene in which Marat is murdered by Charlotte Corday, and I was never certain where to place it. I had to divert such queries to Abel Gance himself, and he was not always sure. (The Marat scene has been in two positions since we first showed the film to the public; it had to be altered when a 'definitive' running order was discovered, in Gance's handwriting.)

Parallel to my own work on the film, Gance decided to create a new version – *Bonaparte et la Révolution* (1970) – a kind of drama-documentary which drastically altered the 1927 material and cast further confusion over the order of the scenes.

I have described the production and the reconstruction of *Napoléon* in a book called *Napoléon – Abel Gance's Classic Film* (Jonathan Cape, 1983). In it I told how Gance intended to span the emperor's life in six massive films; how he spent the money for all six on what proved to be one film; how he brought together many highly qualified technicians – some of whom were directors in their own right; how he struggled to find the ideal Napoléon, overlooking his close friend, Albert Dieudonné, who eventually convinced him by dressing up as Bonaparte and marching into the palace at Fontainebleau where Gance was working; how he succeeded in inspiring the extras – some of whom were strikers from the Renault car factory – into 'becoming the people of the Revolution'; how he caused the most advanced equipment to be manufactured, using techniques of cinematography and editing so sophisticated they have yet to be surpassed; how he caused a sensation at the première at the Paris Opera House with his triptych screen – cinerama, no less, twenty-five years before the Americans 'invented' it; and how the film received a muted reception, there being a short version at the première, a much longer version shown to the press a month later, and a number of different – and sometimes jumbled – versions thereafter. The film was not a financial success, and Gance tried to recoup some of the losses by producing a sound version – *Napoléon Bonaparte* – in 1935. Although it incorporated some of the silent footage, it was a completely different film, lacking the triptych finale (which was put back for a reissue in 1955).

This script of *Napoléon* is written with all the passion that animates the film. If the film did not survive – and much of it still does not – the script would do a lot more than hint at its quality. Few film scripts qualify as literature. Most of them are hard for the uninitiated to read. This one is as exhilarating and riveting as a good novel.

There were several drafts of the script, and some have detailed technical instructions in the margin as to how Gance intended the scenes to be shot. This, however, is the only version to have been published. An important discovery was made recently by Bambi Ballard in the Gance papers, preserved at the Centre National de la Cinématographie in Paris: at my request, in the 1960s, Gance had listed those scenes he had shot and those he had not, but for some reason he never sent me the letter. That list has served as an invaluable guide in preparing this first English edition.

Although some historians quarrelled with the script on strictly historical grounds, it is a breathtaking achievement in every other respect – as is the film itself.

In the final analysis, a script is merely a means to an end. How the director translates those instructions on to celluloid is what counts. Anyone who has seen the restored *Napoléon* will be aware of the brilliance which Gance brings to virtually every scene he tackles.

Images from the surviving scenes will be conjured up by the script, and equally vivid will be those evoked by the descriptions of the missing scenes. I have never felt that the Battle of Toulon, as we know it now, represents Gance's original intention; read the script and watch, in your mind's eye, the scenes as they once existed! Even episodes that Gance rejected, on which he never turned a camera, have a dynamism which makes me sad that I will never stumble across them in some forgotten vault.

I first encountered the film when I was a schoolboy. I saw two reels on my 9.5 mm home movie projector. I was stunned by the cinematic flair – I had never seen anything comparable – and I set out to find more of it, and more about it. I was puzzled by the antipathy the film aroused among critics and historians who remembered the original release. I expected with each rediscovered sequence that they would be proved right, and the quality would take a plunge. But the more I added to the film, the better it became. And eventually I discovered that most of those writers had seen one of the many butchered versions.

When I became a feature-film editor, I began to earn enough to do a proper restoration. I was given facilities by the National Film Archive (who eventually took the project over). Whenever the work-in-progress was screened at the National Film Theatre, the place was always packed, the reaction always very strong. People stayed up all night to watch it at the Telluride Film Festival, Colorado, in 1979, even though it was projected outdoors in freezing temperatures. Watching from his hotel window was Abel Gance himself, then in his ninetieth year.

The climax came in 1980, when David Gill and I staged the first performance with live orchestra for Thames Television and the British Film Institute at the Empire Theatre, Leicester Square, London. Carl Davis created the massive score in three months and he conducted the Wren Orchestra. We were all intensely nervous before the show. What right had we to expect the public to sit still for an old silent film lasting five hours? Of course, they did not sit still. They rose to their feet and gave it a standing ovation. It was the most moving occasion I have ever attended in the cinema.

The American presentations, staged by Francis Coppola with Bob Harris, were also triumphant, with Radio City Music Hall packed night after night. At one performance we telephoned Gance, who was ill in his apartment in Paris, and let him listen to the waves of applause from 6,000 New Yorkers.

I never stop receiving letters from people who say their life has been changed by *Napoléon*. (I am almost relieved to learn that one or two people actually dislike the film, although I imagine H. M. Bateman could have done a cartoon entitled 'The Man Who Failed to Rave About *Napoléon*'.)

Working with the Cinémathèque Française, Bambi Ballard has found additional scenes – no more than five or six minutes, but significant none the less. And, equally important, she has found better-quality material to replace some of the battered material in my restoration. A partially tinted print has been found in Corsica, giving us a template for a tinted version. (Nothing to do with colorization, tinting was a convention of the silent era – amber for day, blue for night, red for fire or battle. *Napoléon* was elaborately tinted and toned.) This sort of commitment is rare. Thanks to the Cinémathèque, in 1983 *Napoléon* returned triumphantly to Paris, at the Palais des Congrès, in the presence of several of those who had worked on the original production. Since then it has been shown all over the world, and to celebrate the bicentennial of the French Revolution, the City of Paris constructed a 2,500 seat auditorium outside the Hotel de Ville and showed *Napoléon* free, accompanied by an orchestra conducted by Carl Davis.

It is hard to find sponsorship for films that have already been shown. Sponsors prefer to back new events, even if the 'new' film is actually very old. But sponsorship is needed for a yet more impressive version of *Napoléon*, not only to restore it to even greater glory on the screen but to make sure that it is shown, at least once a year, for ever.

Editor's note

Gance first planned *Napoléon* as a vast fresco comprising six films of about an hour and a half each. By the time he finished shooting the Corsican sequences (intended, with the Prologue and Part One, to be about 30 per cent of the first film), he had enough material from Corsica alone for a complete film. He had also spent half the budget of the entire series. On 21 June 1925, the major financier of the series withdrew, and Gance was left with an unfinished film and 3.5 million francs' worth of debts. After many months of searching he found new backers who were, however, only prepared to complete the first film in the series.

The first roughs of the script date from 1923. Gance's notes indicate that the great moments of the Revolution were to be shown through parallel scenes in the life of the 'man in the street'. He felt that the cinema-going public would relate more easily to people and events that they could identify with. As he developed the script and became more and more knowledgeable about the subject (he was to read over 250 books before the script was finished), he added more and more major historical scenes. However, the final script, which is the one we have here, still contained many scenes of what he called '*la petite histoire*', such as the children playing at sans-culottes and aristocrats (scenes 347 to 357) which Gance was never to shoot, and lacked some of the most important scenes in the film. Equally, the script is literary rather than technical. Only the Triptych (triple-screen) Section of the present volume, brought up to date after the film was completed, contains detailed instructions as to lenses, frames, tinting, editing, etc. To give a further example of how the shooting script must have looked, we have included a surviving section (which was never shot) in an Appendix.

Despite the copious notes that have survived, there is no indication of when Gance decided to cut the many scenes that were never shot and add or develop the major historical scenes such as the night of 10 August or the death of Marat. One can assume, however, that this happened after the withdrawal of his first backers. The Société Générale de Films, a group of French aristocrats (Comte de Béarn, Duc d'Ayen, etc.), formed in order to make films about the greatness of France, completed *Napoléon*. They also produced *The Miracle of the Wolves* (Raymond Bernard, 1924) and *The Passion of Joan of Arc* (Carl Dreyer, 1928). It is probable that Gance developed the major historical events at the request of these producers.

As Kevin Brownlow has recounted in his book about the making of *Napoléon* (*Napoléon – Abel Gance's Classic Film*), no two surviving prints are the same. Each one lacks some major scenes, each one contains some small scene, or even a few shots, that none of the others have. It was from these unpromising beginnings, and armed with a script that never matched any of the versions in the first place, that he undertook the reconstruction of the film. For the last two years I have been cataloguing every reel of *Napoléon* held by Cinémathèque Française and other French archives. The more I see of the original prints, the more I admire Kevin Brownlow's achievement, for, indeed, no two reels are quite the same and many are totally incomprehensible! Another discovery, among Gance's papers, was a list of what he shot and what he cut that he had prepared at Brownlow's request twenty years ago and never sent; unfortunately, he started off full of enthusiasm and went into great detail, then the list more or less peters out.

In editing the script I have used my incomplete catalogue and Gance's notes in order to indicate scenes that were cut from the script, others that appear lost and some that Kevin Brownlow intends to add to his restoration. These include some short scenes which he intentionally omitted, all of them shot by night, since, without tinting the print, they would not match their accompanying shots.

Most silent-era films were in fact tinted. There were standard colours such as blue for night exteriors and amber for night interiors, plus a range of sepias, mauves, greens and reds where applicable. Abel Gance went a step further and used colour to heighten the dramatic effect of a scene. For instance, during the *'Marseillaise'* sequence, it is made clear in the script that the scene starts at dawn, then, as Rouget de Lisle teaches his song to the crowd, the rising sun '. . . in its turn shares in this great enthusiasm and shines in through the windows. . .' In the recently rediscovered Corsican print the sequence goes from black and white to the spectacular gold of the rising sun on the shot specified in the script: a close-up of a stained glass window.

Where further clarifications about lost material or of the text itself appeared necessary, they have been given in a footnote.

In his footnotes detailing his historical sources Gance made scant reference to the editions and titles of the books he consulted. Therefore there is no way of checking their content. We have included only those footnotes that contribute to the narrative. On the other hand, the occasional mistakes in the text that were not dealt with in 1927 have been corrected for this edition.

Finally, we would like to thank Jayne Pilling for her lucid translations of Gance's footnotes, and John Denny for the care with which he has edited an often intractable script.

BAMBI BALLARD

NOTE ON THE TEXT

In preparing this edition of Abel Gance's film script of *Napoléon* we have attempted to present it in a form that can most easily be read and enjoyed by readers whether or not they have seen the film itself. In its original French edition it luxuriated in a plethora of typographical variations of a kind that is highly expressive of the enthusiasm of Gance's writing but which strikes us today as eccentric and overemphatic. We have therefore reduced the use of special typefaces to a minimum: bold is reserved for titles (captions) intended to be displayed on the screen, and italic is used primarily to distinguish editorial footnote commentary from Gance's own footnotes. (Within the main script italics are used in the normal way, for emphasis, French words, and so on.)

A second consideration has been to try to indicate, for those who know the film, the extent to which the script forms the basis of the film as it was originally made, and the proportion of it that has been so sadly lost. Scenes that we know were cut during shooting are enclosed within double square brackets – ⟦ thus ⟧; scenes (or, more often, titles) that were added are enclosed within single square brackets – [thus]; scenes that are assumed lost, since no trace of them has yet been discovered, are indicated by their scene numbers being printed in italics rather than the normal roman.

Appeal to the collaborators on *Napoléon Bonaparte*
by Abel Gance

[Posted on the door of Abel Gance's studio at Billancourt before the shooting of the film in 1925.]

Artists, technicians, extras.

It is imperative – please understand the deep significance I place upon these words – it is imperative that this film should allow us to enter once and for all into the temple of the arts by way of the huge portals of History. An unspeakable anguish grips me at the thought that my will, and the gift of my life even, are nothing if you do not all give me your undivided loyalty and devotion. Thanks to you, we shall bring to life again the Revolution and the Empire. The task is without parallel. You must rediscover within yourselves the flame, the madness, the might of those soldiers of the Year II. Personal initiative is going to be of the utmost importance. On looking at you, I want to feel a great surge of force capable of sweeping away all critical barriers, in such a way that from a distance I am unable to distinguish between your hearts and your red caps. Swift, crazed, tumultuous, gigantic, mocking, Homeric – pauses and climaxes which render the silences more formidable: this is how the Revolution, that runaway horse, wills you to be. And then, a man who looks it in the face, who understands it, who desires to make use of it for the good of France, and who, suddenly, leaps upon it, seizes it by the reins and little by little calms it, is able to make of it the most miraculous instrument of glory. The Revolution and its laugh of agony, the Empire and its giant shadows, the Grand Army and its suns – upon you falls the duty of recreating their immortal figures. My friends, all the screens of the world await you. From everybody, collaborators of every order, lead players, secondary players, cameramen, painters, electricians, stage-hands, above all from you, humble extras, who will have the heavy burden of rediscovering the spirit of your ancestors and of giving by your unity of heart the formidable face of France from 1792 to 1815, I ask, nay, I demand total forgetfulness of petty personal considerations, and absolute dedication. Only in this way will you truly serve the already illustrious cause of the finest art of the future through the most marvellous of the lessons of History!

To the spectators of *Napoléon*

[*1927*]

Ladies, gentlemen, my friends,

And under the heading of 'my friends' I should like to include you all, for it is only through the secret door of sympathy that one can penetrate deeply into a work like the one you are going to have to judge.

With *Napoléon* I have made what I believe to be a tangible effort towards a somewhat richer and more elevated form of cinema; and this has not been achieved without creating additional hostility and incomprehension towards myself. I should not like you to be mistaken on this point by forming too swift an opinion.

Let yourselves go completely with the images; do not react with a preconceived point of view. See in depth; do not persist in confusing that which moves with that which trembles, discern behind the images the trace of the tears which often imbue them, or the trace of the flames of the spirit which precipitate them, violent, tumultuous, self-destructive. It is only after this effort that you will know whether or not the journey into history that I have made you take comprises a lesson or a poem.

My aim has been to offer to all weary hearts the most wholesome, the most sustaining and the most pleasant nourishment, that bread of dreams which, to our age of harsh necessities, becomes as indispensable as the other kind, that music of light which, gradually, will transform the great cinemas into cathedrals.

I aim above all at attracting to the cinema a large section of the population which does not go there for two reasons: either because the childishness of films in general, the lack of soul in the themes, have finally disposed them against it and made them consider the cinema a cheap entertainment; or because it is ignorant of this new language of the cinema.

I did not want to serve any political party. I say simply that Napoléon Bonaparte is one of the most outstanding figures of humanity. The angle one views him from will not affect the psychological and dramatic interest. I say simply that Napoléon was a fervent republican throughout his entire youth, and the quotation of the great historian of the French Revolution, Alphonse Aulard, is significant:

> I wish to underline that in his youth Napoléon was a man of his times, a revolutionary, a republican. What better praise could we give him?

It is not my purpose, in this film, either to judge or to prejudge Bonaparte's evolution after the Italian Campaign. It could well be that from 18 Brumaire onwards I might be among his detractors. I do not know, and what is more I do not wish to know it in this film. My Bonaparte, up to the point at which I present him, remains in the great line of idealistic republicans, of whom Christ was the first.

From the dramatic point of view, I have made the minimum of concession to the romantic, to anecdote, and, consequently, I have had to break that elementary law of melodramatic continuity without which, it seems, the cinema cannot live. I wanted to try to prove with this version that a 'story' was not necessary in History, and I should like to believe that the thinking public will share my view.

In certain paroxysmic sequences, I created for the first time a new technique, based on the strength of rhythm, dominating the subject and violating our visual habits. I speculated on the simultaneous perception of images, not only of a second's duration but sometimes of an eighth of a second, so that the clash of my images against one another would cause a surge of abstract flashes, touching the soul rather than the eyes. Then, an invisible beauty is created which is not impressed upon the film and which is as difficult to explain as the perfume of a rose or the music of a symphony.

You must pardon my audacity in this sphere. It stems from the sincerity and ardour of my researches; and, if you do not understand entirely, do me the favour of believing that maybe your eyes do not yet have the visual education necessary for the reception of the first form of the music of light. It is the future of the cinema which is at stake. If our language does not extend these possibilities, it will remain no more than a dialect among the arts. It will become a universal language if you make the effort to try to read the new letters which, little by little, it adds to the alphabet of the eyes.

Thank you.

In aiding my *Napoléon Bonaparte* you will aid our national film once more to take the place due to it, which should be, and soon will be, first.

Napoléon *was first screened in Paris on 7 April 1927 at the Opéra. The orchestra was under the direction of M. Szyfer. The main themes were composed by Arthur Honegger.*

The work of reconstructing Napoléon *was done by Kevin Brownlow. The reconstructed film was first presented in public during the London Film Festival on 30 November 1980. The orchestra was under the direction of Carl Davis, who also arranged the score and composed new music for the film.*

The cast included:

NAPOLÉON (as a boy)	Vladimir Roudenko
(as an adult)	Albert Dieudonné
Joséphine DE BEAUHARNAIS	Gina Manès
Tristan FLEURI	Nicolas Koline
Violine FLEURI	Annabella
BARRAS	Maxudian
Caroline BONAPARTE	Pierette Lugan
Élisa BONAPARTE	Yvette Dieudonné
Jérôme BONAPARTE	Roger Chantal
Joseph BONAPARTE	Georges Lampin
Laetitia BONAPARTE	Eugénie Buffet
Louis BONAPARTE	Fernand Rauzena
Lucien BONAPARTE	Sylvio Caviccia
Pauline BONAPARTE	Simone Genevois
Thérésa CABARRUS	Andrée Standard
CARTEAUX	Léon Courtois
André CHÉNIER	Vonelly
Charlotte CORDAY	Marguerite Gance
COUTHON	Viguier
DANTON	Koubitzky
Eugène DE BEAUHARNAIS	Georges Henin
Hortense DE BEAUHARNAIS	Janine Pen
Vicomte DE BEAUHARNAIS	G. Cahuzac
Rouget DE LISLE	Harry Krimer
Camille DESMOULINS	Robert Vidalin
Lucile DESMOULINS	Francine Mussey
Pozzo DI BORGO	Acho Chakatouny
DUGOMMIER	Alexandre Bernard
DU TEIL	Dacheux
Marcellin FLEURI	Serge Freddy-Karll
FOUCHÉ	Guy Favière

FRÉRON	Daniel Mendaille
GREEN EYE	Boris Fastovich-Kovanko
HOCHE	Pierre Batcheff
JUNOT	Jean Dalbe
LA BUSSIÈRE	Jean D'yd
LA MARSEILLAISE	Maryse Damia
Mlle LENORMANT	Carrie Carvalho
LOUIS XVI	Louis Sance
MARAT	Antonin Artaud
MASSÉNA	Philippe Rolla
MOUSTACHE	Henry Krauss
MUIRON	Pierre Danis
MURAT	Genica Missirio
PECCADUC	Roblin
PHÉLIPEAUX	Vidal
Mme RECAMIER	Suzy Vernon
ROBESPIERRE	Edmond van Daële
SAINT-JUST	Abel Gance
SALICETTI	Philippe Hériat
SANTO-RICCI	Henri Baudin
SCHÉRER	Mathillon
TALLIEN	Jean Gaudray
Mme TALLIEN	Andrée Standard
TALMA	Roger Blum

Assistant directors: Henri Andréani, Pierre Danis, Henry Krauss, Anatole Litvak, Mario Nalpas, Viacheslav Tourjansky, Alexander Volkoff. *Chief cameraman*: Joseph-Louis Mundwiller (Brienne, Corsica), Jules Kruger. *Cameramen*: Paul Briquet (triptychs), Léonce-Henry Burel, Marcel Eywinger, Roger Hubert, Georges Lucas, Émile Monnoit, Émile Pierre, Lee Planskoy (Toulon). *Editing*: Marguerite Beaugé. *Art direction*: Alexandre Benois, Pierre Schildknecht, Alexandre Lochakoff, Georges Jacouty, Meinhardt, Pimenoff. *Chief technical director*: Simon Feldman. *Casting director*: Louis Osmont. *Production manager*: William Delafontaine. *Production staff*: Constantine Geftman, Grégoire Geftman, Edmond T. Gréville, Hoden, Leonid Komerovsky, Georges Lampin, Grégoire Metchikoff, Henry Pauly, Ivan Pavloff, André Pironet, René Rufly, Michel Scripnikoff. *Script girl and A. Gance's secretary*: Simone Surdieux. *Special effects*: W. Percy Day, Edward Scholl, Eugen Schüfftan, Nicolas Wilcké, Minime, Segundo de Chomon. *Make-up*: Wladimir Kwanine, Boris de Fast. *Armourer*: Lemirt. *Electricians*: Albinet, Doublon, Graza. *Costumes*: Charmy Sauvageau, Mme Augris, Mme Neminsky. *Josephine's costumes* designed by Jeanne Lanvin. *Trainees*: Jean Arroy, Jean Mitry, Sacher Purnal. *Studio*: Billancourt. *Disribution*: Gaumont–Metro–Goldwyn, M–G–M, UFA.

Prologue
Napoléon's Boyhood

BRIENNE, DECEMBER 1781

[During the memorable winter of 1781 when the snow was heaped up in the courtyard of Brienne College.*]

Snow everywhere. A wall of snow in the foreground. Little by little 1
the famous hat emerges like a black sun rising above the horizon of
the wall. When the hat is almost completely visible there is a shower
of snowballs; the hat disappears. The third time the hat rises higher
and we can make out for two or three seconds the young head wearing
it. It is small, thin, so tanned, so tense, so comical in its precocious
authority that one can understand it being used as a target. The hail
of snowballs increases. Bonaparte – everyone has recognized him by
now – has only just time to duck, and, for lack of anything better to
aim at, the exercise with the hat as a target begins all over again.

Twenty against sixty.

The child is in the centre of a fort made of snow; he is surrounded 2
by nineteen comrades. He is seen from behind. He turns around,
gives orders to his companions, who have just made a great heap of
snowballs, and then he tells one of them to raise and lower his hat on
a stick to make it look as if he had not left his post. He takes advantage
of this to see what is going on in the enemy camp from another
position.

The assailants – more numerous – prepare their white artillery and 3
make ready to attack.

Bonaparte's comrades, each armed with a snowball, wait for the 4
signal.

Bonaparte: 'Fire!' he shouts. 5

All the snowballs are thrown with the same disciplined movement. 6

The assailants' rush is cut short by this salvo. 7

The Minim brothers and the billeting officer Pichegru watch the 8
battle from the porch.

---

* *We see about a hundred little boys run joyfully out of the main building into the snow-covered grounds of Brienne College.*

9 Bonaparte commands; he does not fight. Near him in the snow a mysterious-looking path is being dug. The snowballs rain down.

10 School kitchens. The head cook at his fire. The window closed. The scullion in a white apron, Tristan Fleuri, is looking through the window, beside himself with delight; he opens it to see better. A snowball falls on to the range. A terrible cloud of steam billows up. Another explodes on the head of the furious cook, who closes the window and orders Fleuri to take the cauldron of soup. The latter goes out holding it by the handles.

11 The Bonaparte camp. The boy detailed to raise and lower the little hat raises it too high, his attention elsewhere.

12 The enemy camp. Phélipeaux is watching and points out to his comrade Picot de Peccaduc:

13 The hat rising and the stick showing beneath it.

14 Phélipeaux runs his eye along the fort and spies

15 a gap in the wall of snow. Bonaparte peeping through.

16 Phélipeaux points this out to Peccaduc. Treacherously he takes a pebble and puts it in the middle of a snowball, which he flings at the gap.

17 Bonaparte is hit on the forehead by the snowball and starts to bleed. Some of his friends run to him. He wipes the blood away with his handkerchief: 'Leave me alone, carry on.'

18 A door on to the yard. Tristan Fleuri, carrying his steaming cauldron, watches the battle, laughing. His expression changes, for he sees

19 Phélipeaux, delighted at having hit Bonaparte, putting more stones into his snowballs.

20 Tristan Fleuri cups his hand round his mouth and shouts:

'Look out, Bonaparte! Phélipeaux is putting stones in his snowballs!'

Scarcely are the words out of his mouth than he is hit by twenty or so snowballs, which strike his nose and fall into the cooking-pot. He only just has time to hide behind the door.

21 Bonaparte hears Fleuri; he is filled with rage. In a trice he leaps over the wall of the fort, leaving his friends standing dumbfounded.

4

Completely alone, he races between the two camps towards the 22
enemy, despite a hail of snowballs.

He falls like a bomb into the enemy camp and seizes Phélipeaux. 23
Peccaduc comes to his rescue, but before anyone has a chance to
intervene Bonaparte picks him up, pushes him over the wall of the
fort and drags him off.

Between the two camps. Peccaduc has followed. A struggle begins 24
between the three.

The adversaries no longer dare throw any snowballs for fear of hitting 25
their champions, but they spur them on with their shouts.

Bonaparte concludes his victory. He leaves the other two sprawled 26
on the ground.

The teachers laugh and applaud behind the window-panes. 27

Bonaparte comes running back to take up his position again, pausing 28
at the half-open door from where Fleuri is watching and,

without a word, gives Fleuri a brief handshake.* Fleuri's honest face 29
lights up.

Bonaparte drops back into his camp with a bound. 'Listen, my 30
friends!'

The enemy camp. The leader produces a whistle and gives the signal 31
to attack. They all sally out, determined to avenge Phélipeaux and
Peccaduc, who are crawling painfully back on all fours.

Bonaparte keeps his men in check. 32

The assailants draw close to the fort. Battle. Stronger in numbers, 33
the assailants take prisoners.

In the enemy camp, where two sentinels have stayed behind, prisoners 34
are brought in.

Bonaparte is everywhere at once. His men are faltering around him. 35
He gives an order to five of his comrades, who disappear through the
trough which was seen being dug earlier.

The teachers see the stratagem. A portly Minim brother starts to 36

* *Napoléon pauses briefly as he runs past Fleuri to say* 'Thanks!' *with a triumphant smile,
then he runs on.*

laugh. His smile is stopped by a snowball which all but chokes him.

37 The battle rages fiercely. Bonaparte's camp is gradually weakening and the fortress is about to be stormed. There is consternation all about him.

38 Bonaparte, face inscrutable, forehead bleeding, watches and waits.

39 The porch. The snowballs are pelting down so hard on to the group of Minim brothers that they are forced to retreat. In retreating, a fat Minim brother is hit on the behind. He turns round, protesting: he gets one in the eye. The other teachers pull at him to prevent him wreaking vengeance.

40 *Battle.**

41 Behind the window-panes, their faces pressed to the glass, the Minim brothers now follow the fight from under cover. Snowballs burst on the panes in front of them.

42 The fort is about to fall into the hands of the enemy. Five or six boys, standing round Bonaparte, are still holding their ground. He waits, with arms folded, taking no part in the fighting in order to maintain his freedom of spirit.

43 Enemy camp. The five cadets emerge from the snow like moles, to the amazement of the two sentinels. The prisoners are freed and they all pelt the enemy, yelling savagely.

44 The assailants, flabbergasted by this attack from the rear, are panic-stricken and surrender or run away.

45 The teachers applaud and come out.

46 Tristan, beaming, opens the door.

---

* This single word was developed into the celebrated snowball fight using mobile cameras, fast cutting and superimpositions, which Abel Gance described thus: 'I wanted above all to expand and enliven the screen: I asked my team to use every imaginable means to make the camera walk with a man, run with a horse, slide with a sled, climb up and down, spin round and turn somersaults at will. I also used a lot of superimposition for the climactic scenes . . . There are frames with up to sixteen images one upon the other. I knew that nothing would be visible beyond the fifth image, but they were there; and, once they were there, their potential was there. As in music, when you have fifty players and you cannot distinguish the individual sounds of the instruments, it is the organisation of those sounds which counts – the superimpositions were similarly organized'. (Abel Gance Hier et Demain, a film by Nelly Kaplan, 1963.)

6

*Brienne: (from left) Simon Feldman, Jules Kruger, Alexander Volkoff and Abel Gance
filming the snowball fight*

Phélipeaux, still whimpering on the ground, hurls a snowball at him   47
in his fury.

Fleuri. The snowball lands right in his eyes. He drops the cooking-   48
pot. The soup spreads over the snow and steam begins to rise.

The teachers come up to Bonaparte and congratulate him. The   49
billeting officer says:

‘What is your name?’

Bonaparte replies: 50

‘Napoglioné.’ [With his Corsican accent he pronounces it ‘Napeyeony’.]

The billeting officer, who has not understood because the boy’s   51
Corsican accent distorts the words:

‘What’s that? *Paille-au-nez*?’*

Everybody bursts out laughing. Bonaparte wheels round. His auth-   52
ority is so strong that . . .

* ‘Straw-in-the-nose’.

53 the laughter stops abruptly.

54 Bonaparte repeats, stressing each syllable:

'Napo-léyonné Buonaparté!!!'

55 The billeting officer:

'Well, young Buonaparté, you will go far! Remember it was Pichegru who said so.'

56 A feeling of mingled admiration, envy and rage – and of curiosity. ⟦Tristan Fleuri, who has come up to the group, applauds Pichegru. They turn towards him. A Minim brother says to him severely:

'Tristan Fleuri, attend to your own business in the refectory!'

Tristan turns away, abashed.⟧

57 Phélipeaux and Peccaduc, their clothes in tatters, snivelling. Their eyes are full of hatred for Bonaparte, who puts on his famous little hat again, watching them with one eye. We sense a hatred which goes beyond childhood quarrels. It will resurface again and again on most of the battlefields of the Empire.

A geography lesson

58 A schoolroom. Desks. The pupils are writing. A blackboard. On the board, the heading: 'Study of the climate of islands', and rough sketches of Malta, Cyprus, Madagascar, New Zealand. The teacher is dictating as he draws Corsica:

'As for Corsica – that half-civilized island . . .'

59 Bonaparte rises, pale. The boys look at him. They openly make fun of him. He is in torment. He sits down again, controlling himself, and writes, with heavy underlinings, in his notebook:

As for Corsica, the most beautiful island in the world . . .

60 Phélipeaux and Peccaduc, who are sitting on either side of Bonaparte, surreptitiously kick him. Bonaparte kicks back. The teacher comes up and reprimands them.

61 The teacher concludes the lesson. The boys close their notebooks. A thought occurs to the teacher, who says:

8

> **'Oh! I was forgetting. A little rock lost in the ocean:
> St Helena.'**

He rubs out the islands which are in his way on the board, and leaves 62
– by chance! – only Corsica in one corner of the board, while he
quickly sketches St Helena.

Napoléon's notebook, the end of the last line: 63

> **St Helena, small island**

Bonaparte. His eyes roam, with a strange expression, from Corsica 64
to St Helena. He reads the phrase over again. His anxiety is acute.
He does not know why. He sinks into a dream, so absorbed that he
no longer responds to the redoubled kicks from either side. Text of
his last line:

> **St Helena, small island . . .***

In Tristan Fleuri's garret

Bonaparte talking. His face is all tenderness; he looks transformed. 65
A cage comes into view; in it an eaglet seems to be listening to his
words.

> **Proud companion in misfortune, a present from his Uncle
> Paravicini, the great eagle hunter in Ajaccio.**

Bonaparte speaks lovingly to it. He laughs. He softens as if he were 66
speaking to a creature of exceptional sensibility.

We are in Tristan Fleuri's garret. Bonaparte and the young eagle are 67
in one corner.

Phélipeaux and Peccaduc, in shirt-sleeves, are spying at the half- 68
open door. Malice and envy. They are making fun of Bonaparte.
Bonaparte goes out with a water pot to fetch his pet something to
drink. He passes in front of his two enemies without seeing them.

**Between scenes 64 and 65 in the film there is a short sequence in which Bonaparte sits in
his dormitory, writing of his unhappiness at Brienne:* I am very unhappy here, and my heart
is not made for these people who surround me . . . I force myself to be patient for I
want one day to restore liberty to my country. Who knows? The destiny of an
empire often hangs upon a single man. *Phélipeaux reports him to one of the fathers, who
seizes the letter and destroys it.*

They slip quickly into the room.

69 Bonaparte begins to fill his bowl at a water pump.

70 Fleuri's garret. Peccaduc opens the window. Snow and wind blow in.

71 Phélipeaux opens the eaglet's cage. The bird flies out.

72 It escapes into the snow-filled night.

73 Bonaparte leaves the water pump.

74 Phélipeaux and Peccaduc leave the room just in time to hide. Bonaparte passes without noticing them. Phélipeaux and Peccaduc take to their heels.

75 Bonaparte standing, stricken, by the cage. He runs to the window.

76 The eaglet disappearing into the night, a black speck amid the whirling snow.

77 Bonaparte. A child's despair. This eaglet is his heart being torn from him.

78 Brienne dormitory. The pupils are in bed. Phélipeaux and Peccaduc are the last to slip between their sheets, laughing spitefully. An elderly supervisor is dozing over his paper.

79 Bonaparte. His face takes on a grim expression. He leaves the room.

80 Doorway of the dormitory. Bonaparte bursts open the door and demands:

'Who let my eaglet out?'

81 The boys sit up in bed. What? What's the matter? Your eaglet?

82 Phélipeaux and Peccaduc laugh into their bedclothes.

83 Bonaparte advances, growing increasingly grim. 'Who?'

84 Denials.

85 Bonaparte. A silence. Then, since no one speaks:

'Then you are all guilty and you will all be punished.'

His determination shows in the set of his jaw. Careless of the odds, he peels off his jacket to give him more freedom of movement and springs.

A row of boys sitting up in bed. With the speed of lightning, Bonaparte   86
falls on them and cuffs them. The boys he has punched get up in a
fury.

All the boys leap out of bed in their nightshirts. Pandemonium. Epic   87
battle, for the young Bonaparte holds his own like Cyrano on the
Pont-Neuf. Infernal din; already pillows are flying and bursting, and
the feathers whirl in the dormitory like the snow which is still falling
outside. The Minim fathers in nightcaps and dressing-gowns arrive
with their candles, astonished, adding comically to the scene.* At
first they are powerless to stop the battle and receive a good few
punches, but then they manage to seize Bonaparte and pull him into
the corridor.

Staircase. Bonaparte. Ten strong hands are roughly dragging him   88
along.

Outside door. Night. Snow. The door opens. He is thrown out.   89
The door closes again. Bonaparte stands raging and furious, then,
suddenly, his temper abates, for he sees before him

a tree. The eaglet is perching in it, dejected, its wings folded, its neck   90
drooping under the snow.

Bonaparte. His eyes light up; the tears flow. He speaks to his eaglet.   91

The eaglet seems to understand and beats its wings.**   92

* *First appearance of Polyvision, or multiscreen, as the pillow fight reaches its climax; the
screen splits into four sections, then nine, with different action in each. Abel Gance said of
this: 'I was becoming obsessed with the idea of a fourth dimension, with the possibility of
abolishing time and space: the concept of Polyvision was gradually seeping into my
consciousness'* (Abel Gance Hier et Demain).
** *In the final film this scene is expanded. Bonaparte is thrown out into the snow. He stands
outside the door; inside, the monks extinguish the lamps. At the other end of the porch is a
cannon. Bonaparte walks over to it, sits on it, and buries his head in his arms. Cut away to
Phélipeaux, peacefully sleeping in the dormitory, a feather fluttering over his mouth. Tristan
Fleuri creeps silently out to Bonaparte, drapes his cloak over his shoulders, and puts his hat
on his head. Bonaparte manages a wan smile. Cut to close-up of his tearful face; he spots
his eagle in a tree. It flutters down to join him on the cannon. Bonaparte smiles through his
tears and strokes the bird. Cut back to long shot and fade to white.*

Part One
Napoléon and the French Revolution

NINE YEARS LATER – JUNE 1792 – AT THE
REVOLUTIONARY CLUB DES CORDELIERS

93 An old worm-eaten door, guarded by a grim sans-culotte* leaning on an enormous Louis XIII gun. On the ground, lying across the door, another sans-culotte, Laurent Basse, a pistol in each hand. A delegate of the people, a petition in his hand, asks to go in: 'Impossible! No one! It's a strict order.' A woman in tears: same refusal. Two officers, carrying documents: turned away. Several petitioners jostle and shove: 'Now then! I shall lose my temper!' shouts the fierce sans-culotte they have been trampling on the floor. He rears up like a wolf, his pistols at the ready. 'Nobody, do you hear! Nobody!' Everyone retreats. Hundreds of men and women are seen – on benches, clinging to the shafts of pillars, on beams, perched in recesses, near the ceiling, on the windowsills, stretched out on the floor.

A great swarming crowd which has survived three years of revolution but which bears the marks of those years. Sans-culottes, prison lags, mystic dreamers, fallen nobility, market women and women of the streets, extraordinary figures, in whom are joined all the goodness, anguish and malice of humankind. They laugh, they cry, they eat, they sleep, they drink, but above all they wait: that is the most obvious of all.

The empty platform awaits its speaker. A young man is writing beside his young wife, Lucile.

Danton's secretary: Camille Desmoulins.

She passes notes to him; he kisses her hands. Laughter, youth, energy.

Astonished eyes stare at someone coming in. It is a printer, with a bale on his shoulder and an enormous package of leaflets in his arms. He puts his bale down on the ground and, after a brief exchange with a distinguished-looking captain who is following him, he makes ready to distribute the leaflets among the crowd. Camille Desmoulins intervenes, snatches the paper from the printer's hands and says: 'I want to read it first.' And he reads.

94 Desmoulins's face. His eyes light up. He questions the printer, who points out the captain being given a buttonhole of dog roses by a

---

* *A Parisian partisan of the 'Montagnards' (the hard-liners), led by Danton, Robespierre and Marat, who were to initiate the Terror. Despite the name's connotations, the sans-culottes were by no means destitute; they were mainly petty craftsmen.*

sans-culotte. Desmoulins looks at the captain admiringly. He says to the printer: 'Wait before distributing them.' He hurries out.

The door guarded by the grim sentries. Desmoulins, the leaflet in his hand, arrives. This time the sentries draw respectfully aside, saluting him. He does not respond, for he is preoccupied. 'Ought I to go in? Should I disturb him for this?' A swift glance at 95

the crowd. 96

Another glance at the leaflet. It is worth it; abruptly he opens the door. 97

The three gods!

A small low-ceilinged room with Romanesque vaulting, which once served as sacristy to the church. A confessional to one side; above the confessional a broken crucifix. Round a table piled with papers and covered by a huge map of France – the triumvirate. Standing with his back to the door, Robespierre; to the right, Danton; to the left, Marat; both seated. They have not heard Camille Desmoulins enter; none of the three turns round. Desmoulins raps with his knuckles on the door to attract their attention; in vain. 98

Danton.

He is shaking with irrepressible, Homeric laughter. It is enough to say that it is Danton's laugh. He is laughing so much there are tears on his cheeks. He is dishevelled, wearing a voluminous cloth coat; his throat is bare, an unknotted cravat dangling below his jabot; his coat is hanging open and some of its buttons have been torn off. His hair is standing on end, although vestiges of styling and grooming can still be discerned; his wig is somewhat reminiscent of a horse's mane. His face is pock-marked, with an angry furrow between his brows, laughter lines at the corner of his mouth, thick lips, porter's hands, blazing eyes. 99

Marat.

A sallow, dwarf-like man who, when seated, looks deformed: his head is thrown back, eyes bloodshot, livid spots on his face, a handkerchief knotted over his lank, greasy hair, no forehead, a huge and terrible mouth. He is wearing long pantaloons, sloppy shoes, a 100 waistcoat which looks as if it was once white satin, and over this waistcoat a loose jerkin among the folds of which a hard, straight line suggests a dagger. His mouth rasps out harsh words aimed at Danton.

101   Danton's roar of laughter. He is laughing too heartily to perceive all this vented spleen. Every now and then he throws in a word, but his laughter overwhelms him.

Koubitzky as Danton

Marat grimly gets to his feet. He thrusts his face close to Danton, 102
who is still laughing; his words are increasingly caustic. Danton turns
and says, laughing:

[['You decide, Robespierre!']]

Robespierre, cold, pale, young, serious, with thin lips and stony eyes; 103
powdered, gloved, brushed, buttoned; his pale blue coat has not a
single crease. He wears nankeen knee-breeches, white stockings, a
high cravat, a pleated jabot, shoes with silver buckles. He never looks
directly in front of him. One scornful word falls from his lips:

'Chatterers!'

Marat and Danton. They stop, the one laughing, the other shouting. 104

Camille Desmoulins at the door, knocking to attract attention, 105
succeeds at last.

'What is it?' says Danton. 'Come in, my boy.' Desmoulins enters, and 106
says to Danton:

'Your friend Dietrich, mayor of Strasbourg, has sent you a
captain of the Rhine Army with a song called the *Marseillaise*
– can copies be distributed while they wait for the meeting?'

Danton shouts: 'Go to the devil! You must be mad to disturb us with 107
such nonsense!' And he emphasizes his words with such a heavy
thump of his fist on the table that

[[the two sentries at the door jump.]]   108*

Camille knows his master. He insists: 'Read it!' Danton grumbles; 109
he reads, and in a moment his hand is trembling, but his face betrays
nothing. He finishes and, without a word, suddenly bounds like a
lion for the door and opens it. Desmoulins runs after him.

Cordeliers' Hall. Door. Danton is standing there. Camille at his side. 110
He closes the door behind him.

The hall. The entire crowd rises and applauds. 111

Danton: 'Where is the man?' he says to Desmoulins. Desmoulins 112
brings him over. The captain introduces himself. He is young, thirty-
two. Danton asks him something; the captain hesitates. He is ill-at-
ease in the face of

* *This shot does not appear in the film: instead, a cloud of dust rises from the table.*

113   the frenzy of this mass of people cheering Danton.

114   Danton makes a sign.

115   The hall falls silent.

116   Danton speaks:

'[[Sit down and]] listen!'

117   All obey. Silence. Danton has extraordinary authority over the people and knows how to use it.

118   Small staircase and tribune. Formerly a pulpit, it now bears the insignia of the Revolution. Danton, followed by the captain and the printer with his leaflets, mounts the rostrum.

119   Sacristy. Marat insidiously vents his spleen about Danton into the ears of the Incorruptible One. He laughs in his turn, but it is a poisonous, chilling laughter. Robespierre's face remains inscrutable.

120   In the pulpit. The captain looks round. Deep silence.

121   The crowd, attentive, but as always ready to gibe.

122   The captain. Hesitation. Another long silence. Danton gives him a look of encouragement. An important event in the history of the world is about to take place.

123   A window. The morning light is grey.

124   The captain begins:

'Allons, enfants de la patrie!
[[Le jour de gloire est arrivé]].'*

125   He continues: *'Contre nous de . . .'* His exaltation increases, seeming to add to his stature.

---

* *Allons, enfants de la patrie! / Le jour de gloire est arrivé! / Contre nous de la tyrannie / L'étendard sanglant est levé. / Entendez-vous, dans ces campagnes, / Mugir ces féroces soldats? / Ils viennent jusque dans nos bras / Egorger nos fils, nos compagnes! / Aux armes! Citoyens, formez vos bataillons! / Marchons! marchons, qu'un sang / Impur abreuve nos sillons!*

     Forward, children of the Nation! The hour of glory has arrived. The bloody standard of tyranny is raised against us. Can you hear the roar of these ferocious soldiers in our fields? They are coming even to our arms to cut the throats of our wives and sons! To arms! Citizens, form your battalions! Let us march! Let us march, that impure blood be made to water our furrows!

Danton leading the Marseillaise

Crowd. It is already won over. Religious silence.   126

The captain roars out: *'Aux armes!...'*   127

The crowd can contain itself no longer. It rises, electrified, eager.   128

The sun in its turn shares in this great enthusiasm and shines in   129
through the windows, gradually spreading over the people's faces,
which light up simultaneously from within and from without.

The captain: *'Marchons, marchons!'* The sun reaches him, and he is   130
transfigured.

Danton. The people's eager response can be seen reflected in the   131
powerful face which, in its turn, is flooded with sunlight.

Exultant face of Lucile Desmoulins standing close to the radiant   132
Camille. The sun spreads over them.

The captain: *'Qu'un sang impur...'* We read his lips: *'... abreuve nos*   133
sillons!'

Fantastic ovation. There is a surge towards the pulpit. One of the   134
most beautiful moments of the Revolution.

The pulpit. Desmoulins holds back the crowd. Danton looks at the   135 captain and embraces him violently.

136   The ovation redoubles. Danton asks the captain:

'What is your name?'

137   The captain replies:

'Rouget de Lisle.'

138   'Distribute them,' says Danton to the printer. The man throws his leaflets into the assembly. It rains copies of the *Marseillaise*; people scramble for the sheets.

139   The sun now fills the immense hall, shining in the hearts and on the faces of the crowd.

140   Danton says to the crowd: 'Sit down.'

141   The crowd sits.

142   Danton says:

'Let us learn it [[, my children]].'

143   The crowd. These creatures – for the most part brutal and blood-thirsty – become like diligent children once more.

144   Danton, reminiscent of a tamed lion, sets the example.

Indescribable communion. 145

Rouget de Lisle conducts. Beating time, he begins again, as one does 146
when teaching songs to schoolchildren. Then he shouts:

[['Everyone, everyone on their feet for the chorus!']]

The crowd rises. 147

He intones: *'Aux armes, citoyens! . . .'* His ardour and authority, 148
exaltation, eloquence, mastery.

The whole crowd sings. 149

Sacristy. Marat watches at the door. He shrugs his shoulders 150
scornfully. He closes the door again and comes back to Robespierre.

At the table. Marat says: 151

'They're braying like donkeys out there.'

He slumps down dejectedly. Robespierre remains thoughtful. A
forbidding expression of scorn.

The crowd piously begins again. This time there is unison. Faces 152
wet with tears. Now it is Danton who is acting as conductor: *'Le jour
de gloire est arrivé.'*

Rouget de Lisle, behind Danton, smiles radiantly. His work is done, 153
his moment of glory passed; he slips away quietly, as he came,
followed by his printer, to take his magnificent hymn and distribute
it elsewhere; he vanishes into the crowd.

Marat stumbles against the crucifix. 154*

A colonnade. A young man, back view, poorly dressed, the song in 155
his hand, sees Rouget de Lisle passing, stops him. We do not see the
young man's face, just a glimpse of his profile. He says to the captain:

'I thank you on behalf of France, monsieur. Your hymn will
save many a cannon.'

Rouget de Lisle looks at him: 156

'Thank you, lieutenant. What is your name?'

'Napoléon Bonaparte.' 157

* *Gance remembered shooting this scene, but it has yet to be found.*

158   A moment's silence. The two men shake hands.

159   The crowd sings. *'Entendez-vouz dans les campagnes . . .'*

160   Bonaparte, back view, is leaning against the pillar again and, returning to his songsheet, continues to learn the *Marseillaise* along with the others.

161   A glorious figure of a woman, the *Marseillaise* by Rude, wearing the red Phrygian cap, cries: *'Aux armes!'*

162   A sans-culotte carries on: *'Citoyens!'*

163   Another says: *'Formez . . .'*

164   An old man says: *'Vos bataillons!'*

165   A grim-faced man: *'Marchons!'*

166   A child: *'Marchons.'*

167   The entire Cordeliers' Hall: *'Qu'un sang impur . . .'*

168   The glorious woman: *'Abreuve . . .'*
      Solemn communion in the rhythm.

169   Danton weeps for joy.

170   The crowd.*

[[AT THE TUILERIES THE SAME EVENING
11 JUNE 1792

171 [[Louis XVI's office at the Tuileries. An air of great luxury. Louis XVI is seated at a small desk to one side of the room, by a great window which is closed. Beyond the window-panes, darkness, night. Monsieur de Servan, his Minister of War, is standing next to him, gathering up the commissions which the king is signing without looking at them, since he is busy smiling at what is going on in the middle of his office – namely, a chaconne being danced with grace and sweetness by two young abbés and two charming girls. Marie-Antoinette and the Dauphin, sitting at the other side of the room, watch them. Marie-Antoinette looks extremely downcast. Through the great bays at the end of the room can be seen, on the right, a whist room, where several gentlemen are playing; on the left, another salon,

---

* *Superimposed, a symbolic figure of 'La Marseillaise' appears.*

where a magnificent supper table has been prepared and the nobility of France jostle and throng.

The king is about to sign a captain's commission. His hand is poised to sign, but the ink falls from the pen and spreads in a large blot over the name on the commission. The name becomes illegible. Nothing can now be seen but 'BUO . . .' and 'TE' on either side of the blot. 'What name is this?' Louis XVI asks Servan, who looks and then consults a card in his hand. 172

'Buonaparte, sire'

is the reply.

Louis XVI's hand begins to rewrite: BUONA . . . 173

The storm breaks the tree seen from the window, and an enormous branch crashes down on to the balcony. 174

Louis XVI starts, and then, seeing how the wind is making the heavy curtains, which Marie-Antoinette has had drawn, dance in sinister fashion, he laughs and turns back to his work, saying: 175

'What a squall, Monsieur de Lafayette! What a squall!'

Lafayette seems to say: 'You do not realize the significance of your words, good my lord!' The king carries on signing, signing. No one in this brilliant assembly suspects that the final act of the royal tragedy has begun. 176

[ON THE EMBANKMENT

A corner of the embankment. Moonlight. Wind still blowing. Some oil lamps. Occasional patrols. 177

A woman selling fried potatoes; a little farther on, a second-hand-book seller. Near the fried-potato seller is a round-faced, healthy looking woman with laughing eyes, who is fascinated by the scene unfolding before her. 178

Like Buridan's ass, torn between two bundles of hay – the fried-potato seller on the right and the bookseller on the left – two young men, very shabbily dressed, are arguing as they pool their money. The taller of the two is for buying sausages. 179

A string of sausages, suspended, tossing about in the wind. 180

181 [[The other is for buying a book.

182 [[Bookseller's stall.

183 [[The smaller of the two has his way. They buy the book.

184 [[The tragedy *Cinna* by Corneille. The taller one casts a last lingering look at the sausages.

185 [[He heaves a sigh, and moves off with the other young man to devour the book.

186 [[But the good-natured woman with the laughing eyes is touched to the heart. She buys some sausages.

Thus it was that the future king of the stage, Talma, and the future king of the world, Bonaparte . . .

Wandering along the embankment, the two young men declaim. Talma tries in vain to snatch the book from Bonaparte. He says to him:

'This is too much! It's always you who wants to play the emperor.'

'Naturally!' says Bonaparte. And he carries on.

187 [[The woman with the laughing eyes, not giving up, embarrassed in spite of the self-possessed air she has at first sight, follows them, the sausages in her hand.

188 [[The two young men stop. Talma is correcting Bonaparte's faulty pronunciation.

189 [[Lips pushed forward to make the '*ch*' sound, which Bonaparte pronounces badly.

190 [[The woman with the laughing eyes, who has also stopped, smiles as she watches and listens. 'How charming they are!' she thinks. 'But how can I give them my sausages?'

191 [[Talma adjusts Bonaparte's gestures.

192 [[The woman makes up her mind. As if taking the plunge, she advances.

193 [[And just as Bonaparte, in the full flood of lyrical fervour, strikes a solemn pose, she offers him her sausages in a greasy paper.

24

He is not a man who is easily surprised, but he is nevertheless   194
surprised.

The woman leaves her sausages with them and quickly makes off.   195

'What's your name?' shouts Talma through cupped hands.   196

She turns round beneath a lamp and calls back, with a smile: 197

'Madame Sans-gêne.'*

She runs on. The two friends abandon *Cinna* for the sausages. They
devour them as they walk along, laughing. They come to an abrupt
halt.

Bonaparte. What he sees must be strange for him to register such   198
keen interest. He calls Talma, who comes to stand next to him, and
the two friends look together.

Interior of brightly lit house. Impression of happiness in the midst of   199
poverty. The light is soft and gentle, the atmosphere warm. Near the
window, beneath the lamp, a very young boy, who is reading something
to an old man.

The ten-year-old, a songsheet in his hand, is teaching the *Marseillaise*   200
to his blind grandfather of eighty. The old man, with his lifeless eyes,
repeats the dazzling words:

'L'étendard sanglant . . . est levé . . .'

Bonaparte. Moved, he grips Talma's arm.]]   201

IN A POOR HOUSE

Two Corsicans: Pozzo di Borgo and Salicetti

Dingy landing. To the right in the foreground a half-open door; at   202
the far end two doors. Two men, one of them in his shirt-sleeves, are
laughing as they peer through the half-open door and down the
staircase; then they hide behind the door.

Violine climbs the staircase. One of the men, Salicetti, blocks her
way, but the frightened Violine scurries to the second door at the far
end and goes into her room, slamming the door in the face of Salicetti,
who is pursuing her, while Pozzo laughs mockingly in the doorway
in the foreground. The two men go back into their own room,
laughing.

* *'Madame Free-and-easy'*.

203   Interior of Violine's room, and Fleuri's lodgings. Her heart pounding, she stands at the door which she has just locked, seething with anger at the behaviour of these two imbeciles as she removes her hat.

204   Interior, shabby lodgings. Two rooms in one, in which the two men live. Soup is steaming on the table, which is already laid. The disorder that inevitably accompanies the military life. Interesting faces, but exuding (Pozzo's) brutality and (Salicetti's) treachery. Pozzo says to Salicetti:

'I wager twenty sous that I'll be the first to kiss our neighbour.'

Salicetti takes on the wager. They must be exchanging coarse, bawdy jokes to judge by their eyes, their expressions and their loud laughter.

Violine's fear of her neighbours on the right was compensated for by a secret passion for her neighbour on the left.

205   Violine's room. She crosses to the wall and looks at it with emotion. Her eyes shine with tender passion.

Her neighbour.

206   Dilapidated room. Utter poverty. A stove, with a pipe that stops in mid air, is being used as a store for parchments. On the trestle table, books, dividers, maps, notebook, and a scrap of dry bread and some water. Bonaparte is in the middle of putting on a boot which is so worn at the seams, so old, that his foot goes right through it and he only just manages to keep his balance. He pulls it off his leg and thinks for a second. 'I can't go out like this at any event. I'll go and see if they will lend me one.' He goes out, a boot on one foot, a stocking with a hole in it on the other.

207   Landing. He knocks at the door of the two men.

208   Their room. 'It's Bonaparte! Oh, damn! He is a nuisance.' Hatred, envy, anger, malice. Salicetti puts the tureen under the table; then they act as though they had just finished their meal. Bonaparte comes in. They do not get up or greet him. Bonaparte shows them his stockinged foot and says, pointing at three pairs of boots lined up in a row, 'Would you lend me a pair?' Pozzo quickly puts the boots away in a drawer and says, 'No! Impossible!' 'Very well!' says Bonaparte, who is looking out of the corner of his eye at

209   the soup steaming under the table.

26

Before leaving, he drinks some water from their carafe, and at the 210
same time he furtively

kicks over the soup under the table. 211

He puts the carafe back on the table and goes out, leaving the door 212
ajar.

The two friends make fun of Bonaparte and prepare to eat their 213
dinner. Disgusting! Their feet are paddling in the soup. Their anger
with this joker.

Bonaparte has come back into his room. What can he do? There's 214
some cardboard! That's it! He will make a cardboard boot, and he
takes measurements of his foot, comparing it with the cardboard;
then, going on with his tragedy whilst he does his cobbling, he
declaims: 'Take a chair, Cinna, take a chair! And on every matter
observe the rules I give you.'

Violine's room. She is listening at the wall. Her emotion. Adorable 215
smile. She begins to talk to someone . . . But who is it? It is a little
pot of flowers – and amongst them one particularly sensitive blossom
opens its petals at the sound of Violine's voice.

Petals opening and closing as if they were speaking. Empathy. 216

Violine chatters on, and now Bonaparte's feverish face, very large, is 217
superimposed over this scene; and then another on the right and
another on the left, here, there, everywhere. She closes her eyes,
overwhelmed by unspoken love; then she sings.

Bonaparte has been declaiming, his boot almost finished, when 218
Violine's singing makes him go wrong; he curses his neighbour.

Violine's room. To dispel these over-tender dreams, she has decided 219
to water her flower, and she goes out on to the landing.

Landing. She goes to the fountain, singing so that He will hear. 220

Bonaparte's room. He goes wrong in the middle of his speech and 221
puts his fingers in his ears.

The room of the two men. Pozzo listens, runs to the door and bursts 222
out.

Landing. She sees him and runs back to her room, but too late this 223
time; Pozzo's foot is in the door.

224 In the doorway of the two men's room, Salicetti grins and then moves closer.

225 Violine's room. She tries to close the door. In vain. Apprehension, then terror, for Pozzo is forcing his way in. She backs away. He seizes her by the waist. She struggles. He laughs, determined to win his wager; Salicetti in the doorway smiles complacently. Pozzo holds her fiercely. She scratches him. Now he is on his mettle and grows brutal. She shrieks for help, for he is gradually overpowering her.

226 Bonaparte gives a start and leaves his room.

227 Landing. Salicetti in the doorway. Bonaparte gives him a questioning look. Salicetti does not respond, as he wants to keep the door shut. Bonaparte shoulders him aside and in a flash

228 (interior) he draws himself up on the threshold and shouts:

> **'Are you raving, Pozzo di Borgo?'**

Pozzo, taken by surprise, tears himself away from his kiss, looks round with a sneer and turns back to the luscious flesh. Bonaparte draws his crop from his boot and lashes Pozzo's face with a sharp blow. Pozzo straightens, his face pale and cut by a thin red weal. He makes to leap on Bonaparte. Bonaparte does not budge; his eyes quell Pozzo, who goes out, grim-faced.

229 Landing. Pozzo and Salicetti. Pozzo tries to take Salicetti's pistol and go back into the room. Salicetti drags him away.

230 Violine's room. Trembling with fear and joy, Violine stammers her thanks. With a cool little bow, Bonaparte withdraws. She kisses the spot where he was standing and talks to him as if he were still there.

231 Bonaparte's room. He finds a note pinned to the table by a dagger:

> **To the death, Napoléon.**
>
> *Pozzo di Borgo*

Bonaparte looks thoughtful, then tears it up.

⟦THE WATER-SPRINKLER

Tristan Fleuri, father of Violine and Marcellin, has just been appointed 'Public Water-sprinkler to the King', and, burning to freshen up His Majesty's pavements . . .

Shed. Tristan Fleuri. A face which paradoxically combines the 232
expressions of Sancho Panza and Don Quixote. It has a kind of
charm, good humour, and the lustre of an enthusiast. All the rude
poetry of the French peasant in his blue eyes. The naivety of a
Memling with the expansiveness of a Jordaens. He is finishing
harnessing himself like a horse to the right side of a shaft with a bar
in front of him. On the other side of the shaft, his son Marcellin, a
little eight-year-old wisp of a man, his face open and intelligent, his
garments in tatters.

In front of Tristan, a general overseer in a braided tricorne hat,
conceited, self-important and mean, a long staff in his hand. A pipe
is filling the barrel of the water-cart, but Tristan has not taken into
account the law of gravity which, suddenly acting against him, makes
the barrel tip towards the ground, lifting Fleuri skyward.

A lantern-lighter bursts out laughing as he adjusts his lantern. 233

Fleuri cannot unfasten the straps holding him up in the air. Marcellin, 234
whose outstretched arms reach only as far as his father's boots,
catches hold of a foot and tries in vain to pull him down to earth
again. He dangles with both feet in the air, the boot comes off and
the child falls to the ground.

The lantern-lighter, choking with laughter, comes to Tristan's 235
rescue, while the stupid representative of authority does nothing but
stand by, ranting. The lighter takes out the water-pipe, opens the
sprinkler-valve, and little by little Tristan Fleuri sinks earthward,
babbling out his thanks. He moves off with a struggle.

Street. They meet a group of sans-culottes, who look at them and 236
gather round the overseer.

One of them holds out a revolutionary cap to him. The overseer, 237
puffed up with pride, pretends not to have seen it and says, 'Make
way, you wretches!' Fury of the sans-culotte, who grabs hold of him,
snatches off his tricorne and jams on the cap. The overseer, choking
with rage, throws it in the sans-culotte's face. This gesture seals his
fate. The sans-culottes seize him and within six seconds he is tied
up.

Fleuri. His uneasy smile. He grabs his tricorne, puts it in his right 238
pocket, and takes out a cap from his left and puts it on his head.

Laughter from the terrifying sans-culotte. 239

240 [[Fleuri's smug laugh, which freezes as his eyes focus on

241 [[the overseer's feet leaving the ground and kicking as they rise into the air.

242 [[A rope. Hands pulling.

243 [[Fleuri puts a second cap on over the first, then, as

244 [[a patrol of king's soldiers passes at the double,

245 [[he quickly whips off his caps and puts his battered tricorne back on. Once His Majesty's troops have gone, jeered at by the sans-culottes, Tristan puts on his cap again and, turning his cart about, he sprinkles all the people queuing at the baker's. They hoot at him.

246 [[Fleuri moves away. Three men pass by, all of indeterminate appearance – neither revolutionaries nor aristocrats. Tristan hesitates and changes his hat three times, grinning stupidly in his confusion, which sends the three men into fits of laughter.]]

247 Street. Bonaparte goes by. Fleuri's water-cart in action. The street is narrow. Bonaparte stands right back on the footway, but cannot avoid being splashed. Tristan carries on without noticing.

248 Bonaparte glares after the water-cart, then he takes stock of the disaster: his cardboard boot has collapsed and, ruined by the water, has slipped down round his ankle. He has to carry out a makeshift repair, his foot on a bollard. His breeches are also in tatters.

249 A carriage drawn by two horses, the driver wearing a carmagnole,* comes towards Bonaparte.

250 In the carriage, Joséphine de Beauharnais beside Thérésa and between Barras, Servan and Tallien. Tallien is placing a crown of roses on her head.

251 The carriage comes to a halt in front of Bonaparte. Joséphine, Thérésa and the men get down. Barras looks at

252 a sign on the door:

MADEMOISELLE LENORMANT
PALMIST

253 Barras bangs the knocker while Joséphine, smiling, watches

* *A short jacket worn by revolutionaries in 1793. Gance confuses it throughout with the Phrygian cap.*

Bonaparte, truly comical with his ill-kempt side-locks, his broken boot, his tattered clothes, trying to minimize the embarrassing, almost indecent, state of his outfit. 254

Joséphine laughs mockingly as she removes the crown of roses, which she throws into the street. 255

Bonaparte catches sight of Joséphine laughing at him. Admiration makes his heart miss a beat. 256

Joséphine laughs more than ever and says in her charming exotic accent, pointing to the young man: 257

[['What a droll young man!']]

She goes into the house, followed by Thérésa and the amused gentlemen.

Bonaparte, pale and inscrutable, watching the door through which she has just vanished . . . 258

Mademoiselle Lenormant's

A veiled light filters down from a dome. At the end of the room, a large glass table in the style of an ancient altar. On the end wall the 259 outline of a twelve-pointed star is seen. On the left, a hermetic astrolabe projecting twelve rays and a large zodiac circle. Prism globes revolve. Little earthenware demons bob up and down behind crystal walls. The two young women, pretty and seductive, clad only in light gauze tunics, and the three men are grouped round the sibyl.

260 The young fortune-teller is reading the lines on the palm of one of the women. Suddenly she raises her eyes and looks at her in amazement.

261 General silence. Uneasiness.

262 Mlle Lenormant says:

'An amazing fortune . . . You are going to be *queen*, madame!'

263 A moment of shock, then general laughter which grows wilder and wilder.

264 [[Barras throws himself down before the young woman and says, mimicking the affectation of a courtier:

'Yes, Joséphine! Queen of my heart!'

265 [[Vice. Elegance. Parisianism. Insouciance.]]

266 Bonaparte, inscrutable, is still gazing at the point where the young woman disappeared. On the ground he sees

267 the wreath of flowers which she threw away.

*268 He toys with it thoughtfully with his foot. He walks away without picking it up. He retraces his steps and picks it up.

269 [[Mlle Lenormant's house. While the sibyl reads one of the men's palms, Thérésa (the future wife of Tallien) and Joséphine kiss one another. On the mouth? A deft fan screens possible licentiousness.

270 [[The shop of Fauvelet the pawnbroker. Someone, of whom we see nothing but the arms, is offering a watch to the pawnbroker. He looks at it, sniggers and says scornfully:

'I can't lend more than three francs on this watch.'

271 [[The man accepts, for Fauvelet produces three francs, which he puts into the man's hand. We see Bonaparte for barely a second, but

* *This scene survives in fragments and appears in flashback when Napoléon meets Joséphine at the Victims' Ball (1431ff).*

32

it is indeed him. In his left hand he is still carrying the flowers which he picked up in the street. He goes out, embarrassed.]]

Landing. Fleuri is on the lookout. Bonaparte's door is open. Violine is holding a beautiful lily in her hand. 'You can go in,' says Fleuri. She slips into Bonaparte's room. 'Quickly! Quickly!' Fleuri calls her. *272*

She comes out, closing the door. Fleuri and his daughter go back into their own lodgings. Just in time: Bonaparte returns to his room. *273*

Violine's room. Fleuri and Violine are standing next to one another in great agitation. *He* will be pleased. 'I'm going to listen.' She climbs on to her bed to listen at the wall. *274*

Bonaparte in his room. He looks for a container for his flowers. He has only an old chipped pot. He is about to pick it up when he notices the lily in it. He turns round as if to look for whoever has brought it for him, then, because he does not like people doing things for him so mysteriously, he takes the lily and throws it out on the landing through the door which he has left open. *275*

Violine says to Fleuri: *276*

'Father, this time, when you thank him, perhaps you might dare to remind him that you were scullion at Brienne.'

Fleuri takes his courage in both hands and makes to go out. He sees the lily on the landing. 'No, no, Violine! I can't.' 'Yes, Papa, yes! Go on!' She opens the door again, giving him a push; suddenly she stops, for she too has seen the lily. Sadly, she closes the door again. Fleuri kisses her as if she were a small child. *277*

Bonaparte's poverty was nothing compared to that which reigned in the suburbs

Scenes of frightful poverty, which explains but does not excuse the horrors of 10 August which we shall see.* *278*

---

* The sequence from scenes 278 to 284 was greatly expanded to take in the major events of the fatal night of 10 August 1792, which divested Louis XVI of his powers after the sack of the Tuileries, and saw the first of the massacres of the Revolution. Intercut with the scenes at the forge (also much expanded), we see the king's plea to the Assembly and Bonaparte watching the events taking place in the streets outside from his little room. The Declaration of the Rights of Man, pinned to the wall behind him, forms a stark contrast to the flickering shadows of the mob outside. The hanging described in scenes 241 and 242 is incorporated

33

[[A blacksmith's forge.]]

279   Horses in the shadows. Everywhere sans-culottes, men and women, leaning against beams, are listening to Danton holding forth. Sparks are flying. Never has Danton been so terrifying.

280   Faces, apocalyptic visions. Danton takes a horse-shoe from the wall.

281   The horse-shoe.

282   He shows it to everybody and says:

> **'The Monarchy! . . .'**

283   He takes the horse-shoe with both hands and breaks it. Roars from the crowd.

284   Danton's laughter.

POZZO DI BORGO'S REVENGE

285   Bonaparte's and Fleuri's landing. Pozzo is skulking with a man bearing a package; he points out Violine's door to the man, who goes up to it, knocks and enters. Pozzo watches anxiously with Salicetti. The man comes out again, closing the door behind him. Pozzo gives the man some money and he goes away. Pozzo keeps a lookout.

286   Violine's room. Marcellin is with her. She has just opened the package. It contained a superb court dress with a note which she holds in her hand.

> **For the beautiful Violine.**
>
> *An admirer*

287   Violine. Smile. Emotion. Hesitation. Laughter. She does not dare touch it. It is beautiful, so beautiful! Should she try it on . . . ?

288   Her door. Exterior. At the keyhole. Pozzo watches.

289   She finishes dressing. She looks adorable. Marcellin cannot get over it.

---

into this section. The intercutting between these three scenes gets more and more frantic, culminating in a fast-cut sequence in which Danton, the forge, the mob and Bonaparte are superimposed one upon the other, reminiscent of the celebrated runaway train sequence in Gance's La Roue *of 1922. The sequence ends on a close-up of Bonaparte's exalted face, haloed in light, and the title:* And from second to second, as the Monarchy crumbled, Napoléon had the vague feeling of a source of light growing within him.

Pozzo scurries down the stairs at top speed.   *290*

Street. Activity. Some *tricoteuses** are passing. Pozzo hails them as he   *291*
comes out of the house.

'There's some "quality" hiding here!'

The *tricoteuses* burst into the house like Furies.

Violine's room. Violine has made herself a fan from a newspaper, and   *292*

* *This was the name given to the working-class women who knitted during meetings at the*
convention, heckling the speakers. They were also to be found lining the route to the scaffold,
and they took an active part in the 'red masses', dipping their handkerchiefs in the blood of
the victims.

fashioned a makeshift lorgnette. She has powdered her hair with flour, stuck a beauty-patch on her chin and she is putting on airs in front of a piece of looking-glass, laughing, while Marcellin makes her a bow. The *tricoteuses* burst in. In a moment she is seized and borne away.

293 Landing and stairs. She struggles furiously. She scratches. Her dress comes open, revealing her breast, but the *tricoteuses* hold on to their prey and drag her away, followed by Marcellin, who beats one of the shrews on the behind with a broom in helpless fury and topples her down the stairs. When they have all disappeared, Salicetti emerges from his room, watches them struggling with Violine on the stairs and smiles fiendishly.

294 Outer door of the house. Violine is being brought out, fighting like a lioness. Pozzo hugging the wall. She calls to him to help her; he sneers and follows the group. Marcellin follows for a short distance and then runs back up the road in the opposite direction.

[[His orders are to sprinkle.*

295 [[Tristan Fleuri has been getting ready to leave his shed with his full water-cart, in spite of the brawlers yelling in the street. He cautiously pokes his nose out. Yes! Today it's the cap. He puts it on. At this moment, Marcellin comes dashing in and explains what has happened. Fleuri is devastated. He sets off at a run.

296 [[Street. He is running. He stops. He goes back, runs on again, goes back and finally runs into his water-cart.

297 [[Shed. He says to Marcellin:

'You're sure it was La Force prison?'

'Yes!' says Marcellin. Fleuri stops, looking desperate. An idea comes into his head. Yes! Yes! 'A bayonet, Marcellin, a bayonet.' He snatches it and . . .

298 [[End of the shaft. We see him preparing a Machiavellian invention.]]

299 Violine swept along, half unclothed, putting up no more than a feeble

* *In his notes to Kevin Brownlow (see Introduction, p. xi), Gance is not very clear. We deduce that he did film Violine's imprisonment and release, but that the water-cart was dropped. Apart from a few stills, there is no trace of this entire sequence. We can only assume that Gance found some other way of having Fleuri rescue Violine.*

struggle now. It is a miracle that her head is not already at the end of a pike.

Fleuri has finished his work. His expression is grim. 300

The shaft. He operates a little trigger and fifteen centimetres of a 301
bayonet flick in and out at will.

He storms out, helped by Marcellin, the sprinkler-valve closed. 302

Street, slope. Marcellin is perched astride the shaft, while Fleuri in 303
harness pulls, but the slope makes the cart gain speed.

Bottom of the street. Barricade. Some Swiss Guards, bunched 304
together, are defending themselves; the crowd is about to finish them
off. Shots are about to be fired when

the water-cart comes hurtling down the hill. 305

Concern, then fright as the sans-culottes become aware of the 306
headlong rush of

the runaway water-cart. Breakneck speed. Wheel. Water. Feet being 307
crushed.

Fleuri, face ablaze. 308

The water-cart crashes down like a meteor, overturning the barricade, 309
flooding everything, men, powder, guns. Epic and comic at the same
time. Completely dazed, the sans-culottes still have not quite realized
that the water-cart has gone through, scattering the bunch of soldiers
who were about to fire on them, and putting them to flight in a torrent
of water.

A drenched sans-culotte tries to shoot. His gun does not fire, nor do 310
others. He says philosophically:

**'Ten water-carts would stop the Revolution more easily than
ten thousand guns.'**

The water-cart careering along at top speed and people fleeing before 311
it like terrified ants.]]

The La Force prison. Aristocrats, men and women, some of them 312
badly wounded, are being pitched brutally into prison.

The band of *tricoteuses* arrives with Violine, who is gasping and 313
practically unconscious. Seething crowd escorting her and others
doomed to imminent massacre.

314 [[Fleuri's water-cart, at normal speed as there is no longer any slope.

315 [[Fleuri seems mad to be preparing so calmly to attack this crowd which is bearing down upon him.

316 [[The shaft.

317 [[Fleuri has almost reached the crowd.]]

318 Sans-culottes telling him: 'You're mad! Turn back, you fool!'

319 Tristan, his face grim. His eyes search everywhere and he shouts 'Violine, Violine!'

320 Violine hears and calls back: '*Help me!*'

321 Fleuri has heard her. He tries to move forward. In vain! So he noses his shaft into the crowd again. The hostile crowd closes in round the water-cart. But he opens the valve and the threatening sans-culottes, soaked to the skin, fall back. They form up again on both sides of the cart; he opens the side valves. More dousings. He takes advantage of the confusion to flick out the bayonet from the shaft, and he begins to jab all the thighs and buttocks he can reach.

322 He prods a buxom revolutionary's bottom.

323 She yells.

324 Fleuri at fever-pitch, mad, drenched, sweating, manages to reach the door of the La Force prison just as Violine is about to be thrown in. Bringing all his skill and strength into play, he rescues her by dint of stabbing the posteriors of a vast number of *tricoteuses*. Violine throws herself into his arms. He explains that she is his daughter. The people, with feminine capriciousness, do a complete *volte-face*, suddenly changing their attitude, and shout: 'We must save her!' They all want to be the first to carry her in triumph, though they had been wanting to slaughter her only a few seconds before.

325 Violine and Fleuri hug one another with tears of joy.

326 Pozzo does not dare intervene, but cannot restrain a gesture of rage.

327 Marcellin behind Pozzo. He has seen this gesture. The shaft is in just the right position.

328 Shaft and Pozzo's leg. A flash of the bayonet, and then it is gone, hidden under the shaft.

Pozzo howls with pain. He whirls round in a fury, and, thinking the   *329*
jab came from a mountainous *tricoteuse*, who is smiling tenderly as
she watches Violine and Fleuri and who happens to have a knife in
her hand, he cuffs her. She yells. Pozzo is attacked, tooth and nail.
He runs off under a hail of blows.

Marcellin laughs till he cries.   *330*

Violine and Fleuri are borne in triumph on the water-cart, pulled   *331*
along by the singing crowd.

〖Dies Irae

Interior, Tuileries. Staircase. Delirious joy. People are embracing,   *332*
laughing, stealing, looting. Movement of the crowd abruptly halted
by something. They listen intently.

Corridors. Same action.   333

Some sans-culottes listen at a door. The noise is coming from behind   334
it. Gently they open the door and stand motionless in the doorway.
They see:

The chapel, the great organ. A man, straight out of an Edgar Allan   335
Poe story, terrifying, ghastly, face drained of blood, is playing the
strange, terrible *Dies Irae* on the organ.

The organ. Score of the *Dies Irae* open before him. His hand turns   336
the page and the fingers leave red imprints. Shot of the keys. The
man runs his fingers slowly over them and his hands, red with blood,
leave stains on the ivory. A dead man's arm hangs over the keys at
one side of the keyboard.

Great organ-pipes. We sense the thunderous roar of its heavy,   337
lugubrious voice.

It is spine-chilling. Uneasiness, an atmosphere of remorse. The   338
chapel is full of dead men, corpses draped over the balusters or piled
in the wooden pews.

The sans-culottes advance close to the enigmatic musician, not   339
daring to make too much noise. One of them finally asks:

'What are you doing?'

340 ⟦ The organist looks up with strange, terrible eyes; the men stand petrified, as if the exterminating angel of the Last Judgement were looking at them. He stops playing momentarily, and says in solemn, terrifying tones:

'I am burying the Monarchy!'

And he continues playing.

341 ⟦ One of the sans-culottes leans over towards another and says:

'Do you know his name?'

342 ⟦ The other says, 'No!' – 'Do you?' – 'No!' – 'Do you?' – 'No!' – 'Well, then! . . . Let's kill him! He's driving us mad!' They are about to murder him, when a woman comes running up, pushing them aside to look at him. She recoils in horror, dragging the sans-culottes away, and she says to them in a low, trembling voice:

'It is the Marquis de Sade!'

343 ⟦ They all recoil as if it were Leprosy personified playing the organ. She adds:

'The ghastly secretary of the pike section!'

The aura of terror widens about the infamous marquis.

344 ⟦ The score.

345 ⟦ De Sade, at once ecstatic and satanic, plays on. The chapel. The organ gleams in the background. The sans-culottes leave hurriedly.

346 ⟦ Shot of de Sade.

Dona eis requiem.

Marcellin too was overthrowing the Monarchy!

347 ⟦ Courtyard of Fleuri's house. A dozen urchins, ranging from two to nine years old, boys and girls, some dressed as sans-culottes, the others, dressed with greater care, representing the aristocrats. They arrange the costumes and then split up into two groups.

348 ⟦ Tristan Fleuri's room. Standing on chairs, three children, one of them Marcellin, are surreptitiously and with infinite precaution taking down the model set-piece of the Bastille which is under a glass globe. They carry it off, globe and all.

In the courtyard. The arrival of the Bastille is received with shouts 349
of delight. They put it in a slightly raised position at the top of the
hand-rail of an outside stone staircase.

The little aristocrats take up their stand on the stairs to defend it. 350

Marcellin gives orders. 351

The urchins join battle. Bleeding noses, scratched behinds, little 352
mites squalling, lost in the scuffle, tears pouring down their faces. A
small girl defends the Bastille with fierce desperation, but some piece
of treachery brings the fortress tumbling down to shatter into a
thousand pieces: victory, a comic massacre. Parody of the great events
that have gone before. Marcellin is acting out love's young dream
with a lovely young aristocrat, in defiance of political passions.

Entrance of Fleuri and a neighbour looking for her daughter. Fleuri, 353
thunderstruck, furious: 'My Bastille!' He sees

the two children embracing. 354

The mother spanks her daughter, Fleuri his son. 355

Marcellin, during the spanking: 356

> **'I love you, Camille. Long live the Republic.'**

Camille, being spanked, her face wet with tears, her voice broken 357
with sobs:

> **'I . . . love you . . . Marcellin. Long live the . . . Repu . . . oh!
> Ow! Ow!'**]]

IN CORSICA*

Until now the axis of the dramatic action has been the crowd, and 358
the Revolution its leading player. Bonaparte has been no more than
a drop of water lost in the turbulent ocean, but a drop of water gifted
with independent thought and capable of resistance where all others
were obeying the blind thrust of their passions. His character has
been tempered. The crystallization of his spirit has taken place amid
the collapse of the Monarchy, and from now on he will have but one

---

* When the film was edited, the part filmed in Corsica was drastically cut down; it is also
the section that has suffered the most from the passage of time. There are tantalizing
fragments of some sequences, and even more tantalizing stills of others. Because of this, it is
difficult to deduce what was actually shot. In his notes for Kevin Brownlow, Gance rather
unhelpfully states that he shot the whole of it.

idea: to impose order upon this chaos. In Corsica, the time for contemplation is over: he passes on to action. The play of muscles and defences, physical trials, bodily resilience, feverish activity. A Corsican Robin Hood pitted against Paoli, like the great Armorican* he will develop his powers of resistance and decisiveness and put them, from Toulon onwards, at the direct service of glory.

359   In Ajaccio, 15 October 1792, at his parents' home, his sisters Pauline, thirteen and the most beautiful, and Caroline, eleven; his brothers Joseph, twenty-five, Lucien, eighteen, Louis, fourteen and a half, and Jérôme, nine.

Bonaparte arrives unexpectedly in Ajaccio, entrusted by the Convention with an official mission to study ways of defending the country against the English.

360   Aboard a boat. View of the country. The high mountains of La Force covered in snow, then the blue waters of the gulf.

361   Bonaparte in the boat. His sister Élisa leaning against his breast, he murmurs:

'Mother . . .'

The azure sea slips rapidly away before them.

(All the scenes in Corsica were photographed in the exact locations where the incidents occurred.)

362   Garden fence. Élisa and Bonaparte. No one is expecting them. Élisa, no longer able to contain her joy, wants to run in. Bonaparte holds her back: 'Not so fast, little sister!' His immense, deep, inner joy. He moves forward towards the Casone Grotto and caresses the stones.

363   His emotion. His eyes rove through Milelli's delightful garden.**

364   Élisa respects his emotion. However, she is impatient to open the green front door, but he calms her and quietly opens it himself.***

* A reference to Vercingétorix, who mobilised ancient Gaul against Caesar. He was not, in fact, from Brittany (armoricain) but from the Auvergne in central France.
** In the 1920s Corsica was a practically unvisited island. Gance, who had never been there before making this film (his note in scene 361 notwithstanding), did not realize that the grotto is in fact about half a mile away from the Bonapartes' town house in Ajaccio, and nowhere near Les Milelli, the Bonapartes' farmhouse in the hills, where all these scenes were shot.
*** Bonaparte's sister goes in ahead, finds Laetitia alone. She points to the door, where Bonaparte is silhouetted against the sunlight; the mother is overcome with emotion. Bonaparte comes forward and they embrace. Then the rest of the family floods in.

Interior, his mother Laetitia's house. In it, absorbed in different tasks, are his Uncle Fesch,* Pauline, Caroline, Joseph, Lucien, Louis, Jérôme, the nurse and Laetitia, who is tending the fire. The door has just opened. Pauline catches sight of her brother and lets out a cry. Everyone turns round. Bonaparte stands on the threshold. A silence. For several seconds their impulses are suspended by emotion; then there is a burst of violent movement from everyone at once, and there are frenzied embraces, while Louis goes out to announce the news. Bonaparte can move no further into the room, and Laetitia, separated from her son by this deluge of brotherly affection, has difficulty in reaching him. 365

Louis, at the door, explains to two children that his brother has come back, then he leaves. The children call out to others with their news; they peer in at the windows; the group of children grows; there are ten, fifteen, twenty. They stream in. 366

The children rush at Bonaparte. One says: 367

> 'Hello, cousin.'

The next one says:

> 'Hello, cousin.'

The third says the same. Wrangling with one another to embrace him, they all say: 'Hello, cousin.' Bonaparte laughs till the tears come into his eyes in the midst of this gigantic family, which is especially appreciative of his uniform. The children try on his hat, his sabre, his gloves.

The old shepherd Santo-Ricci de Bovognano, who has been warming himself near the fire, rises like a scarecrow and waves his arms in a terrifying manner. 368

This gesture puts all the children to flight, scrambling and shoving each other in a panic. Bonaparte is astonished. 369

Santo-Ricci says: 370

> **'This is no time for laughter, Napoléon. You must know the appalling truth at once.'**

General anguish. Laetitia puts her head in her hands; Bonaparte goes up to Santo-Ricci. 371

* *Uncle Fesch was dropped from the script throughout.*

372　The skin of Santo-Ricci's face is wrinkled and leathery. As if an ancient oak were splitting open its rough bark to let out the grimmest of secrets, he says:

> **'Paoli, our old and great Paoli, the revered father of us all, is about to sell us to the English.'**

He hides his face as if tainted by the picture he evokes.

373　Bonaparte. Apparent impassivity, but his nostrils quiver. He turns questioning eyes to

374　his mother, who raises her tear-stained face to him. She bows her head again, confirming the shepherd's words.

375　Bonaparte appeals to Joseph who, with his head in his hands on the table, makes a dispirited gesture in confirmation. Then Bonaparte turns back to Ricci. He looks at him with burning intensity and, putting into his words all his suppressed, seething energy, says:

> **'As long as I am alive, Corsica shall never be English!'**

376　The fire flickering in the hearth suddenly leaps up like an enormous flower of flame.

377　Joseph, Laetitia, Élisa, Lucien and Pauline. Their emotion and mingled joy and apprehension on seeing their brother display such decisiveness and strength.

378　His energy. The leaping flame.

379　Ricci, seated, takes Bonaparte's hand and kisses it with tears of gratitude.

*380　Garden. Tranquillity. Flowers. Sunshine. We become acquainted with the whole family.

* *This scene and the ones immediately following it are an example of changes made in the cutting rooms. For once all of the prints agree on the running order: just before the garden scene, there is a long and beautiful sequence which introduces us to the Bonapartes' town house, then takes Napoléon on horseback in superimposition over travelling shots of the Corsican countryside and coastline. It ends with him sitting contemplatively by the Casone grotto. In the garden scene itself, while the family sits gossiping and laughing together, Napoléon wanders away from them to reflect on his future. Should he choose a quiet family life, or, sacrificing his individual happiness, should he try to become one of the leading actors on the world scene? The title* The Bonaparte family found itself up against the fierce jealousy of Pozzo di Borgo, who had become Corsica's attorney general and Paoli's secretary, *accompanied by a menacing close shot of Pozzo di Borgo with a snake crawling on his shoulder, answers the question and sets the mood for the scene*

Iles Sanguinaires. Pose as at St Helena at the end of his life. He gazes   381
at the horizon from the top of a favourite rock.

> **Bonaparte, official representative of France, soon found himself estranged from all those inhabitants still blindly attached to old Paoli, 'the Father of our Nation', who was demanding English rule.**

Paoli's imposing office. The great man is there: sixty-eight, very old,   382
an extraordinary face, a Corsican Charlemagne, now almost unable
to move. Next to him, Pozzo di Borgo, sworn enemy of the Bonaparte
family, whose hatred, passed on through three generations, will
secretly shadow the Second Empire and triumph in 1871 at the fall
of Napoléon III. Pozzo di Borgo says to Paoli:

> **'Through his secret correspondence with the Convention, Bonaparte is at present the most serious obstacle to our alliance with England. In the name of the Corsican fatherland, give me his life.'**

Paoli. He starts back, then he reflects a moment and signs the paper   383
which Pozzo di Borgo is holding out to him.

> **Order to the civil and military authorities to pursue Napoléon Bonaparte, traitor to his country. A reward of five hundred livres to whoever brings him in, dead or alive.**
> **On behalf of the Corsican Council,**
>
> > ***Paoli.***

Pozzo leaves with fierce satisfaction. He sets about inciting the   384
population against Bonaparte.

Bonaparte's home. He comes out on to the step. The human wolves   385
drop back before his gaze.

---

that follows, where Pozzo di Borgo incites the population of Ajaccio, and which ends on scene
number 385. After this, Ignoring the wise advice of his family, who warned him to
flee the hatred of the people, Napoléon came every day to the deserted headland of
the Sanguinaires to discuss the future with his friend the Ocean, *followed by scene*
381. We then move on to the first scene in Paoli's office (scene 382).

From this moment on, and until his departure from Corsica, the life of this young officer became the most incredible of adventure stories.

386 ⟦ Interior, Laetitia's house. Old Uncle Fesch is trying to console Laetitia, who is crying on a chair. Élisa, Pauline, Louis and Jérôme are huddled around her, apprehensively. The door opens. She starts. Men and women spew insults; others, cursing likewise, at the windows, which they push open. They are about to come in. Laetitia takes refuge by the hearth.

387 ⟦ A door. Bonaparte appears, adjusting his collar. He sees the intruders forcing their way in and shouting insults; he advances grimly. They back away, and scatter on reaching the door. He starts to go out; his mother comes over to him, closes the door again and, sobbing, begs him to stay.

'Do not go out, my darling son. I feel it in my heart: they want your life.'

388 ⟦ He smiles, kisses his mother, gently puts her from him and goes out. Laetitia cries; her children try to comfort her.⟧

*389 A secret meeting of old shepherds in the mountains. A scene of classical grandeur; a great fire of branches glows on their faces. The golden tints of the setting sun linger on in the fleeces of their sheep. Santo-Ricci exhorts the shepherds, who take their oaths with hands outstretched over the flames.

390 He declares:

'We, the last supporters of the persecuted Bonaparte family, swear to defend them to the death!'

391 The old, gnarled hands stretch out over the flames for the oath.

Napoléon's brothers, Lucien and Joseph, set out in disguise for Calvi to seek help from the French authorities.

392 Evening. Interior, Laetitia's house. They are making their last farewell embraces and giving their disguises a final examination: Joseph as a

---

* *None of the sequences involving the shepherds have survived, so we cannot know if the following sequence was actually shot. Judging by the description, it would have been tinted red; from here to the end of the Corsican episode, as the events happen at night, the exteriors would have been tinted blue and the interiors amber.*

tramp and Lucien as a hawker. Bonaparte, in captain's uniform, gives them secret letters which they hide in their hats and shoes. Nobody outside; they go out. They disappear into the night. Bonaparte sits, thinking. All eyes turn towards him; his features show the utmost determination. He rises and picks up his voluminous cloak, wrapping it round himself. Laetitia clasps her hands in horror and cries:

'What are you going to do?'

Bonaparte. He is animated with inexpressible energy. He replies: 393

'I am going to take action!'

Before she can intervene, he goes out. This time the son's firmness   394
has communicated itself to the mother and, struggling with her grief, she draws herself up with true Corsican pride. She stands on the threshold, exalted, and watches him disappear into the night. [[A star twinkles in the sky.]]

Rowdy groups of people in a Corsican inn. Politics inflames their   395
minds. The talk is violent and accompanied by much wild gesticu-lation. [[The innkeeper is carrying bottles up and down through the trap-door to the cellar.]] Two Corsican gendarmes put up the following proclamation:

**ORDER TO THE CIVIL AND MILITARY AUTHORITIES TO PURSUE
NAPOLÉON BONAPARTE, TRAITOR TO HIS NATIVE LAND.
A REWARD OF FIVE HUNDRED LIVRES TO WHOEVER BRINGS
HIM IN DEAD OR ALIVE.
IN THE NAME OF THE COUNCIL OF CORSICA,
ITS SUPREME CHIEF,**

Paoli.

As they read it the men cross themselves, and discussion around the proclamation starts up again with more heat than ever.

Pozzo di Borgo shouts: 396

'Our fatherland is England with Paoli: Death to Bonaparte!'

Another Corsican retaliates spiritedly: 397

'No, it's Spain with Buttafuoco. Death to Bonaparte.'

398 A third Corsican yells:

'No, it's Italy with the Duke of Savoy. Death to Bonaparte.'

399 A man climbs up on to a chair and throws open his cloak; everyone falls back. He says with an authority which brooks no opposition:

'Our fatherland is France, with Bonaparte.'

400 Stupefaction, for it is he, Bonaparte, who has dared, in person, to speak out at the very moment when a price is being put on his head. The temerity of this gesture momentarily disarms all hatred.

401 Pozzo di Borgo runs out.

402 The men get over their shock. They are about to fall on him and arrest him, but his eloquence holds even the fiercest at bay, and they listen to him:

[['Madness has possessed the spirit of your people, and a fatal blindness is leading you to your ruin!']]

403 People listening.

404 Bonaparte. His power of persuasion is beyond expression. He says:

'If you could understand the dream that fires my soul, you would all follow me! Believe me. . . A man will come who will unite in himself all the hopes of the nation, and then . . .

      'For France, you see, is the mother of us all! . . .'   405

⟦ Map of France.⟧   406

They listen to him reverently; hatred melts like snow in April.   407

A woman kneels.   408

The mounted gendarmes arrive with Pozzo di Borgo and surround   409
the inn.

The gendarmes enter and level their guns at Bonaparte.   410

Bonaparte on his chair. He says nothing.   411

Cowardice all about him. Everyone runs away.   412

Exterior. The shepherd Santo-Ricci, on his way back with the other   413
shepherds, is attracted by the noise and watches the scene through a
window. He makes the shepherds hide in the shadows and goes back
into the inn.

Bonaparte. His contempt for the cowardice around him. He gets   414
down from his chair. He folds his arms and says: 'I am your prisoner.'
They seize him and tie him up. They are about to lead him away
when Pozzo di Borgo says:

      'He is to be shot in the courtyard.'

Pozzo goes out.

Near the prisoner, an old man is acting particularly violently towards   415
him, cursing him with extraordinary vehemence. Bonaparte, who is
not easily surprised, appears astonished by this. It is, in fact the old
shepherd, Santo-Ricci. The gendarmes, seeing this zealous hostility,
slacken their attention a little, all the more so when they are handed
something to drink.

Santo-Ricci picks up a rope that was lying on the ground and begins   416
to bind it round the other ropes.

The gendarmes laugh at this superfluous precaution and turn away.   417

Santo-Ricci and Bonaparte. Santo-Ricci, as he coils his rope, cuts   418
Bonaparte's bonds and looks meaningfully towards

49

419 [[the trap-door through which the innkeeper was going up and down earlier.]]

420 Bonaparte returns the look to show that he has understood.

421 Santo-Ricci goes to the window, opens it, whistles and disappears.

422 The gendarmes turn round: 'What's going on?'

423 The shepherds emerge from the shadows and arrive on the scene.

424 The gendarmes in the courtyard. Alarm!

425 The gendarmes inside the inn go towards the window and load their guns. Bonaparte takes advantage of the confusion to slip away* [[through the trap-door.]]

426 Struggle between shepherds and gendarmes.

427 Interior. The gendarmes realize: 'He's gone!' [[They try in vain to raise the trap-door.]] They run right and left. Disorder. Fury.

428 Battle outside between the shepherds and the gendarmes.

429 [[End of a garden. The battle is seen raging thirty feet away. Bonaparte emerges from a small staircase leading up from the basement. Moonlight. Santo-Ricci is waiting with a horse. He embraces Bonaparte, who gallops away. Pozzo di Borgo comes running up. He wounds Santo-Ricci and calls the gendarmes.]]

430 Bonaparte gallops past.

431 Forty gendarmes on horseback leave in a cloud of dust and disappear into the moonlit night.

432 Bonaparte galloping along.

433 Pursuit. The gendarmes lose track of him.

434 Paoli's office. Night session of the insurrectionary council. All the

---

* *The stills and fragments of the scenes at the inn show that they were filmed with a certain number of changes: Napoléon jumps off what was in fact a table, not a chair, and escapes through the main door of the inn, jumping on to his horse from the terrace overlooking the road instead of using the trap-door leading to the garden described in the script. It is probable that none of the shepherds, apart from Santo-Ricci, appeared in the scene. Although Kevin Brownlow's restoration made this section coherent, it did not show Napoléon's actual escape. A shot showing him leaving the inn has recently been found and will be restored to the print.*

Corsicans of note are gathered round the aged leader. Paoli solemnly draws himself up.

'War with France is declared!'

Window. Bonaparte appears so suddenly in the window, in the light 435 of the moon, that it is impossible to know how he got there. The enormous tricolour flag draping the façade of the town hall where the meeting is being held streams behind him.

All those present turn round and are appalled. 436

Swift as lightning, Bonaparte seizes the immense flag, which is within 437 his reach; he tears it down and says:

'I am taking it away. It is too great for you!'

And he vanishes as swiftly as he appeared.

Sensation among those present. Pistols are aimed at the window. 438 Too late.

The men rush to the window and make out 439

Bonaparte on horseback, already a long way away in the moonlight. 440

Exterior, town hall, torches. Uproar. More horsemen set off in 441 pursuit.*

Paoli has not moved, but his majestic face is blazing with anger. He 442 writes:

Order of exile for all the Bonaparte family. Power of life and death to every Corsican patriot over the members of this family.

Approval from all round. 443

Exterior, Laetitia's house. Shepherds keep a lookout from under 444 cover.

Interior, Laetitia's house. Old Santo-Ricci's wound is being dressed. 445

Terrible distress. Élisa, Pauline, Caroline, Louis, Jérôme, old Uncle 446 Fesch and the shepherds. Defences are being prepared. They are priming the guns, and piling up the mattresses.

* *This scene, comprising half a dozen shots, was actually shot at night (as opposed to 'day-for-night'). It therefore does not match the rest of the scenes which were shot in daylight and would only have harmonized once all the exteriors were tinted blue for night. All the night shooting will be restored to the proposed tinted version of* Napoléon.

447   Exterior. Riding flat out, a horseman arrives; the shepherds' guns are aimed and then lowered; it is Bonaparte. Without dismounting, he pushes open the door and says:

448   **'We meet in five days on the beach at Aspretto. You must all leave immediately. *Questo paese non è per noi.'**

And he disappears.

449   Just in time. The gendarmes storm past in hot pursuit.

450   Laetitia resists. 'No, no, I am a Corsican. I shall die here!' Santo-Ricci, despite his wound, gets up and pleads with her. He touches her weak spot when he says to her:

'Flee for Napoléon's sake. Think of his despair if he has to blame himself one day for the death of his whole family!'

This thought overcomes Laetitia's resistance. Preparations are made for the family's departure.

451   Bonaparte gallops past. Close on his heels the gendarmes, same pace. They fire but miss him.

452   Bonaparte dashes past. The gendarmes pass several seconds later. Pozzo di Borgo pulls up with the last ten and says:

[['We'll cut off his retreat at Sarrola.']]

They take a track off to the right.

453   Breakneck ride.

454   The track comes out on a road. Pozzo urges them on. They arrive at the road. Pozzo takes a long mountaineering rope from the shoulders of one of the gendarmes, and with another he stretches it across the road, one and a half metres from the ground, securing it round two sturdy trees.

455   Bonaparte galloping at fantastic speed.

456   Pozzo's men wait for him to fall. In the darkness he will be unable to see the rope.

457   Bonaparte at full speed, still pursued by the other gendarmes. He seems to be heading for certain disaster.

---

* *'This country is not for us.'*

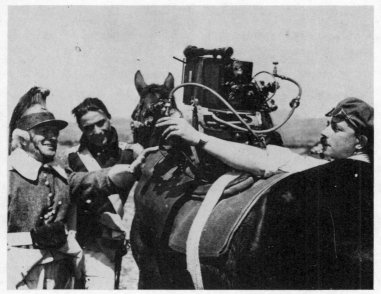

Simon Feldman preparing to shoot the chase across the marshes

Bonaparte at the gallop. He fires his last pistol shots at some riders who are gaining on him. Two riders fall. Having nothing but his sabre now, he draws it, ready to fight to the death. 458

He is approaching the rope. He sees the danger. He slides forward onto the horse's neck and, clinging to it with one hand, leans down as the horse gallops on and slices the rope with his sabre the second before it would have touched the horse's nostrils. 459

Fury of the disappointed pursuers. They set off again, fuming with rage. 460

⟦ Bonaparte, on the point of being taken, makes his horse jump a bank and disappears into a thick wood. The gendarmes' horses hesitate. One skilled rider takes the same path; the others are about to follow. Pozzo stops them and says triumphantly: 461*

'This wood ends in a precipice and will deliver him into our hands. He will have to come out this side.'

* This sequence was replaced with the exciting chase across the marshes to the sea, treated almost entirely in travelling shots, in which the camera was at one point lashed to a horse's back.

53

The horsemen block the exits to the wood.

462 ⟦ Bonaparte advances through the branches, opening up the path with his sabre. Suddenly he comes to a halt, for in front of him:

463 ⟦ A precipice.

464 ⟦ He is on the point of turning back when the other rider arrives and fires.

465 ⟦ Bonaparte falls. The rider jumps to the ground. The two men are on the edge of the precipice.

466 ⟦ The gendarme turns round, his hands cupped round his mouth, to shout to the others that he has succeeded. Bonaparte, who had been shamming, leaps on him. A struggle begins on the brink of the precipice.

467 ⟦ They fight desperately back and forth.

468 ⟦ Bonaparte gains the upper hand; he succeeds in pushing the gendarme over the cliff, whilst retaining his cloak. He seizes the cloak, flings it round himself and puts on the gendarme's hat. In the struggle, the eyepatch the man was wearing has fallen to the ground. Bonaparte picks it up and pulls it over one of his eyes, leaps on to his victim's white horse and makes off, leaving his own black horse beside the chasm.

469 ⟦ Bonaparte fools the gendarmes completely, bursting out of the wood at full gallop and motioning towards some imaginary point, urging the gendarmes to follow him.

470 ⟦ The gendarmes and Bonaparte in pursuit of himself. He directs them by gestures. They follow him.

471 ⟦ A strand, rocks, a beach.

472 ⟦ Bonaparte, only a little ahead of the gendarmes, shouts to them:

'I've just seen him dive into the sea.'

He points to

473 ⟦ a small boat fifty metres from the shore, moored to a rock surrounded by water.

474 ⟦ The men's fury. Bonaparte says: 'I will bring him back alive!' He dives into the water.

The gendarmes watch him anxiously.   475

Bonaparte swimming.   476

Gendarmes on the shore.]]   477

Bonaparte reaches the boat, jumps into it and cuts the mooring-rope.   478

The astonished gendarmes look on.   479

Bonaparte. His horror.   480

No oars! Only the little mast for the sail; but no sail!   481

An idea comes to him. He takes out from his tunic the great flag from   482
the town hall at Ajaccio and begins to make a sail out of it.

On the shore, the gendarmes become perturbed. Suddenly there are   483
shouts of rage. They have realized, too late.

The boat is fitted with its tricolour sail, which billows in the wind.   484
Bonaparte [[takes off his eyepatch and]] shouts to the gendarmes,
pointing to his flag:

'I shall bring it back to you.'

Pozzo di Borgo fumes. The gendarmes, up to their knees in the   485
water, fire uselessly in the direction of the boat.

486   The little boat draws farther and farther away in the moonlight.

487 [[The man whom Bonaparte had pitched into the ravine appears, his clothes in shreds, on Bonaparte's black horse. He jumps to the ground, questioning his comrades. Cursing and swearing, they point to the horizon at]]

488   the boat, which is now a long way off.

489   Pozzo di Borgo. The very depths of human hatred. He brandishes his fist and says:

[['To the death, Napoléon.']]

490   The boat is now no more than a tiny French flag set upon a vast expanse of blue.

[**Thus, on 26 May 1793, after an epic chase, Napoléon set sail in Ucciani's dinghy.**]

The outlaws

491   The Bonaparte house in flames. Dawn. The Corsicans, their anger out of control, feed the blaze. A band armed with scythes, picks and staves sets out in search of Laetitia.

492   A hillock. Laetitia with Caroline, Élisa, Pauline, Jérôme, Louis and old Uncle Fesch and five old shepherds, who drop behind, one after another, too weak to cope with the arduous pace of the flight. Only Santo-Ricci will remain until the last minute. A shepherd comes running up and says to Laetitia, 'Go quickly. They are coming!' She still does not want to leave. She watches

493   the distant blaze of her house.

494   Laetitia. She is in anguish. Her grief at leaving this land she loves so much, at leaving in this fashion, hounded, banished. She falters. She falls to her knees. She sees all her children round her, and Santo-Ricci begging her to go. She thinks

495   of the pack of wolves at her heels.

496   With a fierce movement she straightens up: 'Come!' And they all hurry down the hill.

The sky becomes overcast. Black clouds scurry across the sky and begin to pile up. 497

The little party struggling through the maquis. Covered with briars, scratches; weariness. An old shepherd stops, unable to go any farther, and says, 'Have courage! Go on without me.' He embraces the children, weeping. 498

Élisa walks along, her shoes in shreds. She throws them away; she would rather walk barefoot. Her legs are bleeding. 499

Louis pulls Pauline along with Caroline and Jérôme in tow. Laetitia helps old Uncle Fesch. 500

The pursuers torture the old shepherd to find out which way the fugitives have taken. 501

The sky completely black. A flash of lightning. 502

Torrential rain, a morass. The wretched little party goes by. They sink into the mud up to their knees. Laetitia is carrying Jérôme. Two shepherds carry Caroline and Pauline. 503

In the downpour the Corsican wolves continue beating the maquis in search of the outlaws. 504

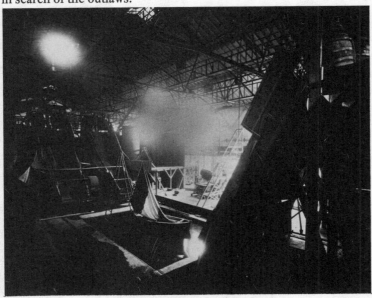

Billancourt studios: the studio tank

505 Out at sea, gale blowing up, pouring rain; the boat with its tricolour sail.

506 Bonaparte looks at the sky and around him.

507 Sea, nothing but sea everywhere, with the great waves breaking.

508 Bonaparte's anxiety begins to show. He trims his makeshift sail.

509 He is driven before the wind. The rain comes down harder than ever.

510 ⟦ Maquis. Bleak country. The storm is raging. An absolute deluge. The outlaws pass, huddled together in a tight little band, like a broken wreck at the mercy of the storm.⟧

511 At sea. The hurricane is unleashed. Bonaparte is performing fantastic feats with his sail. He is tossed up and down in swirling clouds of spray, countering each danger skilfully with his improvised sail.

That same day, at the same hour, another mighty storm was unleashed at the Convention, destroying the Girondins*

512 In the words of Victor Hugo: 'To be a member of the Convention was to be a wave on the ocean.' Souls at the mercy of the wind. The eye takes in the entire hemicycle from top to bottom. There are three thousand people present. 'A vast entrenchment of humanity menaced on all sides by shadows – immense bivouac of souls on the edge of an abyss. Nothing in history can be compared to this gathering, bending in the wind that issues from the mouths of the people and is the breath of God. Nothing more misshapen, yet more sublime. A band of heroes, a horde of cowards. Wild animals on a mountain, reptiles in a marsh! Titanic census.'[1]

This is a brief visual impression, in the same rhythm and movements as those of the storm. Tight correlation between the two storms. The deep significance becomes apparent. The boat appears to sink. The eye plunges from the galleries down on to the Girondins gripped with

1 – Victor Hugo, *Quatre-vingt-treize* (1873).
* *For the première at the Paris Opéra in 1927, the 'double tempest' sequence, which starts here, appeared as a triptych. It subsequently disappeared – according to Gance he burned it in despair some time in the 1940s. The film-maker Jean Dréville, then a journalist, watched all the Opéra showings from the projection booth. He was so impressed by the double tempest triptych that he was able to restore it, from memory, in 1985. It now forms part of the print that is shown in France.*

horror before the fury of the Assembly. Ten times the boat is on the point of sinking under a sky lit up with lightning flashes. The tumultuous Assembly rising and falling in a terrifying swell, streaked with flashes from the blade of the guillotine, a head falling with each flash.

Words can no longer describe the parallels. Can music be put into words? Indescribable double storm. Inner dynamism. Suggestion rather than evocation. Paris, surging crowds, tumbrils. The Girondins advance. The soldiers drive them back. Flash from the guillotine.

Mountains of water bear the boat upwards. It falls again vertiginously. 513

On the rostrum, a furious Marat* steps forward. 514

The Girondins; a surge of collective hatred towards him. 515

Marat takes out a pistol; guillotine flash. 516

Young girls throw him flowers. Marat catches them, and his smile is horrifying.]] 517

Boat. Bonaparte battles desperately against death, manoeuvring his sail. Lightning blinds him. 518

The outlaws on the run. The wind is blowing twice as violently as before, and they have to cross a raging torrent. Lightning. 519

Difficulties. General feeling of hopelessness. Laetitia's energy.]] 520

Boat. The danger has never been so great. 521

The Girondins try to escape. 522

The people flood into the amphitheatre. 523

Henriot has a cannon trained in their direction. Guillotine flash. 524

Boat. Bonaparte is exhausted. His hands are bleeding. No human force could endure it. 525

He takes down the sail and collapses in the bottom of the boat. 526

The boat, adrift like an empty nutshell, tosses up and down among the towering waves. 527

* *Robespierre in the film.*

528   The Girondins, hemmed in on all sides, still try to defend themselves. The soldiers and the crowd surrounding them. Guillotine flash.

529   Danton roars.

530   Wave of Girondins pulled by the crowd in one direction. Flow.

531   Robespierre smiles.

532   Wave of Girondins pulled by the crowd in another direction. Ebb.

533   Saint-Just* impassive.

534   Wave of Girondins rolling to port.

535   [[Couthon in his wheelchair abuses them and spits in their direction.]]

536   Wave of Girondins pitching to starboard.

537   Bonaparte's boat, tossing crazily.

538   Girondins being led away, great commotion. Guillotine flash.

539   Bonaparte's boat, tossing crazily.

540   [[Sans-culottes rushing past; wild eddying, with several heads on the ends of pikes.

541   [[A compact mass on a plain in the midst of the hurricane. It is the exhausted fugitives who have collapsed together in the downpour to wait until the storm abates. One shepherd lies dead on the ground near them.]]

542   The whole of the Revolution shown in very short tableaux simultaneously with the tossing boat; then fusion of the two. Climax. We are no longer dealing simply with the Convention, but with the Revolution as a whole.

[Thus, all the giants of the Revolution were swept one after the other into the raging whirlpool of the Reign of Terror. And a man, the defiant sport of the oceans, his tricolour sail opening to the wind of the Revolution, was being triumphantly carried to the heights of History.]

* *Robespierre.*

60

[[The sailing-craft *Le Hasard*.]]

The sea has grown calm.* A xebec, a large boat with six rowers and 543
two small lateen sails, a one-piece mast and a jib, sails by.

The name of the boat, *Le Hasard*, on the stern. 544

Joseph and Lucien in the boat. Joseph is looking through a spy-glass 545
and calls to his brother. He points out

a small dismasted boat drifting aimlessly. 546

Joseph points it out to the rowers; they strike out towards the boat. 547

They bring the small boat in with a grappling-hook. The men look 548
into it.

Astonishment of the two brothers. They see 549

Bonaparte unconscious in the bottom of the boat, clutching the torn 550
tricolour.

They prepare to lift him from the little boat aboard the larger one. 551

The exhausted outlaws drag themselves along. They are in a pitiful *552*
state; the two shepherds are with them, ever vigilant. Suddenly their
poor faces light up; hope springs anew, for before them

the beach at Aspretto!

A lonely cove and the sea. *553*

The outlaws find new courage. *554*

Large boat. Bonaparte comes to as they tend to him. 555

He stares about, as if waking from a nightmare, sees the tricolour in 556
his clenched hand, remembers, looks at his brothers and murmurs:

'Quickly, quickly, to Aspretto!'

Joseph gives an order to the rowers, who change course. Energetic 557
activity around Bonaparte, who is recovering his strength.

Cove at Aspretto. Laetitia's family. Great delight. A sailing-boat *558*
appears on the horizon, coming towards them.

* *In the print it is now dawn, the epic 'double tempest' having taken place at night.*

559   Santo-Ricci, who has been keeping watch, sees in the distance the townspeople of Aspretto, who have learned of the outlaws' presence and are coming to the attack with scythes and hammers.

560   The shepherd warns Laetitia. Renewed despair. Are we to perish within sight of safety?

561   Simultaneously the boat approaches.

562   Laetitia and the children utter cries of distress.

563   The clamouring townspeople draw nearer.

564   The boat is very close.

565   The townspeople fire on the family, who take shelter in the hollow of a rock; one of the shepherds fires.

566   One of the townspeople falls. The momentary confusion gains time for the fugitives.

567   The boat is close inshore. Up to their knees in the water, Laetitia and her children wait anxiously.

568   Santo-Ricci refuses to follow them; his duty is done.

569   A villager fires.

570   Santo-Ricci falls from his rock and rolls on the ground. He still refuses to follow them.

571   Santo-Ricci raises himself to his knees and watches, his face haggard.

572   The family boarding the boat.

573   The furious townspeople burst on to the beach and fire.

574   The old shepherd smiles and falls dead.

575   The rowers fire back.

576   Some of the townspeople fall. The others take to their heels.

577   In the boat, joy at their reunion.

578   Tears on Laetitia's face.

579   Bonaparte, with a fire burning in his eyes that we have not seen before, says:

'Now the Bonapartes have one country and one country only: France!'

Prophetic expression on Bonaparte's face.

A cruising English sloop. 580

English flag at the mast top. 581

A young officer is peering intently through a spy-glass. He goes 582
eagerly up to the captain and says:

> **'Captain, permit me to sink that suspicious-looking vessel to
> starboard.'**

The senior officer takes a look.

The sailing-boat bearing Napoléon and his family. 583

Name of the boat: *Le Hasard*. 584

The senior officer says to the young officer: 585

> **'No, young Nelson, don't waste powder and shot on such an
> insignificant target!'**

And he moves away. Nelson clenches his fists. His instinct warns him
that his captain is wrong and that the cannon at his feet, if only he
were permitted to use it, would be doing sterling work. Fuming, he

once more picks up in the sights of his telescope

586 Napoléon's boat drawing farther and farther away.

587 Nelson thoughtful.

588 *Le Hasard.*

589 Nelson musing.

Caesar and his destiny. A future emperor, three kings and a queen on a few square metres between sky and sea.

590 ⟦ Starry night; the boat scuds along, its sail bellying; the sea is calm as a mill-pond. Moon.

591 ⟦ Bonaparte watches at the tiller alone, for everyone has fallen asleep. Caroline and Jérôme at his feet. Picture of peace and serenity contrasting with the turbulent movement of the preceding scenes. The six rowers strike the water with a regular beat.

592 ⟦ The old pilot near Bonaparte observes him in silence.

593 ⟦ He crosses to the rowers and indicates

594 ⟦ Bonaparte at the helm.

595 ⟦ The old pilot cannot hide his astonishment from the rowers. He says:

'That young captain is amazing. I have been watching him these two hours now. He is making straight for France without ever looking at the compass.'

596 ⟦ The rowers stop rowing and stare at him.

597 ⟦ Bonaparte puts the tiller over to compensate for the drift produced by the halt in the rowing.

598 ⟦ The old pilot shows them the compass: 'You see, I'm right!' The rowers agree.

599 ⟦ Bonaparte, his eyes raised.

600 ⟦ The rowers raise their eyes in their turn and look at

601 ⟦ the starry sky.

602 ⟦ The rowers' eyes return to Bonaparte, more and more astonished.

603 ⟦ Bonaparte, his eyes focused upon

one star among all the other stars. 604

The pilot, awestruck, suddenly points out to the rowers 605

the gigantic shadow of Bonaparte, projected in the blue sky by some 606*
miraculous effect of inverse parhelion.

The rowers, agape, cross themselves and mumble prayers. Reveren- 607
tial silence.

Bonaparte, motionless, his eyes piercing deep into the sky, seeing 608
nothing apart from his star, towards which he is steering.]]

An eagle flies down and alights on top of the main-mast, from which 609
a flag flutters.

* *This shot was filmed and included in the final triptych.*

Part Two
Bonaparte and the Terror

'Am I then at the end of the world?'
Bonaparte

TOULON*

[In September 1793, the port of Toulon, where 20,000 English, Italians and Spaniards were entrenched, was besieged by a French army under the command of General Carteaux.]

Having taken refuge in the outskirts of Toulon to escape the September Massacres, Violine and Fleuri had soon realized that the provinces were not left unscathed by the fury of the extreme factions.

610 A band of soldiers in cast-off garments, leading away ten hostages, men, women and children, who are crying, weeping, pleading or singing. Some of the Toulon townspeople try to free them. They come to blows; the relay horses are startled and paw the ground. The soldiers take another ten hostages and drive them along with a whip.

Exterior of a hostelry, which at any other time would be a poet's dream, it is so pretty and picturesque. A large sign: ÇA IRA HOSTELRY. Violine watches from the window. Her face bears a new expression, thoughtful and grave.

611 Interior. Fleuri's inn at Toulon, as charming and picturesque as the exterior. Three or four alarmed citizens come in to take refuge. Commotion. Merchants, farmers, several soldiers of the siege garrison. Nervous excitement. Tristan Fleuri, as innkeeper, is serving. An old woman helps him, along with young Marcellin.

612 Violine, from behind. She has been looking out of the window; she turns round, listening. She is wearing a pretty Arlésienne costume. She pays particular attention to the words of the man who is talking.

* *The Battle of Toulon has survived in several slightly different montages, none of which match the script; also, when Gance made the sound-track version of 1935, he cannibalized unique reels and negatives (including an earlier Pathé Napoléon, the remains of which have just been discovered hidden amongst the Gance reels at the Cinémathèque Française) for superimpositions suggesting all the different Napoleonic battles. Except for sections which we know with certainty were never shot, we have not gone into the myriad subtle changes that Gance made during the shooting of the battle, since the overall events are the same. The major addition is the inclusion of the murder of Marat by Charlotte Corday, which took place shortly before the Battle of Toulon. Charlotte Corday visits Marat on the pretext of bringing him a list of suspects. Marat, in his bath, orders the housekeeper to leave them alone. Corday starts to read the names, then, as he writes, pulls a dagger and stabs him. She tries to escape, but is captured before she manages to leave the apartment. The scene ends with a long, beautifully lit close-up of Marat's face. It is one of the most celebrated scenes of the film, as well as being the scene for which Antonin Artaud, who played Marat, is best remembered.*

Her face registers every shade of anguish and distress.

Violine and a group of three men. One of the men is sketching 613
something. She moves closer to look. The man does not hide what
he thinks, but shouts in reckless excitement:

**'Civil war, however horrible it may be, is nothing, my friends,
compared to the ghastly tragedy of our undefended frontiers.'**

And, indicating the map on the wall, he proves his point. A map of
France. Animated drawings, showing the dire situation of the frontiers
and the retreat of the French armies.

Violine and Fleuri before the map of France. Reverently they make 614
the sign of the cross; they look at one another. Their hearts could
suffer no greater pain. They say nothing.

A mud-caked horseman arrives, exhausted. They all rush to him. 615
They ply him with questions. He replies, his morale utterly destroyed:

'They're retreating everywhere! It's a disaster. France is lost!'

Violine. Her face radiates a grave strength. She goes out. 616

Violine's room leading off the inn. It is very neat. Flowers everywhere. 617
Engravings of heroic subjects on the wall. Violine furtively bolts her
door, pulls out her bed and searches.

A hiding-place from which she brings out three books, two mysterious 618
pictures and a distaff with her spinning-wool. To take them out she
has had to move a crusader's sword, which she replaces reverently in
its hiding-place. She pushes back the bed, hides her books and
pictures in an apron and goes out, while

(interior, inn) the excited Fleuri, leaving the discussion and carried 619
away by his warlike enthusiasm, goes into another room.

[[Waiting from day to day for his call to the army, Tristan Fleuri, already a soldier in spirit . . .

Fleuri's room. A dummy figure made up from a bolster, with 'Enemy 620
of the Republic' written across the top. Three sabres, some guns,
some cartridge-belts; it is more like a miniature arsenal than a
bedroom. A panoply of arms clutters the whole of one wall, with old
guns, ancient suits of armour, knives, pistols.

621 〖 Tristan is nervously reading through his gun handbook. He levels his gun, puts it down, goes through the motions of reloading, all the time running on the spot.

622 〖 Marcellin watches from the doorway. His eyes are gleaming. He slips into his father's room. He is carrying a tray with a stew-pot on it.

623 〖 Fleuri, still running on the spot, plunges his bayonet into the bolster with such violence that the bayonet drives into the wood on the other side, and he has difficulty in pulling it out again. Brandishing his gun above his head, he belabours the head of the bolster with his bayonet, still running on the spot.

624 〖 This heroic spectacle sends Marcellin into transports of admiration and he begins to beat the charge on his stew-pot with two spoons.

625 〖 Fleuri turns round, smiles at him, and mimes: 'Louder!'

626 〖 Marcellin doubles his efforts. The old woman, astonished at such a din, comes running in on her shaky legs and totters back in bewilderment.

627 〖 The bolster is now no more than a cloud of down, the table is overturned, and the victorious Tristan Fleuri is banging on a tin wash-tub to show his son how the drumsticks are held; his son tries to copy him on his stew-pot. Suddenly Marcellin breaks off and shoots a question at Fleuri: 'How old was the little drummer-boy Agricole Viala when he died?' Fleuri replies, 'Thirteen.' Innocent, charming smile. He counts on his fingers and says, 'What luck! I've still got six years to live!'*

**628 〖 Dusk, pastoral scene of great beauty. An atmosphere of intense, profound poetry arising from the time of day, nature, the people and the setting. Hundreds of sheep are grazing, all facing the same direction. An old shepherd is dozing. Near him Violine, kneeling, is

* *Marcellin, in one of his attempts to join the army, appears as a little drummer boy during the Battle of Toulon. He is given these lines then, in the only scene in which the character Moustache, who appears so often in the script, actually appears in the foreground of the film. This scene, with the dialogue as titles, immediately precedes scene 827.*
** *In his notes for Kevin Brownlow, Gance says this sequence was not shot; however, Mme Annabella, who played Violine in the film, remembers it as the 'Joan of Arc' sequence, and at least one still of it survives. Albert Dieudonné, in his book Le Tzar Napoléon, published in 1927 and loosely based on the filming of* Napoléon, *also mentions the shooting of this sequence. Perhaps Gance tried it, then abandoned it. It appears in no other documentation of the time.*

fervently praying, her hands folded, her face raised towards an old oak tree, through which filters the setting sun. A bird on a branch is silhouetted in the foreground.

⟦ Violine. Her face wet with tears. Her expression is one of infinite purity and her eyes gaze at a fixed point with remarkable con-centration.   629

⟦ Nothing moves. Only the prayer rises like incense, almost visible, so deeply does she feel it.   630

⟦ Fleuri at the inn. At the door he says to Marcellin: 631

'I'm sure I'll find her still playing shepherdesses, same as every other day.'

Fleuri goes out.

⟦ Flock of sheep. Fleuri comes up and stops. He looks, smiles, is about to speak, then changes his mind for, to his surprise, he sees   632

⟦ Violine's face running with tears, ecstatic, in prayer.   633

⟦ 'What can this mean?' he wonders. His eyes are drawn towards the ground by   634

⟦ Violine's books and pictures behind her.   635

⟦ Fleuri bends down. His surprise increases. He looks at the books, then   636

⟦ at Violine, who has not noticed him and is still praying.   637

⟦ Fleuri looks at the books again.   638

⟦ *Life of Joan of Arc*   639
The Divine Mission of Joan of Arc
The Deeds of Joan of Arc
Two Popular Pictures
The Clothes Worn by Joan of Arc

⟦ Fleuri raises his head. Intense emotion. He looks at one of the pictures. It is   640

⟦ *Joan of Arc at Domrémy*. A distaff at her side, she is praying beneath an oak tree.   641

⟦ Fleuri raises his eyes and sees   642

643 ⟦ Violine beneath the oak tree, in the same pose as in the picture, her distaff at her side.

644 ⟦ Fleuri turns his head.

645 ⟦ On the road, in the distance, soldiers forcing peasants to give them what they want. This is reminiscent of the Burgundian hordes.

646 ⟦ Fleuri calls: 'Violine!'

647 ⟦ She turns round, shocked, sees her father, smiles in embarrassment, furtively wipes away her tears.

648 ⟦ She walks towards him, looks for her books, does not see them. He brings them out from behind his back. 'I saw!' he says to her. She pretends astonishment: 'What did you see?'

649 ⟦ Fleuri looks at her with intense, inexpressible emotion. She lowers her eyes. She sees that he has understood. Golden silence. He is lost for words; two tears well from his eyes. She throws herself into his arms, crying out:

'At all costs someone *must* save France, Papa!'

She sobs. He clasps her to his breast and rocks her. A long silence. Their grief. They embody the tragedy of France. Tristan asks her gently:

'Have you heard the voices, then?'

650 ⟦ Violine raises her tear-drenched face to her father and replies sadly:

'No, they haven't come yet.'

651 ⟦ She adds:

'It's a long way to come, Papa. It takes time!'

This thought disarms Tristan Fleuri, but Violine, suddenly excited, motions to her father, her hand on her mouth, to be quiet. She looks eagerly towards the oak tree.

652 ⟦ The oak. The crimson glow of the sunset lingering among the softly stirring branches.

653 ⟦ Violine, overwhelmed, murmurs:

'Listen!'

654 ⟦ A nightingale on a branch.

Fleuri smiles and says:

'It's only a nightingale.'

Violine. The shadow of the nightingale on a branch gently swaying 656
in the wind flickers across her face. She sees that it is so. 'Yes, Papa,
it's only a nightingale!' she says sadly.

They must go back home. He helps her up and they move away, he 657
carrying the books, and she the distaff.

The pastures. They are walking along. Suddenly she stops, clutching 658
her heart, and in the greatest agitation points to something in front
of her.

Between the branches, tossing in the wind, a white apparition. 659

They move forward softly. Suddenly Tristan's expression undergoes 660
a rapid change, for

it is only some sheets drying between two trees. 661

She realizes that she was mistaken. Her dejection. She cries softly, 662
like a tiny brook. 'Come, little one, come.' He leads her away, holding
her close, trying to console her. The sheep follow her right up to the
fence.]]

Bonaparte had just been appointed captain, second in command, to the artillery at Toulon . . .

Bonaparte walking along. He is carrying an enormous volume of 663
Jean-Jacques Rousseau under his arm. He looks quite bizarre. The
Duchesse d'Abrantès described him thus: 'At this period of his life
Napoleon was ugly. Since then, a complete transformation has come
about. I am not speaking of the dazzling radiance of his glory, I mean
no more than the physical change which has developed gradually
over the last seven years. Thus, everything about him which, at
Toulon, was bony, sallow, sickly even, has filled out, grown clear and
more beautiful. Features which were almost all angular and pointed
have now filled out, for his face now has some flesh on it whereas
before it was all skin and bone. His look and his smile are as attractive
as ever. His hairstyle, so strange to us nowadays in the Pont d'Arcole
engravings, was quite simple in those days, for the dandies he railed
against so strongly wore theirs much longer; but his complexion was

so sallow at that time, and he took so little care over his appearance, that his unkempt, ill-powdered hair made him look most unpleasant. His hands were thin, long and black. He walked with an awkward, tentative gait, a frightful round hat worn down over his eyes, his two ill-powdered side-locks escaping from under it to fall over the collar of his coat, wearing one boot without a top, the other badly polished.'*

He stops in surprise.

664 A battery among the vines. The sea in the background. One might think this was a grape harvest rather than a war. Indolence, carelessness. Men are playing cards. The dominant feature of these scenes is the excessive, shameful poverty and the complete lack of discipline. Let us take a brief look at the state of the army France was about to put under Bonaparte's command. He walks by, dumbfounded, and looks to the right. He sees

665 a soldier sitting among the vines, his great puffy face stained with black grapes.

666 Bonaparte looks to the left. He sees

667 two cannon, muzzles pointing skyward; between them is suspended a cord on which socks are drying.

668 Bonaparte turns round. He sees

669 men playing boules with shot.

670 Bonaparte leaves.

671 A mortar filled with grapes. It is being used as a press to make rough wine. Two soldiers are engaged in this rustic work. Bonaparte passes by. Nobody takes any notice.

672 〚 Bonaparte walks along. A leg dangles in front of him, with a filthy, bare foot. He raises his head. It is

673 〚 a soldier asleep among the branches of an olive tree, one of his legs dangling in space.〛 Bonaparte looks to the right and, although rarely moved to surprise, is flabbergasted. He sees

674 a colossal soldier watering some nasturtiums, which have climbed over a peaceful cannon and have clearly been entwining their flowery arms around it for some months.

* *Duchesse d'Abrantès*, Mémoires.

74

Bonaparte can stand it no longer. He folds his arms and glares so   675
fixedly at the man that he drops his watering-can. Bonaparte walks
on, [[but the soldier, Moustache, furious at having been unnerved by
that glare, shouts:

**'By Moustache's honour! I, Moustache, will eat that greenhorn
for salad!'**

He means what he says, and he turns slowly and threateningly in
Bonaparte's direction, revealing a part of his anatomy, for his uniform
is too small and has been cut open at the back and is held together
with laces like a woman's corset.

His comrades look fearfully in Bonaparte's direction, for it is well   676
known that gunner Moustache always keeps his word.

Fleuri's room at Toulon, more cluttered than ever with arms, trophies   677
and military engravings. Tristan Fleuri is lying on the floor. On his
stomach and chest a vast assortment of very heavy objects, among
them a wash-tub which Marcellin is filling with all kinds of objects.

Inn. Violine is pulling the enormous firedogs from the hearth. They   678
are too heavy for her. She calls Marcellin, who comes to help her;
the two carry the firedogs out.

Fleuri's room. Violine and Marcellin come in and place one of the   679
enormous firedogs on top of the other objects on Fleuri's chest.

Fleuri's apoplectic face. Absolute sincerity – like Don Quixote. He   680
gropes for a book, which is open at a particular page, and he gets
Violine to re-read it for him, to convince himself of the efficacy of his
method:

GREAT MEN

**To harden himself, Caesar slept with lead weights
on his chest . . .**

'Yes, yes. Put on the other firedog, children!' – 'But, Papa, you'll   681
burst!' – 'Violine, please, do what your father tells you. Look! Caesar
did it!' And Violine, with much misgiving, dumps the other enormous
firedog on to her father's chest, with Marcellin's help.

Fleuri gasps like a carp out of water, but he steels himself. Sweating,   682
panting, smiling, he orders: 'Climb into the wash-tub, Marcellin!'

683 [[The obedient Marcellin, watched anxiously by Violine, who really fears an explosion, climbs into the wash-tub. A noise. They all listen.]]

The painter Carteaux, general-in-chief of the armies besieging Toulon.

684   Inn. Carteaux and his general staff come blustering in. He is dressed in a stiffened blue coat, seamed with gold, his head is thrown back, and he is complacently stroking his big, black moustache which sets off his fair complexion and handsome face to perfection. He has no merit apart from his fine presence and his Jacobinism. His staff officers in brilliant uniforms bow and scrape obsequiously round him. With Carteaux is a dazzling group of members of the Convention – Fréron, Barras, Salicetti, Robespierre the younger, Gasparin. Carteaux is being showered with compliments. He protests with false humility. Horses can be seen outside.

685 [[Fleuri's room. He gets up to run to these illustrious customers and upsets everything that was piled on top of him, including Marcellin, with a noise like thunder.]]

686   Inn. Violine comes to serve. She passes

687   Salicetti, who takes her by the chin. She pushes him away. He sniggers.

688 [[Bonaparte questions a bizarre-looking sentry, who points to the inn.]]

689   Carteaux drinks: a Jordaens. Fleuri is busy serving, here, there, everywhere. Violine is helping him. Carteaux laughs. Fatuousness. Stupidity. Bonaparte appears in the doorway.

690   Violine freezes. Her expression is endearing. She retreats into the shadows, her heart beating fast, and points him out to Fleuri, whose pleasure is obvious.

691   Bonaparte marches straight up to Carteaux. Carteaux, taken aback by this unexpected intrusion of a junior officer, and one of such a sorry appearance, when he has all his generals with him, demands:

'What have you come here for, young man?'

From his pocket Bonaparte produces his commission, presents it to Carteaux and says:

76

'I have come as second-in-command of the siege artillery,
sir.'

A laugh on Carteaux's face, then an ironic pout. He replies with a
theatrical gesture:

'Artillery? Why, we don't need any; we shall take Toulon with
the sword and bayonet.'

Grandiloquently he calls all the officers present to witness; they bow
in agreement, thus underlining the scorn with which Carteaux regards
Bonaparte and his commission.

Bonaparte. A barely perceptible smile flits across his face. He prepares   692
to leave.

Carteaux holds him back by one of his coat-tails and, showing him   693
the ordnance map which is being unfolded by an officer, he asks him:

'If you were in my place, what would *you* do?'

Carteaux winks to the officers to come and amuse themselves at
Bonaparte's expense. They all gather round Bonaparte, who looks at
the map. He appears aloof. With great ease he explains his plan.

Bonaparte's eyes flash.   694

The map, upon which twenty different images merge and melt into   695
one another – geometrical lines, miniature armies, forts blowing up,
diagram of a fleet burning.

Bonaparte's finger moves to the edge of the small anchorage, to the   696
Aiguillette fort.

Bonaparte. His impressive manner. He says: 697

'[[Toulon is there.]] Once this fort is taken the English will
abandon the town!'

Suppressed ironic laughter. Carteaux alone bursts out laughing
without restraint and says:

'Well, Captain Cannon, one can see that geography is not your
strong point!'

Violine, overwhelmed with love, standing motionless, and Fleuri,   698
overwhelmed with admiration.

Carteaux says to Bonaparte with an authoritative air full of patronizing   699

77

bonhomie and conceit:

> 'I trust you will concede, young man, that first of all artillery
> is useless, and secondly . . .'

700   A red-hot cannonball crashes into the room. Everyone takes to their heels in confusion. Some come back in, some go out through the doors, the windows. Smoke.

701   Bonaparte has not moved a muscle; he raises his eyes; he sees (with a smile on his face):

702   General Carteaux sitting on the ground like a big, terrified child.

703   Bonaparte kicks the cannonball with his boot into the ashes of the hearth and concludes the general's sentence:

> '. . . secondly, it is most unpleasant!'

704   Carteaux struggles to his feet and runs out, while Bonaparte sits down, unfolding the map of Toulon.

705   Violine picks up one of Bonaparte's gloves, which has fallen to the ground; she retreats into the shadow next to Fleuri. He, unable to contain his joy any longer, says to Violine:

> 'This time I shall not hesitate. I shall remind him of Brienne.'

706   He composes himself, because this will need courage. He approaches Bonaparte as he bends over his map, and stammers, for at times of great emotional stress he does stammer:

> 'C-c-c . . . c-c-ca-captain . . . I was at B-b-bri . . .'

707   Bonaparte raises his eagle eyes and nails Tristan to the floor with his reply:

> 'Bread, olives and *silence*!'

708   Fleuri, struck dumb, backs away, stumbling over himself.

709   Violine tenderly raises Bonaparte's glove to her face and strokes her cheek with it, lost in thought. Her tears flow.

710/711   Bonaparte paces to and fro. He studies the map.

712   Marcellin has surreptitiously taken Bonaparte's hat and put it on his

78

head; he has his sword, too, and is walking thoughtfully behind him, copying his movements.

Violine. Her vexation and embarrassment. She scolds him. He puts down the hat. She smiles sweetly through her tears. 713

At Bonaparte's instigation the incompetent Carteaux was replaced by the worthy Dugommier, who was quick to realize the exceptional qualities of his little artillery captain.

Elegant office. A council of generals presided over by Dugommier, 714 fifty-five, noble stature, open face, tanned by the sun, wide, high forehead, keen, blazing eyes, bushy white hair which accentuates the fire of his gaze and gives his features more prominence and vivacity.

The old general of artillery, du Teil, feeble and infirm, scarcely able to walk; General Lapoype, worried; General Marescot and Adjutant-General Victor. They are arguing animatedly over a large map spread out on the table. They appear not to be listening to one another. Through the closed window Bonaparte can be seen, with his back to them, in the barrack square.

Barrack square. One might almost be in hell. Under the supervision 715 of Bonaparte, issuing sharp, precise orders, heavy cart-horses are being trained for the artillery along with the carters, who are no less terrified. Petards are being exploded under the horses' hoofs and in front of them. The square is riven with flashes; the horses paw the ground, kick and rear. The carters run away, come back, run away again. Drums beat deafening tattoos into a horse's ear, while a bugle sounds the charge into the other ear and a soldier pricks its flanks with a bayonet.

Bonaparte keeps everything going with curt orders. The men who 716 address him are extremely respectful. We sense that he has already been accepted. Thunderous noise and activity in the square.

Dugommier's office. They cannot reach an agreement. Dugommier 717 thinks for a moment, calms them down, then goes to the window, opens it, calls Bonaparte and turns back into the room.

Dugommier's office. Bonaparte outside, Dugommier inside. 718 Dugommier shows him the map and asks his advice. Bonaparte gives his opinion soberly and with precision. Dugommier thanks him and returns to the senior officers, having closed the window.

719   They all concur with Bonaparte. General du Teil asks a question. Fresh difficulties arise. Dugommier opens the window and asks Bonaparte. The young captain gives his opinion on this new point with the same incisiveness and rapidity. Dugommier passes on the information. It is received with applause: 'Excellent, excellent, let us continue.'

720   Barrack square. A carter is frightened of his rearing horse, so to show him how, Bonaparte leaps astride the horse and makes it waltz in the midst of the fire as if in a circus.

721   The soldiers and troopers look on in amazement at this display of courage and sang-froid.

722   Dugommier's office. Continuation of the general staff meeting. Yet another ticklish point. For the third time Dugommier opens the window and calls.

723   Bonaparte canters up.

724   His horse rears up on its hindlegs, giving the impression that it is about to come into Dugommier's office. Dugommier backs away. 'Come and join us at the table.'

725   Bonaparte jumps down, climbs through the window and stands waiting. Dugommier invites him to come and sit next to him. Bonaparte salutes respectfully, hesitates; then, since Dugommier and the other generals insist, he sits down. They question him.

726   He begins to expound, inscrutable.

727   They are all attentive and nod in approval while he is speaking.

⟦The mobilization of Tristan Fleuri

728 ⟦   Inn. A gendarme delivers an envelope to Tristan. He calls Violine and Marcellin, who come running to him. He is trembling with joy. He does not dare open it. He gloats over it, and as he looks at it he sees

729 ⟦   the letter. Superimposed, a tiny general, Tristan Fleuri, capering ridiculously.

730 ⟦   His bliss. His hands are shaking too much to open the envelope; he asks Violine to do it, and she reads in astonishment:

Citizen Tristan Fleuri is appointed cook to the armies of the Republic and . . .

[[Fleuri. Expression like Don Quixote's on realizing that Mambrino's   731
helmet was a barber's basin, and two tears well up in his poor eyes.
He is too mortified to speak.

[[Marcellin comes out of his room dragging a long sabre.   732

[[Marcellin. He shows his indignation by stamping his foot, and goes   733
out.

[[Violine and Fleuri. She raises doleful eyes. They look at each other.   734
Long silence, then Fleuri bursts out sobbing. Violine tries to console
him, like a mother.]]

Inspection

Dugommier and his staff pass by. Very nearly the same lack of   735
discipline as in the preceding scenes. Men are smoking, drinking;
they salute and then sit down again; they play cards. The senior
officers move away. Suddenly, on a signal given by a man as he comes
running up, discipline materializes as if by magic. Pipes are put
away, bottles are hidden. Men start working, polishing, standing to
attention, straightening their clothes. You would think that Carnot
himself was about to pass by. It is only Bonaparte, followed by Junot
and Muiron. Bonaparte already wields such authority over the men
that he is feared infinitely more than the generals. He passes in his
poor tattered and patched uniform, pretending not to see this show
of discipline. He stops before a bizarre soldier wearing a bearskin
right down over his eyes.* [[Suddenly the man shrinks about a foot,
as if his feet had sunk into the ground. Bonaparte opens the long coat
enveloping this strange soldier. Explanation: it is Marcellin, who had
climbed up on a drum, his head swamped in the enormous bearskin.

[[The drum has caved in. Marcellin's bare feet are now inside it.]]   736

* *From here the scene differs, and what follows was transferred to the single-screen version
of the film, to the review of the Army of Italy, when poor little Marcellin makes his last
ditch attempt to join the army. What happens at Toulon is: Napoléon lifts the bearskin,
Marcellin looks at him with great, beseeching eyes, followed by scene 737. (The single-
screen ending, which Gance put together in 1928, does not of course appear in this script.)*

737 Bonaparte tweaks his ear, without laughing, and dismisses him, saying:

'Too short!'

Laughter. Bonaparte turns round. They all freeze. Marcellin weeps. Bonaparte leaves. Everyone breathes again and goes back to playing and drinking, when he suddenly reappears. Mad scramble to come to order again. He frowns. He says nothing and leaves. This time they do not relax.

738 Dugommier and his staff in a protected dip in the terrain arrive at a bastion under fire. Dugommier is about to go in. Lapoype stops him and says:

'The bastion is untenable. The army commissioners are having the guns withdrawn.'

And, indeed,

739 the brilliant, gold-braided army commissioners,* among them Salicetti, under cover of the dip in the terrain, are supervising the withdrawal of a piece of artillery, which is proving exceedingly difficult, with men falling like flies. Dugommier and his staff come up to the group.

740 Bonaparte arrives at the bastion. Junot and Muiron try to prevent him going in. He looks at them commandingly; he goes in. They follow him.

741 The bastion. The wall has been severely breached by the enemy shot. Bonaparte commands the artillerymen hauling the gun to about-face. They hesitate and point to the group of Convention members. Bonaparte goes over to them.

742 Salicetti, in a violent temper, speaks peremptorily to Bonaparte. 'We decided the position of this battery!' Bonaparte replies cuttingly:

'Look after your business as deputies and let me look after mine as an artilleryman. This battery stays here, or I go!'

743 Salicetti. His rage and hatred burst out:

'Heads have rolled for less than this, my friend!'

* *Convention members appointed to supervise the army.*

82

The other Convention members intervene. Dugommier wavers. The   744
whole group retreats, for the shells are falling thick and fast.

Bonaparte leaps to the entrance of the bastion and shouts to the   745
gunners: 'About face! Take that gun back inside!' [[They drag the
gun in and come running out, one wounded in the face, the other
falling dead several paces farther on. Bonaparte goes in first, followed
by Junot and Muiron.

[[Interior of the shattered bastion. Twenty or so dead bodies on the   746
ground. Two cannon. The shower of enemy shells continues. Not a
soul alive. The position appears untenable. Through a breach can be
seen the anchorage and, in the far distance, the English fleet.
Bonaparte surveys this scene of horror, impassively. He sees something, calls Junot and speaks to him. Junot goes out immediately.
Bonaparte turns in another direction and calls

[[Gunner Moustache, who has been wounded and is running away.   747
Hearing Bonaparte's shout, he comes back again. Bonaparte questions him: 'How is it that all the men have deserted their posts? You
will stay here!']] The giant Moustache, his face covered in blood,
replies:

'Impossible, Captain!'

Bonaparte: 748

'Impossible is not French!'

Moustache. He is quelled by the famous reply. Now his amazement   749
outweighs his terror. He salutes and returns to his gun.

Junot comes running in with a batten of wood, a plank, a pot of paint   750
and brush. While Muiron sets up the batten, Junot paints in large
letters on a plank, at Bonaparte's dictation:

Battery of. . .   751

He is about to go on when . . .

A flash. A cannonball crashes in and envelops them in smoke. Have   752
they been killed? The smoke clears. Bonaparte continues his scrutiny
of the anchorage; Junot has not budged; he finishes off his notice.

Battery of the Fearless.   753

He is about to get up when another shell falls at his feet and bursts,   754

83

knocking him over and showering him with earth, masonry and all sorts of debris.

755   Junot gets up, unflurried. He looks at

756   his plank covered with earth.

757   He looks up at Bonaparte and says with a smile:

'Fine! I shan't need any sand now!'

He shakes the board. The sand has dried the paint. Muiron fixes the board to the top of the batten, while Bonaparte grasps Junot by the shoulders and looks him full in the face, saying:

'Friend Junot, I like you!'

758   Noticing a dead man's drum, Bonaparte says to Murion: 'Beat muster.' Muiron picks up the drum and goes out of the bastion. He can be seen beating muster.

759   The soldiers rally and move towards Muiron, grumbling and cursing.

760   The men arrive and confer. Shells. Smoke. Muiron points out the inscription raised over the bastion: BATTERY OF THE FEARLESS.

761   French courage blossoms once more. Vying with one another, they all rush to be first at the breach in the bastion.

762 ⟦ Interior of the bastion. Bonaparte shows Junot

763 ⟦ the men jammed in the doorway in their zeal to get inside. They swarm into the bastion like lions. Four words have sufficed to transform them.

764 ⟦ Bonaparte. Flashing eyes.

765 ⟦ Dugommier returning with his staff. From some way off he sees

766 ⟦ the mass of soldiers surging eagerly forward at the very spot where, only a short while before, there had been nothing but death and panic.

767 ⟦ Doorway of the bastion. There are already too many men, and there are still fifty soldiers trying to get in. Sergeant Junot is stopping them. A wounded man is carried out. 'Ah! Room for another one!' says Junot. A man cheerfully goes in. Another casualty: 'One more!' says Muiron. Another man goes in, and the others wait impatiently.⟧

768   Dugommier comes to see for himself what is going on. His officers follow him. Near the breach Dugommier sees the notice and looks inside . . .

Bonaparte is organizing the defence as if he were in barracks, totally   769
calm, precise, without a single gesture. Everything is executed in
perfect order in the midst of cannonballs and corpses.

Dugommier is full of admiration for 'Captain Cannon', as Carteaux   770
called him, and as he leads his officers away, he says to du Teil in a
low voice:

'If we are to take Toulon, we had better leave it to him.'

[Bonaparte. A shell falls at his feet, its fuse burning. Bonaparte quickly   771
seizes it and throws it out through the breach, where it explodes. As
if nothing had happened, he goes out with Junot and Muiron.
Moustache, drunk with joy, climbs up on to his gun-carriage and
shouts:

'On Moustache's honour! The dialogue with glory has begun!'

[[Every man is quivering with suppressed elation.   772

[[Outside the breach. The men waiting impatiently to go in stand aside   773
respectfully for the young captain. There is a feeling that Moustache's
words are true.]]

Dip in the terrain. Dugommier confronts Bonaparte and says to him   774
in front of his staff officers:

**'Captain Bonaparte, I appoint you commander-in-chief of
the artillery.'**

Salicetti burns with hatred and jealousy.   775

Coolly, Bonaparte salutes and moves off.   776

[A cooking-pot; a hand stirring a sauce. It is Fleuri. He is gloomy.   777

[Another cook near Fleuri looks at him and shrugs his shoulders.   778
Marcellin comes in. He is carrying a torn drum and is dragging
behind him the skirts of a light infantryman's jacket. He comes and
sits down. Fleuri tries to embrace him. The child pushes him away
with disdain and flings to the ground the cook's hat which was on the
table.

[Fleuri weeps, and his tears   779

[drip one by one into the sauce which he is gently stirring.]]   780

29 November 1793, when all Europe had its eyes focused upon Toulon, considered the world's most formidable fortress.

*781   It is six o'clock in the morning. Bonaparte on horseback looks through a telescope, then sets off at a gallop.

782   Dugommier, taking his breakfast in a dressing-gown, is laughing with several generals in various states of undress. Bonaparte bursts in and speaks. Immediately

783   there is a commotion. Bonaparte gallops away.

A surprise sortie by the English troops under the leadership of O'Hara.

784   The English troops advance; they make a powerful impression.

. . . Piedmontese.

785   Piedmontese troops advance. General Gravina.

. . . Spanish.

786   Spanish troops advance. General Pignatelli.

. . . Neapolitan.

787   Neapolitan troops advance. General Valdès.

While Sidney Smith . . .

788   Contrast. The English captain, dry, forbidding, unmoving, phlegmatic.

. . . keeps watch over the French fleet trapped at anchor as over some kind of prey.

789   The French fleet at anchor.

790   Sidney Smith. His face is filled with savage delight.

791   Terrible artillery fire. The French retreat.

792   Dugommier on the belvedere panics. His orders are clumsy and, seeing the danger, he orders the charge and leaves.

793   Bonaparte arrives at the belvedere. 'Where is Dugommier's guard?' Gone, is the reply. He bites his lip. The situation is grave. He looks through his telescope and sees

---

* *The following sequence, if it was shot at all, was almost certainly not shot as it appears here. Some fragments of it appear, in a different context, later on in the battle.*

Dugommier in an awkward spot and losing ground. 794

Animated map of the situation. 795

Dugommier. Forced to retreat fighting. 796

Animated map. Bonaparte, motionless, is worried. 797

Animated map. 798

The French troops fall back. 799

Animated map. 800

Dugommier in despair. He retreats, suffering heavy losses. 801

Animated map. 802

Bonaparte's anxiety. 803

Battery of the Convention. It is taken by the English. The French are being slaughtered. O'Hara is exultant. 804

Dugommier is wounded and fights as he retreats. His soldiers rescue him. 805

Belvedere. Bonaparte. The wounded Dugommier is brought in, raging. Bonaparte whispers in his ear: 806

    'You left without an order from me, Papa Dugommier!'

Dugommier acquiesces. 'You command!'

Bonaparte says: 807

    'Order the retreat and call a council of war for this evening.'

Astonishment. Shame on all sides. But his impassiveness commands obedience. Dugommier weeps with rage, but acquiesces and gives the order. The officers disperse in different directions.

Totally unperturbed, Bonaparte says to Dugommier: 808

    'Tomorrow night, General, you will sleep in Toulon.'

Profound impression on the senior officers and the members of the Convention. Dugommier looks at him.

Jubilation and cheers from the enemy. 809

⟦ A cannon overturned on top of some dead men. A movement. A heave. The gun topples and keels over, and from under the bodies 810 the giant Moustache, black with powder and blood, like an epic hero, emerging from his coma as if waking from a sleep, rises up, sneezes, and says simply:

'I must have caught a cold here!'

He sneezes again.]]

811   The French council of war is ending. Candlelight. It is evening. Bonaparte is speaking. Respectful silence. Dugommier nods with approval; he begins to speak, but becomes confused and lets Bonaparte take over again.

812   Bonaparte's hand on the map of Toulon spread out on the table. It points to the Little Gibraltar fort.

813   Bonaparte speaks.

814   Diagram of the Little Gibraltar fort in profile, one hundred and fifty metres across, with its horizontally piled pine trunks, its embrasures boarded up, a double bank of chevaux-de-frise and a line of felled trees as a barricade. A battle of figures and words flashes on and off, a mathematician's exposition of an assault, totally precise. Among other things we read:

> Defence 3,000 men. Attack 2,500, 3 columns:
> Delaborde, Dugommier, Victor.
> Defence 20 cannon, 4 mortars.
> Ditch 3 metres deep, 5 wide.
> Attack 60 of 24, 20 mortars.
> 4 guns of 24 – 17° at 900 toises.
> 2 guns of 18 – 43° at 2,000 toises.

Geometric parabolas show where the French shells are to strike, the figures disappear and, still over the diagram of the fort, these words appear on their own:

> One o'clock in the morning.
> Aiguillette and Faron

and two seconds later:

Three o'clock in the morning.
Victory or retreat.

815   Bonaparte, questioningly:

'I request the attack for midnight tonight.'

And he waits.

Unanimous approval of his plan. 816

Enemy council of war. Candlelight. Present are Admiral Hood, the 817
Sardinian Major Saluzzo, the Spanish Colonel Luis de Ariza, the
Neapolitan Brigadier-General Izquierdo, Admiral Trogoff, Sir Hyde
Parker, Admirals Langara, Gravina, Fortegerri, Generals Dundas,
Valdès, Chevalier Thaon de Revel and Sir Gilbert Elliot.

In contrast with the French council of war, everyone is speaking at 818
once. They lack a leader.

Admiral Hood brings the commotion to order and says, forcefully: 819

**'We are masters of the sea; the French fleet is our hostage.
With 20,000 English, Spanish and Italian troops our forts are
impregnable. I feel no anxiety.'**

And he sits down.

Enemy council of war. The commotion begins again, louder than 820
ever.

French council of war. Everyone is standing. 821

Amid a respectful silence, Bonaparte, with his finger on Little 822
Gibraltar, says:

**'[Toulon has but one weak point – the Aiguillette promontory.
If we take it, the town is ours. We shall therefore storm the
town at midnight.]**

Order, calm, silence.'

They leave quietly. 823

The sky. Black clouds. Storm imminent. 824

Preparations for battle; dark night. The only light comes from 825
flickering lanterns on the ground. It is raining.

A sort of mire or marshy pond. Thirty or so men are standing, 826
motionless, waist-deep in the water. Their leader says:

**'Have patience. It's seven o'clock now. We'll surprise the
enemy tomorrow morning at five!'**

Moustache mockingly says to some recruits, who are blue with cold:

'You can't smoke, but you can sit down.'

He laughs. The leader motions him to be quiet, for Bonaparte is passing by. All stand motionless. The rain comes on harder. Moustache sneezes.

827　Dugommier looks at his watch:

Ten minutes to midnight.

Dugommier looks up at the sky, worried by the storm which is about to break.

828　French column ready for the attack. Impressive, restrained enthusiasm. Admiring, reverent silence as Bonaparte passes by. The rain is torrential, falling in an almost impenetrable curtain.

829　Knoll. Staff officers, illuminated by the lantern. The rain is still falling. Dugommier looks at the time.

Midnight.

830　Knoll. Dugommier exchanges glances with Bonaparte and gives the order to attack.

831　The artillery thunders out. Twenty cannon spit fire.

832　Then twenty more.

833　Then twenty more.

[Now, revealing a magnificent plan of attack, he flung Victor's and Delaborde's columns against the Sardinian and Spanish wings . . .]

834　In the downpour Victor's column charges.

835　Delaborde's column charges.

[. . . keeping for himself the assault on the English in the centre.]

836　The Convention members in a tent torn by the wind. Salicetti shrieks to the others:

'Bonaparte has just committed the greatest crime in history. An assault on a night like this. It is such a folly that even his head cannot pay for it!'

The other Convention members are of much the same opinion.

A road blocked with chevaux-de-frise and sandbags. The French 837
become entangled in the barricade under a continuous hail of bullets
that decimates them.

At the foot of Little Gibraltar. The French are checked. The troops 838
retreat under the downward fire of the English.

Dugommier comes to the rescue; the rain pours down harder than 839
ever.

The cannon sink into the mud. 840

Soldiers' legs sunk calf-deep in mud. 841

Rout of Delaborde's column. General Delaborde is seriously 842
wounded. The French panic.

Delaborde's column rushes headlong into Victor's column, which 843
was running towards it. They fire at each other until they recognize
who they are. They flee together. Panic is everywhere.

Dugommier is repulsed and withdraws. He is dragged away back- 844
wards by force.

Bonaparte beside a battery, trying to see: impossible . . . to hear: 845
impossible.

Dugommier, brought back by some of his loyal men, is in despair. 846
Bonaparte comes to his side. Dugommier leans over to speak in his
ear and says, drawing his hand across his neck, in imitation of the
chop of the guillotine blade:

'We are lost, my boy!'

Bonaparte impassive. He leaves. 847

Bonaparte says to a mounted officer: 848*

'Captain Suchet, have the Ardèche volunteers who arrived
this morning brought up as reserve.'

Suchet is shocked and is about to raise an objection, which must be
serious if he dares to mention it: 'Permit me, Captain . . .' But
Bonaparte cuts in and says: 'Go!' The officer leaves.

The Ardèche volunteers. They are all very young, almost boys, ill 849

---

* The 'volunteers of Ardèche' sequence is one that we know with certainty was shot; all of it
is lost, except for the dying boy in scenes 978 to 980.

clad, poorly armed. They look lost in this deluge of rain and fire.

850 'Forward!' shouts their officer after a moment's dreadful hesitation.

851 They march forward, like obedient sheep, awkward but endearing.

852 A blazing house shows up their movements.

853 Bonaparte watches them through his field-glass and for a moment stands shocked, then his anger shows.

854 For it is plain to see that these young Frenchmen are frightened. They appear cowardly or stupid. The enemy are twenty paces away and raking them with fire. They stay where they are, milling about.

855 Bonaparte. His anger erupts. He covers his eyes, crying out in indignation:

> **'The cowards!'**

856 Not far away from Bonaparte, Moustache looks at Bonaparte, then at the stupid-looking young soldiers, with growing anxiety.

857 The young lads continue to let themselves be massacred on the spot without returning fire; yet not a single one runs away.

858 Bonaparte stops one young man as he retires wounded. Moustache hurries over. Bonaparte raises his crop to the young soldier and says indignantly:

'This is outrageous! Not one of you has fired a single cartridge!'

The young soldier raises his clear eyes to Bonaparte and says:

> **'We don't know how to load our guns, monsieur . . . We've been soldiers only since last night!'**

Bonaparte is greatly shocked. The crop falls from his hands. He says, not wanting to believe it:

> **'But . . . that is impossible!'**

859 Moustache, who has heard, replies, with tears in his eyes:

> **'Impossible is not French, Captain. By Moustache's honour, that's the truth.'**

860 Bonaparte. He swells with emotion, and he embraces the young soldier; then, taking control of himself and making a lightning decision, he shouts to the drums: 'The charge!'

The drums beat the charge in the downpour. 861

There is enthusiasm all round him. He sets off at a gallop, followed 862
by a hundred or so cavalrymen.

The cavalrymen come up to a group of stoical young men, who are 863
awaiting their death at the post assigned to them, without using their
guns.

Captain Suchet is in tears, leaning on a cannon. 864

Bonaparte at the head of the cavalry takes his hat off to them. The 865
others do likewise.

Kitchen. Brouhaha. Wounded soldiers stumble down into the kitchen 866
and collapse. Violine is in a corner with Marcellin, whom she is
holding back. Fleuri, dressed as a cook, a skewer in his hand, is
everywhere at once. The layout of the kitchen is reminiscent of that
at Brienne, and red-hot cannonballs are flying in through the same
window.

Fleuri looks out of the window. 867

A cannonball. He ducks and bobs up again. He is elated. 868

An enemy soldier is knocked over and falls on his rump in front of 869
the little window which serves as a ventilator.

Fleuri jabs his skewer into the soldier's buttocks. 870

The enemy soldier gives a tremendous leap forwards. 871

Fleuri is the heart and soul of the defence. He shouts: 872

'This is nothing. I've seen it all before at Brienne!
Gallant Paille-au-nez!'

Young Bonaparte of Brienne and Bonaparte of Toulon. 873

Bonaparte leads the charge. The English begin to give way. 874

Bonaparte. Wounded in the face, blinded by the blood, he brushes 875
away the handkerchiefs being offered him and gives out some orders.

A tent battered by the wind and rain. Officers moving round it. 876
Concern.

**At this moment the members of the Convention decide to call
off the assault.**

877   Interior of the tent. Council of war. Salicetti is in a rage. Dugommier is present, crestfallen and hesitant. Barras, Robespierre the Younger and Fréron are in open agreement with Salicetti and censure Dugommier, who dispatches an officer to Bonaparte.

878   The officer goes out and gallops off.

879   He speaks to Bonaparte, who impassively addresses a few words to his officers and gallops away.

880   The tent. Bonaparte arrives, his face covered in blood, stands in the entrance, but every eye is on Salicetti berating Dugommier, and nobody sees him.

881   Salicetti says:

'Generals Houchard and Custine have just been guillotined in Paris for lesser faults.'

882   Bonaparte, seeming greater by virtue of his outrage and masterful self-control, utters a single word of contempt:

'Speechmakers!'

Everyone turns round. They start, as if they had been lashed by a whip. Terrible silence.

883   Bonaparte crosses to Dugommier and speaks to him in a low tone. They weigh the gravity of their decision. Dugommier says:

'Will you answer for its success?'

With his eyes Bonaparte indicates 'Yes'.

884   Dugommier once more assumes his air of leadership, turns to the Convention members and says peremptorily:

'The general-in-command assumes personal responsibility for all the operations and decides to continue the attack.'

885   The Convention members are taken aback, then burst out with furious recriminations, while the tent flaps wildly, half torn away by the wind. Dugommier prepares to leave, saying:

[['The meeting is over!']]

Salicetti walks swiftly over to Bonaparte, full of menace, but the officers surround their leaders. The Convention members feel isolated and withdraw.

94

Bonaparte and Dugommier gallop off. The wind has risen to gale 886
force.

The assault on the Little Gibraltar

The French troops arrive with Dugommier. Deadly fire from the 887
English.

The black sky. It is torn by a flash of lightning. 888

Prodigious but useless feats of courage on the part of the French. 889
Futility. A ditch of water six metres wide prevents the men from
crossing. The scaling-ladders are overturned and the men cannot
climb them.

Dugommier is in despair and strikes his forehead in his powerlessness 890
to do anything.

The English cannon thunder relentlessly. 891

The French retreat again. 892

Bonaparte rides up with Muiron, Junot, Marmont and about a 893
hundred men.

His personal courage. 894

Terrific wind. 895

Bonaparte issues orders as the lightning flashes. 896

A veritable human ladder is organized; men climb up on to the 897
shoulders of others. Then still others mount this ladder.

Ramparts of the fort. Twice men are pitched from the ramparts down 898
into the ditch, and the entire chain crumbles, but Moustache has
reached the top and is performing such feats with his gun and sabre
that he gives Bonaparte and Muiron time to climb the moving ladder.

And, 'in the midst of pitch darkness, rain, raging wind, confusion, 899
corpses, cries of the wounded and the dying' – as Napoléon himself
wrote – 'there is no more firing, only hand to hand fighting. Swords
are the only weapons left. The English gunners are hacked to pieces
around their guns. Of all those defending the redoubt and who are
taken prisoner, not one has escaped unwounded.'

The intrepid Muiron is dealt a blow from a pike. 900

901 Indomitable British tenacity. Details. Bonaparte salutes this heroic defence.

902 Bonaparte receives a lance wound in the thigh. Moustache, totally unarmed, seizes a mortar and, lifting it as if it were no more than a cannonball, crashes it down on the Englishman who dealt Bonaparte the blow. Bonaparte binds his own wound and carries on fighting and commanding as he does so.

903 Never, as Chuquet says, will Bonaparte show such fearlessness in the course of his other campaigns. He is everywhere, sees everything, and is equal to everything. Lightning from the sky and flashes from the cannon encircle him. He is in his element, in the thick of fire.

904 Junot's fearlessness.

905 A furnace of red-hot cannonballs is hit by a shell and collapses; a lava of fire and glowing cannonballs spreads over the wounded. Bodies go up in flames. [Bonaparte calls out:

'The drums? Where are the drums of the Sixth?']

906 Five drummers arrive, furiously beating the charge.

907 Moustache laughs, then his face falls, for he sees

908 two drummers fall. Then two more, then the last.

909 Moustache runs to the side of the last drummer, who in one final effort vainly tries to beat the charge, but his arms fall back. Moustache takes the drum and collects up others, and sets them all up on some sandbags.

910 The hail falls and bounces on the resonant drums.

911 Moustache throws a meaningful glance at

912 the last drummer, who understands and dies, smiling.

913 The drums beaten by the hail.

914 Bonaparte has had the cannon turned round; he is firing on the town and on the English squadron.

915 English council of war. Frenzy, feverish excitement, uproar.

916 Shells close by.

917 Admiral Hood turns to Trogoff and says:

'Bring out the English squadron . . .'

He turns back to Sidney Smith, phlegmatic as ever, and says slowly: 918

'. . . and burn the French fleet.'

Sidney Smith bows and saunters out.   919

On the shore the frantic defenders of Toulon begin to embark.   920
Sardinians, Spaniards, Neapolitans mingle together. Women and
children are crushed.

The French steal along the shore and start fighting.   921

The drums furiously beaten by the hail still sound the charge and   922
underline the men's movements with their rhythm.

Embarkation of enemy troops in the storm, pressed hard from all   923
sides by the French.

The wildly tossing sea.   924

An eagle wheels over the sea.]]   925

On a hillock. Bonaparte stands, coolly issuing commands. He no   926
longer takes part in the fighting now that his example has produced
the necessary results. Near by he notices

another captain of his own age, belonging to the Allobroges legion,   927
about an inch shorter than himself but showing the same assurance,
the same fearlessness, the same carelessness in his dress; he is fighting
like a tiger, driving off the Neapolitans and coolly manoeuvring
towards victory.

Bonaparte sends Junot to fetch the man who seems to be his double.   928

Junot asks the young man to come. The man follows him.   929

Bonaparte and the young captain. Bonaparte looks at him and says: 930

'I admire you. What is your name?'

The young captain replies:

'Desaix.'

The two young men. Their fiery gaze. Youth and glory are reflected   931
by each as in two living mirrors. Drunk with happiness at the victory
which is beginning to take shape, they can find no words to say to
one another, and suddenly both burst out laughing, without knowing

why. Bonaparte stretches out his hand; Desaix shakes it warmly. They part. They will not meet again until they are in Egypt.

932   The eagle in the storm.

933 ⟦ Sidney Smith orders barrels of oil and pitch to be emptied over the ships and fuses to be laid.

934 ⟦ Battle at the water's edge in the raging storm. Sloops overturn. The French are fighting waist-deep in the water. Gigantic waves drive back both friend and foe.

935 ⟦ Sidney Smith aboard a sloop. He draws on his gloves fastidiously and then says, as if he were opening a ball:

'Set them on fire!'

936 ⟦ Flaming tow is thrown in, and in an instant

937 ⟦ the *Thémistocles*, the *Centaure*, the *Liberté*, the *Duguay-Trouin*, the *Héros*, the *Suffisant*, the *Tricolore*, the *Destin* and the *Content* are at the mercy of the flames.

938 ⟦ Diorama. One of the most awesome fires in history flares up. This and the fire of Moscow are the two most vividly imprinted on Bonaparte's imagination.⟧

939   Bonaparte comes to the top of a rise. He can scarcely credit an action such as this. But not a sign of his consternation shows on his face.

940   He only clenches his fist.

941   Details of the fire.

942 ⟦ The eagle in the reddened sky.

943 ⟦ Sidney Smith lights his pipe as the sloop is rowed along, as if nothing were the matter.

944 ⟦ The French officers seethe with rage as they follow him through their telescopes. The reflected light from the fire is so great that everything is lit up as if in broad daylight.

945 ⟦ The French sans-culottes swarm down hillsides like demons in the glow of the flames, singing and yelling.

946 ⟦ In vain, English, Spanish, Sardinian, Neapolitan troops try to counter-attack, but they scatter like spume from waves breaking on the shore. They retreat farther. A powerful rhythm is gradually established,

with the following elements:

Bonaparte remains motionless and impassive; everything else about him is caught up in frenzied motion. 947

Battle at the water's edge. 948

Dugommier, laughing grimly, drops with exhaustion, one side of his moustache singed, wounded in the knee and arm. 949

Battle in the last forts. 950

Cannon spit fire from the forts. 951

Trajectory of the cannonballs. 952

Howling wind. 953

Cannon of the English ships. Practically one hundred shots a minute. 954

Map showing the enemy's line of flight. Map intercut with galloping horses and shouts of laughter. 955

Torrential rain and hail. 956

The eagle braving the storm. 957

Fire, details. 958

Fire, general shot. Toulon burns and the sea too appears to burn. 959

Dugommier laughs. 960

Dying men. 961

English vessels getting under way. 962

Sloops overturned by the storm and caught in the flames. 963

Explosion of the fire-ship *Vulcain*. 964

Admiral Hood, alone in the centre of a respectful group of officers aboard the *Victory*, is weeping, his head in his hands. 965

There are no more boats; civilians, women, children and old men, are shot down in large numbers by the fire of the sans-culottes, having no alternative but death by drowning. 966

Bonaparte looks on. 967

Explosion of the fire-ship *Saint-Louis de Gonzague*, and of the *Iris*. 968

969 [[Everything is ablaze. The oil spread over the water burns on the towering waves.

970 [[The sky is red.

971 [[The sea is red.

972 [[The land is red.

973 [[And Bonaparte looks on, motionless.

974 [[Explosion of the *Montréal*, heard as far away as La Ciotat. Napoléon himself wrote: 'The swirling cloud of flame and smoke which rose from the arsenal was like the eruption of a volcano, and the thirteen vessels burning in the roads like thirteen magnificent firework displays. Fire traced the outlines of the masts and the shape of the vessels. It lasted several hours and afforded a unique spectacle. It was possible to gauge the height of the flames because all the masts and rigging were engulfed in brilliant fire and all the smoke rising from it was blood red. On the horizon against the black sky the entire English and Spanish squadrons could be seen drawing away, their signal lamps alight; it looked like a long procession.'

What he saw . . .

975 [[Bonaparte. His face still covered in blood. The blood has dried, his expression is inspiring.

976 [[His forehead and his eyes. Shortened repeat of the preceding shots one over the other, and on top of all this visual turmoil a map of England and, predominating over everything, white numerals rising out of these images, calculations of military strength, of cannon, of parabolas, of cannonballs; the numerals are distinct, but replace one another at a dizzy speed, and the total impression is as if one were at the centre of a typhoon where nothing can be made out distinctly any more.]]
    Bonaparte, lit up by the red glow, and impassive.

977 The senior officers gradually assemble round Bonaparte. He is already the centre of attention.

978 A young soldier lies dying on the ground, and yet his admiration is so great that he asks a comrade who is bending over him, motioning towards Bonaparte (he can barely speak):

'What . . . is the name of . . . that captain?'

The friend bends down nearer still, so that he can hear, and says: 979

[['Bonaparte.'

'Ah! . . .']] 980

he says, his face lighting up in a smile; then his eyelids close. He dies happy.

Fleuri, his face glued to the kitchen ventilator-window. Tears are 981
running down his cheeks. Violine, ecstatic, is standing next to him.
Serene, innocent expression; the people's adulation begins.

Violine crosses to the fireplace, which is being used for roasting meat, 982
and throws some books into the fire. Fleuri comes up to her. What
are you doing? He rescues a book she was about to throw.

The book: 983

The Vocation of Joan of Arc

Fleuri asks: 984

'So . . . you are giving up? . . .'

The future trembles in the expression of her eyes as she replies: 985

'Yes, because this man will save France.']]

The Convention members arrive on the scene now that the fighting 986
is over, flourishing their swords, bright and devil-may-care, resplen-
dent in their new uniforms. They congratulate the soldiers.

The French soldiers enter Toulon singing.]] 987

The Convention members embrace Dugommier, who is delighted 988
and indicates:

'This is the victor of Toulon!'*

Bonaparte deep in thought. His poor captain's uniform is so torn, so 989
black with powder, that he looks like a beggar. His thigh is bound
with a bloodstained cloth. He suddenly notices

Moustache who, with his face smeared with blood and his ear torn, 990

* In the film, after watching the French fleet burn, Napoléon, exhausted, has fallen asleep
with his head resting on a drum. Dugommier points to him, and the Convention members
come up to him and lay the captured standards of the enemy around him. As the sun rises,
the eagle flutters down and settles on the top of a flag pole. Fade out.

is playing cards with a rifleman who looks just like him. Bonaparte takes one of the playing-cards and writes on the back:

991 ⟦ **29 Frimaire, Year II, 7 o'clock in the morning, Toulon taken by General Dugommier.**

He says to Moustache's partner:

'Deliver that on my behalf to the Convention in Paris.'

992 ⟦ The Convention members approach him, then, suddenly overwhelmed by the respect which his greatest enemies will maintain towards him until St Helena, they no longer dare speak to him. They back away like so many children, and merge with the officers and soldiers who are crowding forward to see him. Salicetti comes up to him with outstretched hand and says:

'I wish to be your friend.'

Bonaparte does not offer his hand in return, but says:

'I wish to have five hundred million men as friends!'

Salicetti gnaws his lips and withdraws. Silence. Dignity. Majesty.

Suddenly Bonaparte wraps himself in his cloak and lies down on the ground. He drops with fatigue at the foot of one of the walls of the bastion, his head resting on a gun-barrel. A respectful silence falls as the men jostle to see him sleeping. Then Barras lets out a sudden exclamation and points to something above their heads. They all look up. Intense, apprehensive curiosity. Astonishment.

Bonaparte asleep. Top of the ruined wall: the eagle of the storm, resting. 993

Barras loads a gun to kill it, but Gasparin and Dugommier persuade him against it, indicating Bonaparte. 'Don't make a noise. You'll wake him!' And, gripped by an inexplicable uneasiness, they widen the circle round the sleeping Bonaparte. Total stillness.]] 994

Bonaparte asleep. The eagle. It seems to be watching over the young captain's sleep. 995

AFTER THE CAPTURE OF TOULON

Interior of the inn. There is hesitation over the number of places to be set. Some soldiers are laying the table with Fleuri. Fleuri takes a piece of paper out of his pocket once more to reassure himself: 996

> **Citizen Fleuri will today prepare a dinner for nine
> for the Commissioners to the Armies at the
> Champ-de-Mars Hostelry.**
>
> Signed: *Salicetti*
> Toulon, 6 Nivose, Year II.

He sets the ninth place and goes out, taking with him several empty baskets which had been used for flowers.

Exterior of the inn. Marcellin, practically naked, is splashing about in a tub and having fun flicking water at some soldiers. Fleuri comes out to dump the baskets and to collect some watermelons. There is an atmosphere of bustle and excitement. Ten soldiers are erecting a sort of primitive platform with great planks. Fleuri asks one of the soldiers: 997

'What are you making?' – 'I don't know,' says the soldier – 'What about you?' – 'I don't know either,' says another. 998

Inn. Fleuri returns to work at his table. Gaiety. Violine kisses him as she goes by. 999

1000   Flowers. Fruit. Fleuri laughing. Sunshine. A bird singing. A cock. Fleuri is singing. Violine kisses him. The child in the water laughs.

1001   Violine stops on the balcony as she goes up the stairs, looks out for a moment and cries out in dismay.

1002   Fleuri runs to his daughter.

1003   Violine covers her eyes, speechless with indignation. Fleuri is now at her side, followed by the soldiers who were helping with the table, their curiosity aroused. Fleuri is shocked, and slowly closes the shutters. The soldiers go back down the stairs with lowered heads and go out, closing the door. In fury Fleuri breaks a plate he was holding in his hand. A cloud of gloom descends upon the inn.

1004   Since March 1793, Stanislas Fréron has been administrating Provence like a pasha, causing concern among the Cordeliers, his puritanical friends. He is a weak-minded man, quick to enthuse, but a somewhat sinister figure who makes jokes in the midst of a massacre and plays Don Juan and Torquemada simultaneously.

     The grim army commissioners settle themselves on the improvised platform. There is to be an open-air session of the tribunal. Fréron presides. Present are Salicetti, Albitte, Laporte, Ricord, a clerk. Fréron stops his ears, shouts 'Silence!' and says:

> **'I, Fréron, commissioner to the armies, seeing that
> an exemplary punishment must be administered to the
> citizens of Toulon for having assisted the English against
> troops of the Republic, am therefore bringing to immediate
> trial eight hundred hostages.'**

1005   The hostages. A mass of men, women, old people and children, rounded up indiscriminately, like a herd of cattle. They are several metres from the tribunal, separated by a wall of soldiers, which extends round on both sides, enclosing them in a sort of pen in front of the inn. The mistral is blowing. They have just arrived. Violine looks down on them from the balcony, peeping from behind half-closed shutters, filled with pity. A soldier comes to fetch Fleuri. Violine is frightened, but Fleuri has to obey. He follows the soldiers.

1006   Tribunal. Fréron, more taken up with settling the menu than in passing judgment, talks to Tristan Fleuri, who has just arrived in great confusion. He consults his deputies. He asks Fleuri:

> **'Larks? Pâté? All right, pâté!'**

The Convention members agree. Fleuri is about to leave but Fréron holds him back, and they all start discussing food amid laughter.

Salicetti, seeing Fleuri engaged with Fréron, gets up and goes back into the inn. *1007*

Violine, who has been watching the hostages with beating heart, turns round and suppresses a cry. Salicetti is standing before her. He does not say a word: he takes a list out of his pocket and shows it to Violine. List of hostages. His finger points out the name of Violine Fleuri among twenty others. She looks at him in horror. He folds his list, motioning towards *1008*

the staircase leading up into the darkness. *1009*

He says to her: 'One or the other. Choose!' She panics and tries to escape. He bars her way. She begins to call for help. He says: *1010*

'If you call out, I shall add your father to the list.'

She is dumbfounded. The monster! She begins to sob. He goes up to her and tries to drag her after him. She does not dare resist; she begins to climb the stairs because she is in a state of confusion, or perhaps because she is about to give in? No! It is because she knows where to find the knife-case on the banisters. She snatches up one of the knives to strike Salicetti, but he is the stronger and disarms her. *1011*

She falls back at the foot of the stairs. He opens the shutters; he calls the soldiers and says: 'Take this woman to join the others!' They lead her away, half fainting, by way of the balcony. *1012*

Rear view, Salicetti watches Violine being led away, like a drunken woman, towards the crowd of hostages. He too goes out. *1013*

Fréron has assembled the makings of a conference on the art of cooking, to judge by the tribunal table on which he has piled fruits and Provençal dishes which he is discussing with Fleuri and the members of the Convention. Salicetti returns to his seat. Fréron looks at the time. *Sapristi!* He gets to his feet, blows his nose, adjusts his wig and clears his throat. *1014*

The hostages. A wave of anxiety. Desperation. They are riveted to the spot. Every eye is upon *1015*

Fréron, who begins to speak, simpering and acting as if he were giving out prizes: *1016*

'We decree that the name of Toulon shall be abolished and replaced by the name City of Shame. The whole town shall be razed to the ground. Twelve thousand masons are required immediately to destroy it completely.'

1017 The hostages. Sensation.

1018 Violine. She sees

1019 her father, who has not the remotest suspicion of her drama.

1020 Violine bites her fists to stop herself crying out. Her eyes turn and come to rest with supernatural steadiness on

1021 a group of senior officers, among them the impassive Bonaparte.

1022 Violine. Bonaparte is there! What does the rest matter? She drinks in the dear image and her features regain their serenity.

1023 Fréron rises and prepares to leave, talking gluttonously to Tristan Fleuri and oblivious of everything else.

1024 The hostages. He has forgotten us! They begin to hope again. Yes, yes, he has forgotten us! The sentence has been passed. There is a brief moment of joy.

1025 The tribunal prepare to leave.

1026 The guards begin to move the hostages out when they all become acutely anxious once more. They are petrified.

1027 Fréron, who was on his way out, returns to his seat and says:

'I was forgetting one small detail.'

1028 Nobody stirs for one terrible moment.

1029 Fréron says:

'Eight hundred hostages will be executed on the spot after the sentence has been read.'

He laughs.

1030 The hostages. Wave of horror. A backward surge of terror, then a forward surge of indignation. Women faint.

1031 Salicetti shows his satisfaction.

1032 Violine. She says nothing, but her eyes turn to

Bonaparte, who has remained impassive in the circle of officers. 1033

Violine gazes at him intensely, and two tears run down her cheeks, 1034
although not a muscle quivers.

Fréron laughs more loudly than ever and, triumphant and filled with 1035
greedy anticipation, gives his final decision to Tristan Fleuri, who
keeps a tight grip on himself in order not to faint with terror:

> **'And we'll wash all that down with Chambertin and**
> **champagne.'**

There is a great roar from the hostages.

'*Sapristi!* Silence! Be quiet!' shouts Fréron. But the noise is so great 1036
that it is impossible for anyone to hear. He speaks to Fleuri again and
gets to his feet to go into the inn.

Tribunal. Salicetti also rises and says: 1037

> **'I, delegate commissioner, call upon the commander of**
> **artillery Bonaparte to carry out the sentence immediately.'**

Bonaparte leaps forward to the tribunal, his face pale: 1038

> **'Am I a butcher? I refuse!'[1]**

Sensation among the judges. Heavy silence.

Violine faints. 1039

The Convention members consult together. Glaring at Bonaparte, 1040
Salicetti declares:

> **'We appoint General du Teil in place of Bonaparte. A report**
> **of his refusal will be given to citizen Robespierre.'**

He signs an order. An officer rides away to find General du Teil.

Bonaparte retorts: 1041

> **'Tell him at the same time that if we continue to defile the**
> **Revolution the people will be ashamed of being French!'**

1 – This incident revealed Bonaparte's disinclination to resort to acts of vengeance
in the wake of victory. Marmont claims that he used his influence to save some of
the victims, and Molteno that he remained stern and critical. Has he not himself
testified that he was never party to the shooting of the unfortunate citizens of
Toulon for which the front-line gunners were responsible? In Bonaparte's own
words: 'An outrageous order was given. Appalling measures were resorted to. This
action speaks for itself' (A. Chuquet, *Toulon*).

1042   The stormy meeting is brought to a close. The hostages are dragged away in batches surrounded by soldiers, the swooning women like so many bundles of washing, towards the end wall which encloses the square; on the right a fountain; on the left an olive press, with a blind horse plodding untiringly round and round. An old man of ninety-four is carried on a chair.

1043   Bonaparte rides slowly away so that he will not be present at this massacre. Violine's eyes grow frantic. If he goes, her only hope, her only support is lost. She collapses, sobbing like a little girl.

1044   Interior of the inn. The Convention members are taking their places at the table. Fleuri calls: 'Violine! Violine!' There is no answer.

1045   Fleuri. She must have gone up to bed. He begins to serve. Salicetti goes out again. Toast to Fréron, 'the butcher of the day'.

1046   Fréron. His laughter. A great butcher's knife red with blood. Fréron's laughter.

1047   Flowers. Fruit. Sunshine. Laughter. A bird. Violine, utterly distraught.

1048   Salicetti close by the hostages. He comes up to Violine and says:

'Your hand! You have only to raise your hand!'

She turns away. Salicetti is howled down. The soldiers have to protect him. He retires, seething.

1049   Exterior, inn. Fleuri passes Salicetti as he comes back in. Fleuri goes out to fetch food. He calls Violine.

1050   Violine hears, cries quietly, the tears welling up in an unending flow. She does not answer.

1051   Fleuri says to Marcellin:

'She must have gone off to play at shepherdesses again! Come and fetch some water.'

He goes to fetch water.

1052   General du Teil arrives in a carriage. Infirm. He climbs down. All these men must be shot. Outburst of 'No! No! . . .'

1053   Interior of the inn. A soldier is speaking to Fréron. Livid with rage, Fréron goes to the balcony.

Balcony. Fréron says to du Teil: '*At once!*' Du Teil bows. He takes command of the firing-squads, weeping. *1054*

Fountain. Fleuri approaches. The hostages are yelling. Fleuri, full of compassion, suddenly catches sight of *1055*

his daughter's dress. He goes up to her. Grief and despair. *1056*

Some of the soldiers are drinking to boost their failing courage. The deaf old man of ninety-four has no idea what is going to happen. *1057*

Dinner table of the Convention members. Gaiety. Fréron heartlessly makes jokes which convulse the others with laughter. *1058*

Barras finishes making a paper bird. *1059*

The hostages. Fleuri is violently pushed back, and he runs away. *1060*

Exterior, inn. Fleuri comes running back. Marcellin thinks for a moment and goes running out in the direction taken by Bonaparte. *1061*

Interior, inn. Dinner. Fleuri flings himself down at Fréron's feet. He is thrown back outside. *1062*

Exterior, inn. The soldiers are loading their guns. *1063*

Marcellin running along the road. *1064*

1065   Violine.

1066   Fleuri.

1067   Soldiers. Du Teil gets ready.

1068   Marcellin and Bonaparte. Bonaparte lifts the boy on to his horse and comes galloping back.

*1069   Champ-de-Mars. The soldiers take aim.

1070   Violine. She has regained her composure, but there are still traces of tears on her cheeks. She is praying. She remains serene while all about her storms of despair are unleashed. She is filled with the spirit of Joan of Arc.

1071   The officer raises his sabre and averts his head to avoid having to look.

1072   Bonaparte galloping along.

1073   Violine. She stares unflinchingly at

1074   the hundred guns ready-aimed.

---

* *The reel containing the shooting of the hostages was rediscovered by Gance in 1958 and given to the Cinémathèque Française but it has not been seen since. It may yet be found among the reels that Gance took back from the Cinémathèque in the late sixties and deposited in another archive; in the meantime, here is a contemporary description of what it contained: 'The distraught crowd. The soldiers raising their guns. Fréron's signal. The officer's command. The soldiers firing. The decimated crowd. Soldiers firing, the thinning crowd seen from behind them. The crowd, half of which has fallen. Descriptive close-shots. | The soldiers reload their guns. The camera travels at great speed along the line of soldiers who fire one after the other, each shot appearing to hit the lens as it goes past. The camera travels rapidly along the line of people. The lens is now a gun firing, with people falling at each shot. | An enormous gun fills the screen: fire, flame, smoke. A face in utter terror, impact, blood trickles, the eyes turn up. A giddy whirl. | Another face. An enormous, mesmerizing gun. Fire. A shattered skull. A pitch forward, then back, then forward again; a fall. | Another gun. Another face in paroxysm. Fire. A slide into an endless abyss. | Then the lens becomes a bullet and rushes towards a victim, then another, and embeds itself in their flesh. | Face. Fire. Flame. Smoke. Roll. Face. Fire. Blur. Face. Fire. Vertigo. Gyration. Roll. Gyration. Roll. A slide. Blood. Gyration over a roll, over a slide. Fire. | Superimposition of every camera movement, intercut with red flashes, in a montage that gets faster and faster. Ten-three, eight-three, five-two, three-one, two-one, one-one. Images crackling like sparks. A vanishing cloud of smoke. | Three motionless shots; the dead on the ground; the soldiers leaving in the distance; Fréron, wrapped in his black cape, immobile, gigantic (shot from below), contemplates the hecatomb.' (Jean Arroy, reprinted in L'Écran, April/May 1958.)*

Bonaparte galloping. He comes to an abrupt halt for   *1075*

the officer lowers his sabre.   *1076*

The hundred guns thunder out together.   *1077*

Fleuri, his teeth chattering. His distress is heart-rending. Suddenly   *1078*
he stiffens. Is it with joy or horror?

His daughter Violine, followed by large numbers of victims who,   *1079*
though wounded, have been spared death, is approaching along the
sunlit road.

Fleuri. He cries. He laughs. He no longer knows what he is saying.   *1080*

He tries to embrace her. He is pushed aside. She smiles and passes   *1081*
by.

Violine is helped into the inn. Compassion. Marcellin comes in.   *1082*

Bonaparte sets out again, reading.   *1083*

Robespierre's office*

Salicetti comes to Robespierre to beg the favour of putting Bonaparte on trial.

Robespierre's office. The conversation comes to an end. Salicetti   1084
sitting on the edge of an armchair. Behind him pigeon-holes contain-
ing cards. Salicetti, surly and vindictive, concludes his indictment;
he is choking with hatred.

Robespierre gives him a sidelong look.   1085

Salicetti, in conclusion: 'He deserves to die!' Robespierre approves. 1086
Salicetti smirks. Robespierre beckons; one of his secretaries enters.
He says:

1 – There is something very odd and mysterious about this conflict between Salicetti
and Bonaparte which led to a prison sentence. The court records have been
destroyed. Napoléon is silent on this particular period. The Duchesse d'Abrantès
hints at the truth in her *Mémoires*. She ensures, however, that the deeper [*cont. 112*]

---

* From here to the end of the scenario, Gance's notes on what he shot and did not shoot
become less detailed and reliable. We can only indicate cuts and alterations by making
assumptions based on comparing the scenario with the existing prints. Also, just before we get
to Robespierre's office, there is a short scene between Pozzo di Borgo and Salicetti, where
the former promises to fabricate enough evidence to indict Napoléon.

'Let General Bonaparte be offered the command of the Paris garrison in place of Henriot.'[1]

Salicetti is dumbfounded, and tries to explain. Robespierre stops him and says:

'This Bonaparte is a man of strength such as we lack in Paris.'

'But' . . . exclaims Salicetti. Robespierre cuts in with finality:

'If he refuses, then I will give him to you.'

And he dismisses Salicetti with disconcerting coldness.

1087   Robespierre's secret work-room* over the rue Saint-Honoré (destroyed in 1816). First floor. On one of the walls Gérard's full-length portrait of Robespierre, on the other an extraordinarily beautiful full-length pastel of Saint-Just. These two life-size portraits of the two exterminators face each other like two mirrors.[1] Robespierre is at his desk. He has on his pale-blue coat and green spectacles; his dog Blount is stretched out at his feet. Saint-Just, a rose between his lips as always, is standing behind him, leaning casually against the mantelpiece. Couthon, sitting near the window in his wheelchair, is feeding his white rabbit. One of Robespierre's negro secretaries passes him a dossier; he looks at the name, turns round to Saint-Just, who each time makes a small gesture of approval. [[MLLE DE SOURDEVAL, AGED FIFTEEN, writes Robespierre's hand: DEATH, and his initials: M.R.

Title on the next dossier: DE MONTFORT, AGED NINETY-FOUR.]]**

---

mystery remains and no one has yet been able to penetrate it. We offer the following psychological interpretation which seems to us plausible as it allows us a striking 'short cut' through to this curious coincidence: Joséphine and Bonaparte were both condemned to death, yet both were reprieved at the same time by the mysterious events which neither Joséphine nor Bonaparte nor the historians have been able to elucidate. See Frédéric Masson concerning Joséphine and d'Abrantès concerning Bonaparte.

1 – The Committee for Public Safety rolled on inexorably, sweeping all before it with the aid of the guillotine. Robespierre and Saint-Just gave this death machine its impetus, the one at its head as high priest, the other in the rear as prophet of doom (Alfred de Vigny, *Stello*)

* *The entire scene in the film takes place in this room.*

** *In the film the first dossier has Lucile Desmoulins' name on it. In the recently discovered Corsican print, the scene is completed as follows: a second dossier has the name André Chénier on it and draws the following sarcasm from Saint-Just:* 'A poet? Of no use to the Revolution!' *When Chenier is called to the scaffold, later in the film (scene 1156), all Tristan Fleuri has to say is* 'André . . .' *and we are reminded of this scene.*

The hurdy-gurdy player, Robespierre, St Just

Robespierre's hand writes: DEATH, and his initials: M.R.

Rue Saint-Honoré. Surge of curiosity in the crowd. There they are!   *1088*

A blind old man carries on playing his barrel-organ. A jaunty monkey   *1089*
on a chain frisks about on the organ.

Tumbril. La Bussière and Tristan Fleuri next to the driver. He is   *1090*
smoking his pipe, trying to conceal his violent feelings.]] In the
tumbril, Danton, the most magnificent figure of the Revolution.

Fleuri and Danton. Fleuri, tears in his eyes, whispers in his ear: *1091*

'You could have escaped abroad. Everything was ready!'

Danton looks at him and says: *1092*

**'Is it possible to take one's country with one on the soles of
one's shoes?'**

Emotion in the crowd. Silence. Open mouths. The sympathy of the   *1093*
people can be clearly felt. The troopers threaten the crowd, to get
the tumbril moving. One spark and the prisoners would be free; but
no one dares.

Camille Desmoulins is sobbing; Danton holds him close, like a child.   *1094*

1095 ⟦ In the street his young wife Lucile displays supreme courage, and, biting on a handkerchief, urges him on to the sacrifice.⟧

1096 Robespierre's office. Everyone suddenly stops to listen; they get to their feet and look out through the half-open shutters.

1097 Danton. He sees

1098 Robespierre behind the shutters.

1099 Danton. With all his leonine strength he shouts:

'Infamous Robespierre, the scaffold is calling for you. You will follow me!'

1100 Robespierre, pale and motionless.

1101 ⟦ In the crowd, Violine clutches Marcellin to her.

1102 ⟦ Violine is crying.

1103 ⟦ Violine and Marcellin, who tugs at her arm and asks in surprise:

'Why are you crying when they are singing?'

She clasps Marcellin closer to her and leads him away.

1104 ⟦ Portico of Robespierre's house. The doors are closed. The imploring crowd gathers round it. They raise their hands, fearfully, begging a reprieve for those condemned to death and a halt to these daily massacres.

1105 ⟦ Robespierre listens, understands and gives an order. An icy smile flits across his face.⟧

1106 Violine has joined the group of people begging a reprieve for Danton.

'Mercy for Danton!'*

1107 ⟦ Suddenly the doors are flung open, and the crowd stays where it is, dazed, not daring to venture forward, as if held back by an invisible chain.

1108 ⟦ Violine. Her taut, fierce expression as she looks up towards the green window; then she goes limp and allows her brother to lead her away.

1109 ⟦ The frightened crowd disperses.

This is followed by one last shot of the group in Robespierre's office, then we see Danton standing by the guillotine. He cries: 'When my head has fallen, show it to the people; it will be worthwhile!'

114

A *tisane*-seller carrying his urn on his back looks at the window. Some   1110
small urchins drink from the tap of his urn; he shakes his fist at the
window; immediately two police dressed in civilian clothes seize him
and drag him away. The open tap sprinkles *tisane* in his wake.

The Guillotine Tavern. People standing on chairs. Curiosity. There   1111
they are! There they are! Some are using dainty opera-glasses.
Silence. Emotion. Respect. Admiration.

Joséphine looks on, deeply moved, but at the same time very curious.   1112

Joséphine turns her head away with a cry.   1113

An onlooker embraces a unknown woman who is watching blood-   1114
thirstily, without turning away.

An impressive silence falls upon the group of young beaux. Joséphine   1115
dares not look back again.

A tiny child laughs as he pulls at the skirts of his mother, who is   1116
petrified with fear.

Lucile Desmoulins sees Camille guillotined. The tragedy can be   1117
followed on her face.

The blind man continues grinding out plaintive airs without knowing   1118
what is taking place; his own misery is enough for him. As Stendhal
puts it so well, the Republic dealt itself a heart-wound with Danton's
death. Its death agony will last six years, until 18 Brumaire.]]

Robespierre's office. The citizen-servants come in with candelabra,   1119
for night has fallen. Robespierre appears prostrate, his head in his
right hand, his left hand clenched on a closed book, the title of which
can be read in large letters: CROMWELL.

Couthon has himself carried in a basket by one of the negroes to one   1120 *
of the other negroes. Each time the blade falls, Robespierre registers
the shock with a start. His dog Blount howls at the top of its voice.
Saint-Just comes in and lightly shrugs his shoulders in commiseration.
He signals to one of Robespierre's old secretaries, who under-

---

* *Scenes 1120 and 1121 were changed: Couthon does not appear, and, as the hurdy-gurdy
plays, Robespierre distractedly opens the volume of* Cromwell. *In a close-up we see the
shadow of the guillotine on the cover. Saint-Just points it out to Robespierre, who slams the
book shut in a fright, then looks at the objects on his desk: the illusion had been created by
the shadow of an open inkwell and the ribbon of a cockade. Robespierre brushes them violently
off the desk.*

stands and fetches a hurdy-gurdy from the cupboard. At a sign from
Saint-Just he begins to play a mountain dance.

1121 ⟦ Robespierre raises his head in fright, then smiles, giving Saint-Just
a look of gratitude for having used his favourite remedy.⟧

1122 The hurdy-gurdy player.

1123 A negro announces someone to Robespierre. 'Show him in.' Salicetti
is ushered in. Salicetti's cordiality, deference. He says to Robespierre:

**'Bonaparte has refused the command of the Paris garrison.
He does not wish to support "a man like you".'**

Bonaparte has refused! Robespierre frowns, takes up an initialled
printed sheet; he stamps it and holds it out to Salicetti. On the paper
can be read:

**Since General Bonaparte has lost the confidence of the
representatives of the people through his suspicious conduct,
they hereby suspend him from his duties and decree
that he shall be placed under arrest and handed to the
Committee of Public Safety.[1]**

Salicetti, Albitte, Laporte

Salicetti is triumphant. He has his revenge. One of the negroes writes
in large letters on the dossier:

1124 GENERAL NAPOLÉON BONAPARTE

1125 Salicetti goes out, obsequiously. Saint-Just and Couthon do not
bother to acknowledge him. Robespierre makes a small, patronizing
gesture in his direction.

1126 ⟦ In the street. The shadow of tumbrils on the opposite wall. The fierce
outline of Danton can be recognized in one of the tumbrils.⟧

1 – This was practically a death sentence. A great many generals had already perished
in the same manner (Stendhal, *Vie de Napoléon*). Salicetti was accusing Bonaparte
of being a spy, the object of which was to place Bonaparte's head on the scaffold
(Duchesse d'Abrantès, *Mémoires*). Contemporary accounts of the period state that
Bonaparte was not accused nor arrested for supporting the Terrorist régime
(d'Abrantès). 'I will not conceal the fact that reliable contemporary sources give
different accounts of the extent of the danger facing General Bonaparte' (Stendhal).
See Lenotre, *Tribunal révolutionnaire*, on the consequences of being outlawed.
Bonaparte himself said, at the time of Thermidor, 'Salicetti has behaved abominably
towards me. I'm not yet twenty-six years old and he has snapped off my life at the
stalk' (d'Abrantès).

Robespierre's office. Saint-Just deigns to move from the mantelpiece
from where he has been complacently looking at his portrait. He
opens his little notebook and says:

**'I wish to denounce Vicomtesse Joséphine de Beauharnais to
your Committee of Public Safety. She is capable of seducing
the most virtuous of men.'[1]**

The negro makes a dossier and writes on it:

JOSÉPHINE DE BEAUHARNAIS.

The ink on the previous file is not yet dry, so that the two names of
Napoléon Bonaparte and Joséphine lie one on top of the other.

**[[Through a mysterious accident of Fate, it was thus that
Napoléon and Joséphine met on the threshold of death.**

Shadow of tumbrils on the wall.]] *

LES CARMES

This prison, the walls of which are still stained with the blood of the
September massacres, is one of the most sordid in Paris.

Joséphine, pulled, jostled, thrown into Les Carmes prison. Behind
her, her two children in tears, Eugène de Beauharnais in a very simple
little carpenter's costume, and Hortense. Brutality. Rough, uncouth
guards. The children cling to their mother. They are violently
separated. As a particular favour they allow her to keep her vicious
little dog Fortuné, which has bitten a guard in the arm. The guard
makes light of the wound, but he is bleeding. Semi-darkness.
Prisoners pass freely to and fro, for it was possible to come and go
within the prison during the day, as at the Saint-Lazare prison,
according to André Chénier. A squalid staircase disappears into the
darkness. In the foreground a fanlight. Joséphine sobs distractedly.
There is blood on the walls. It is a sort of squalid hovel, into which a
little light filters at certain times of day through a fanlight, high up in

---

1 – An *anonymous* denunciation warning against the Vicomtesse Alexandre de
Beauharnais because of her inside contacts in ministerial offices led to an order made
by the Committee of Public Safety on 30 Germinal (19 April) (Frédéric Masson,
Joséphine).
* *A shot of the prison fortress at Antibes, with one of Napoléon entering it, immediately
precedes the scenes at the Carmes prison.*

the wall, opening on to one of the corridors. It is above the sacristy through which, a little less than two years earlier, on 2 September 1792, the clergy were led to their death.

1131   On the steps of the staircase a man in the shadows seems to take pity on her.

1132   Joséphine. She raises her tear-stained face and looks up at the fanlight.

*1133   ⟦ Shadows of tumbrils on another wall.⟧

1134   Joséphine. She is overwhelmed and cries out.

1135   The man on the stairs gets up and comes to Joséphine's side.

1136   The handsome young man, who appears from his tunic to be a soldier, contemplates her. She has not seen him. He takes one of her hands. She is so disturbed by her predicament that she takes no notice of this. The man comes closer and speaks gently to her. He has great charm. She stops crying, with a sudden shock, draws her hands away, taking fright at this stranger who has taken advantage of her agitation.

* *Replaced with a shot of a tumbril jolting over the cobbled street; in it a young woman, her hands tied behind her back.*

118

She asks:

'But who are you, monsieur?'

The man replies:

1137

'General Hoche, madame.'

She takes a better look at him, smiles at him through her tears, and when he takes her hand once more she does not resist. He draws closer still.[1] Her eyes full of terror, ⟦she looks at

⟦ shadows of tumbrils on the wall.⟧

1138

Hoche and Joséphine. She abandons herself to her misery and to this unlooked-for comforter, who holds her close as if she were a little girl. In the face of death the barriers of etiquette are quickly overstepped.

1139

⟦ Prison of the fortress of Antibes. Laetitia, in a state of collapse, is crying silently, deaf, blind and dumb with grief. Salicetti passes. She pleads with him, on her knees. He turns away and has her roughly pushed aside by sentries.*

1140

⟦ Prison. Salicetti enters. The jailors' obsequiousness. It is clear that he is in his element.⟧

1141

The spy-hole in the door opens softly, and Salicetti peers through malignantly. The door opens equally softly and Salicetti, having checked his pistol and dismissed the turnkey, who gently secures the door again, enters noiselessly.[2]

1142

1 – Joséphine began a relationship with Hoche who was imprisoned at Carmes around the same time as she was. No one has questioned this fact. But her relations with Hoche did not even last a month. That hardly makes it an affair, simply a short-lived passion – but is it then any the less significant? (Frédéric Masson, *Joséphine*.)
2 – All that is known for certain is that this prison episode remains full of mystery (Duchesse d'Abrantès, *Mémoires*). Salicetti the accuser lost no time in attaching himself to the accused, but Bonaparte never confided in his former enemy (Chateaubriand, *Mémoires d'outre-tombe*, 1860). 'According to my brother, who was at that time Salicetti's secretary, Bonaparte's life was saved for reasons no one has ever discovered' (d'Abrantès).
* *Laetitia, sometimes surrounded by Bonaparte's sisters, appears occasionally throughout the script; her appearances after Corsica were all cut from the shooting script. What now happens in Antibes is: Salicetti enters Napoléon's cell and finds him seated at a table, writing:* 'Preparing your defence?' *he sneers;* 'No,' *Napoléon replies,* 'I'm working out a route to the East, by way of a canal at Suez.' *Crestfallen, Salicetti sneaks away.*

1143   Bonaparte, deeply absorbed in his work, does not hear him coming
to stand behind him. Salicetti folds his arms and sneers.

'Preparing your defence?'[1]

1144   Bonaparte turns his head. The blaze of his eyes quickly subsides, and
he quietly and calmly replies:

'No, I am working out a route to the Indies by way of a canal at Suez.'

He goes back to his work.

1145   Salicetti laughs, but when confronted with Bonaparte's look of grief
and compassion he is gripped by a mysterious fear. Unnerved by such
great calm, he remains silent. Such loftiness of character is beyond
him. He goes out, much disturbed.

[[Tristan Fleuri, recalled to Paris, inherits a new employment, as unexpected as the previous one.]]

1146   Les Carmes. The famous painting by Muller: *The Summons of the
Victims of the Terror*. Beaumarchais and Florian are playing cards,
laughing. Also there as prisoners are de Sade, Santerre and a hundred
others.

1147   The man calling out the names in a strangled voice, the sweat standing
out on his brow, in the uniform of a prison warder, is Tristan Fleuri,
carrying out his new and terrible duties. The guards have enormous
dogs at their sides.

1148   Joséphine in terrible anguish. She is cowering in Hoche's embrace.

1149   Fleuri, 'recruiter of ghosts', calls the roll of the victims with a heavy
heart. [[La Bussière by his side checks them and passes them on.]]
Tall gendarmes with terrible faces, half drunk, urge them on like
dogs. Fleuri says:

---

1 – ' "Salicetti was my evil genius," Bonaparte said to M. Permon. "Dumerbion liked
me and he would have taken me into active service. This report made on my return
from Genoa was poisoned by spite and was then used as grounds for accusing me
whilst it should have been grounds for my glorification. I can forgive it, but to forget
it is something else again. In any case, I repeat, I do not bear him any ill will" '
(d'Abrantès).

[['Sourdeval.'

A young girl of fifteen passes.]]* Fleuri reads:

'De Beauharnais.'

Joséphine. A cry. She staggers to her feet, embraces Hoche, who   1150
supports her.

Joséphine falters at each step. Other prisoners watch her with   1151
compassion. Hoche helps her along. Her face is drawn; she tries to
maintain her bearing, but in vain. She reaches Fleuri at the same
time as a man of tall stature and aristocratic bearing. Astonishment:
'You, monsieur!' she says.

**The Vicomte de Beauharnais, divorced from Joséphine two
years earlier, also had to pay the price of his nobility.**

Fleuri, consulting his list again and blowing his nose, says:

'I only need one head. Sort it out between you.'

Beauharnais bows, very aristocratic, and says:

'For once, madame, allow me to take precedence.'

He kisses her hand, passes on with dignity, and, turning round, says:

'Say farewell for me to our children, madame.'

A tipsy sans-culotte mimics the hand-kissing with a fat old hag.   1152
Coarse, heartless laughter.

Joséphine faints away.   1153

[[La Bussière, who conceals beneath a cold exterior the heart of a child   1154
and whose daily acts of heroism can scarcely be credited, so far are
they beyond the bounds of imagination, follows Joséphine with his
eyes. Joséphine's beauty has visibly moved him.[1]

[[La Bussière leaves Fleuri to follow Joséphine, whom Hoche is trying   1155

---

1 – Fortunately, La Bussière is vigilant. He is a strange character who, out of
compassion, not only stole dossiers but chewed and swallowed them, thereby
risking his own life to save the lives of people he did not even know. If La Bussière
is not simply a figure of legend, then he is surely an extraordinary hero (Frédéric
Masson).

* In the film it is Lucile Desmoulins, not Mlle de Sourdeval, who is summoned; she gets up
and walks bravely towards the door.

to revive, and does all he can for her.]]

1156   Fleuri reads, but his misted eyes and his strangled voice make it difficult for him:

'André . . .'

1157   A dark young man, a dignified expression on his face, some papers in his hand, has been writing. He hears his name. He gets up, holding out his papers to an old man next to him. The old man takes them. Everyone looks at the young man.

1158   On a manuscript can be read the title:

THE YOUNG CAPTIVE

1159   With unfaltering step, the young poet walks away to his death. Fleuri can no longer carry on, his eyes are so blurred, and he is replaced by a gendarme, ruddy with wine and somewhat unsteady on his feet, who continues the 'recruitment of ghosts'. In the foreground, prisoner Rouget de Lisle can be seen. He is composing. [[Manuscript (last verse of the *Marseillaise*):

Nous entrerons dans la carrière . . .]]

The 'thermometer' of the guillotine

1160   A stained-glass rose window. The window is lit from our side and not by light shining through it, for it is night. Apse of a little chapel. Coming into view below it, in place of the expected altar, we see the top of a gigantic set of pigeon-holes with large placards bearing the following titles:

ON TRIAL   NEXT BATCH   BEHEADED   INNOCENT

Our attention is continually drawn to the enormous pigeon-holes. One end of the ancient little chapel of the condemned of the ancien-régime has been converted into a clerk's office and archive, a registry of death dominated by the holy window above. The pigeon-holes labelled 'On trial' and 'Beheaded' have an impressive number of dossiers in them, whereas the pigeon-hole labelled 'Innocent' is empty. A man, or rather a cyclops, Bonnet, nicknamed 'Green Eye', private secretary to Fouquier-Tinville, is in charge of these bloody archives. His good eye is so small and squinting that he could be thought blind; the other eye is so disproportionately large and staring that, like a nightmare, it remains indelibly inscribed in our memory. A ruffle of ginger hairs encircles his head like a tawny crown. His nails are filthy and immensely long. He smokes a long pipe with a skull-shaped bowl. A candle is burning in front of him. He opens the wrought-iron door, after consulting a list he holds in his hand. A scribe comes in, escorted by two gendarmes, carrying a huge pile of dossiers which, with the aid of a small ladder, he stuffs with great difficulty into the 'Beheaded' pigeon-hole, which is already practically full. Green Eye checks that all the dead are present and correct.

⟦ Guardroom of the adjoining Bonbec tower. The same evening.   1161
Candles. About ten gendarmes from the special corps detailed to the condemned; they wear blue coats with yellow cross-belts and tasselled tricornes. Prison warders with large keys and their guard dogs. Among the warders, La Bussière, and, next to him, also dressed in warders' uniform, Tristan Fleuri. Every face expresses terror, submission, denouncement. A heavy silence. They are waiting.

⟦ Fleuri heaves a great sigh.   1162

⟦ Every face turns towards him: he *dares* to sigh!   1163

⟦ Fleuri suppresses a guffaw and winks at La Bussière.   1164

⟦ Green Eye opens the door and calls Fleuri and La Bussière, who   1165
come over to him.⟧

Clerk's office. The pigeon-holes seen from farther off. Some empty   1166
copying desks on one side; in the middle, Green Eye's table heaped with dossiers. Gendarmes at the doors. Green Eye opens the wrought-iron door again. La Bussière and Fleuri are at his side.

The three men by the 'Next batch' rack. Green Eye piles all the 'On   1167
trial' dossiers into their arms and says harshly:

**'Execute all this lot without trial. Copy out your lists
immediately, I need three hundred heads a day!'**[1]

The two men feign submissiveness but, in an aside, they reveal their   1168
loathing for Green Eye. They settle themselves at the high desks to do their work.

⟦ Fleuri points out the almost full 'Beheaded' pigeon-hole to La   1169

1 – Fabricius writes 'F' in front of the names on the lists. 'F' stands for '*foutu*' –
'finished', 'done for' (Lenotre, *Tribunal révolutionnaire*).

123

Bussière. It is like a giant thermometer. In a low voice he says to La Bussière:

'France has never had such a high fever!']]

1170 A stern gendarme lieutenant looks underneath them – their feet are dangling – and around them, lest any of the ghastly files should escape.

1171 La Bussière, his desk, his dossiers and his list. He takes a dossier from the left; he writes the name, then he passes it to the right. He gives a quick glance round him, pulls out a dossier from the left-hand pile; he looks round again to make sure nobody is watching him, tears off a piece of the dossier and eats it.

1172 Dossier:

JOSÉPHINE DE BEAUHARNAIS

1173 Fleuri. Same set-up. He looks up and sees

1174 La Bussière in the process of eating his dossier.[1]

1175 Fleuri copies him but with the difference that poor Tristan, unlike his colleague, does not manage to swallow the scraps of dossier; he chokes, then he sadly says to La Bussière in a low whisper:

'You're lucky you can digest them. I just can't manage it.'

1176 Fleuri. His amazement.

DOSSIER NAPOLÉON BONAPARTE

His distress; he pushes it towards La Bussière, saying:

'Eat this one as well.'

1177 La Bussière in dumb-show; 'Impossible, my friend. I would suffocate!' And he pushes the Bonaparte dossier back.

1178 Fleuri makes up his mind. He tears off tiny pieces and rolls them into small pellets, which he puts in his pocket.

1179 Green Eye looks up and watches them.

---

1 – There is no proof that La Bussière did actually eat Joséphine's file but he did boast of having done so and Joséphine believed him, for on 5 April 1803 she was present with the First Consul at the Théâtre Porte-Saint-Martin for a special benefit performance for La Bussière and she paid 100 pistoles for her box (Frédéric Masson).

La Bussière gives Fleuri a kick. Their feet under the desk. The two 1180
friends carry on assiduously with their task.

Green Eye, reassured, works on. 1181

Fleuri finishes his rescue of Bonaparte by means of his little pellets. 1182
Just in time, for Fleuri and La Bussière give a start, eyes riveted on
a door.

Green Eye gets up obsequiously, while the gendarmes salute as if the 1183
highest personage of the Republic had just entered.

[[**The most fearsome man of the Reign of Terror, Saint-Just.**]]

Saint-Just, followed by Fouquier-Tinville and Dumas the Bloody.* 1184
He pauses on the threshold. His power. We now see the full length
of the chapel; until now we have seen nothing but the choir. It looks
exactly like a court clerk's office. Twelve court clerks, ten copyists
and six ordinary clerks are sitting at high desks, busy with their
morbid work. They are all petrified at the entrance of Saint-Just.
Dead stillness.

The chief clerk runs his finger round his collar and almost passes 1185
out.

Fleuri is in a complete sweat. He crouches so low over his list in order 1186
to write better that he appears short-sighted.

He is so terrified that he makes blots. He clutches his right hand with 1187
his left to stop it trembling.

Everyone petrified. Saint-Just passes. He contemplates the sinister 1188
pigeon-holes, adjusting his hair and examining it in a pocket mirror.
By chance, the tall shadow of a cross spreads over the great wall.**

Antibes

[[The office of the clerk of the court, Antibes. Salicetti speaks to an 1189
officer:

'I do not understand the strange delay in the arrival of

* *Saint-Just in fact enters alone.*
** *The shadow was replaced by the following sequence: after having closely examined the
terrified Fleuri's handiwork, Saint-Just goes over to the set of giant pigeon-holes and stands
before it in rapt contemplation; the last shot is a close-up of his face, wearing a sinister smile.*

> Bonaparte's file. Another must be made up here and he must be shot within three days.'

Salicetti goes out.

1190 〚 Salicetti totally without pity for children.

1191 〚 His anger when his collar is spoiled.

1192 〚 Exterior prison. Caroline, the youngest of Bonaparte's sisters, jumps on Salicetti as he comes out, and like a little lioness scratches his face. He has her thrown some way off like a limp rag.

1193 〚 The little girl sobs, her forehead smeared with blood and dust.〛

THERMIDOR

1194 The great vessel of the Convention, bubbling like a volcano. The galleries full to bursting. The benches of the Right are empty; over there, the 'Montagnard' seats with the gaping hole left by the Hebertists, over here, the enormous gap where the Girondins once sat. Only the 'belly' is crowded, silent, impenetrable, awaiting events. All are leaning forward, taut as bows.

1195 In a gallery. Violine, pale-faced, with Marcellin, whom she is holding by the hand.

1196 We hear:

> 'Death to the two monsters!'

And, almost unanimous:

> 'Death to Saint-Just! Death to Robespierre!'

1197 Robespierre and Saint-Just make their entrance. Awesome and terrible silence. Robespierre, dressed in the blue coat he wore on the 20 Prairial, his head beautifully powdered, walks as though towards some kind of apotheosis; Saint-Just in his chamois-coloured coat with a white waistcoat and pale grey breeches. His earrings give him a disquietingly androgynous look.

1198 Robespierre goes to the rostrum.

1199 Violine furtively brings out a pistol from her bodice. She has come to kill one of the tyrants.

1200 Wild tumult.

Robespierre has been trying to speak; he calls out to Collot d'Herbois, who is presiding:

1201

'For the last time, will you let me speak, president of assassins!'

Now it is Tallien who leaps forward, brandishing a dagger. Robespierre's friends drag him out of reach. Tallien cries out:

1202

> **'I have armed myself with a dagger to pierce the breast of this new Cromwell, if the Convention lacks the courage to indict him.'**

He waves his dagger in the midst of an immense commotion. Passions have reached fever-pitch.

Robespierre approaches his former friends, who disown him; he wanders from the centre to the right. Choking with fury, he tries to speak. He has reached the spot where Danton used to sit; empty row of seats. Garnier de Saintes shouts out:

1203

> **'The blood of Danton is choking you!'**

Robespierre now leaps like a wild animal up the empty tiers belonging to the Right. Fréron thunders at him in a terrible voice:

> **'You're walking on the graves of the Girondins!'**

And he does indeed stumble among the bodies of those present. He collapses in exhaustion.

The kill is about to begin when

1204

Couthon tries to escape in his wheelchair. He is held back.

1205

Saint-Just leaps to the tribune like a wounded tiger and shouts:

1206

> **'Jackals!'**

This abrupt interruption shocks the house into silence. They listen to him. He is totally unlike his usual self; ordinarily so calm and in control of himself, he is now carried away by an insane lyricism which in the course of one minute will sway this crowd to the extremes of mass emotion.

Violine. She cocks her pistol. Nobody has noticed her.

1207

Saint-Just. His expression gradually grows calm and by the end of his speech it will become quite serene. But for the moment his passion raises him to his full stature.

1208

'Yes, we had to have victims, but is not the Revolution a great
beacon lit upon tombs?'

1209   Silence.

1210   His cold prophet's face radiating with lofty dignity, Saint-Just says:

⟦ 'The Terror will partly obscure the significance
of the Revolution, but none the less it is because of us
that there is liberty in the world!'⟧

1211   Everyone is listening.

1212 ⟦ Saint-Just says:

'Certainly, I admit our weaknesses. The executions of the
Terror inured us to crime, as strong liquor dulls the palate.'

1213 ⟦ In the space of thirty seconds we see the following series of shots:

(a)   Ruffians wresting children from their mother.
(b)   The Nantes drownings. The bottom of a boat gives way,
       children sink into the water.
(c)   A bell ringing in a raging hurricane. The name of Tallien
       streaks across a sky wild with hurrying red clouds.

128

(d)   The wheels of a passing tumbril.

(e)   The executioner Samson releasing . . . the guillotine catch; the shadow of the triangular blade falls over him.

(f)   Crater of an active volcano.

(g)   Burst of brutish laughter.

(a1)   Ruffians dragging struggling women.

(b1)   The Lyons massacres, hundreds of condemned prisoners herded together; shot not by firing squads but by cannon at point-blank range.

(c1)   A bell rings. The name of Fouché streaks across the red sky.

(d1)   The wheels of a passing tumbril.

(e1)   The executioner.

(f1)   The seething crater of the volcano, more violent than before.

(g1)   Another burst of brutish laughter.

Then five series of the images we have already seen. At the end of the fifth series, we see six superimpositions all at once.]]

Silence. Saint-Just's act of contrition is received with mingled astonishment and respect.   1214

Saint-Just continues: 1215

'Have you forgotten that during this time we have forged a France that is new and ready to be lived in?'

'. . . passed 12,000 decrees, of which two thirds were dedicated to human ends?

[[Saint-Just remains in the background as: in the space of one minute, flowers, sunshine, laughing grape-harvesters on a bright road and other appropriate images to suggest happiness are superimposed, then a series of animated words, each one trying to gain supremacy over the one before: 1216

EQUALITY
THE ABOLITION OF SLAVERY
PRIMARY SCHOOLS
TECHNICAL SCHOOLS
TRAINING COLLEGES
THE TELEGRAPH SYSTEM
DECIMAL SYSTEMS
STANDARDIZATION OF WEIGHTS AND MEASURES

THE ORDNANCE OFFICE
THE GREAT BOOK OF THE NATIONAL DEBT
HOSPITALS
INSTITUTES FOR THE BLIND AND DEAF-MUTE
ZOOLOGICAL GARDENS
THE CONSERVATORY OF MUSIC AND ARTS AND CRAFTS
POLYTECHNIC COLLEGES
THE INSTITUTE OF FRANCE

THE RIGHTS OF MAN]]

1217   Saint-Just says:

'And we have done all this with that vulture, the Vendée, at our flanks, and on our shoulders that mass of tigers, the Kings . . .'[1]

[[Saint-Just still in the background. Republican armies rush past at the double; a flapping standard bearing the word 'WATTIGNIES', then another standard, 'WISSEMBOURG', another, 'FLEURUS', another, 'JEMAPPES', another, 'VALMY'. Raging wind. All trembling in the sunshine; bugles, drums; the Republic laughs, the end of Danton's *Marseillaise*. All this single, then double, then triple, and quadruple, until it is impossible to see. Everything is carried away by the rhythm.]]

1218   Saint-Just concludes:

'You can now scatter our limbs to the four winds: new Republics will rise up from them!'

1219   General stupefaction. No one knows which side to take any more.

1220   Violine. She is overwhelmed. She drops her weapon; she has lost her desire to kill. She sees that wicked acts are often required of men in order to defend great ideas, and her hatred subsides.

1221   Saint-Just descends from the rostrum amid a tremendous silence and rejoins Robespierre, who embraces him. Just as the two great tribunes are preparing to leave, the deputies begin yelling as before: 'Death!' They shriek like men possessed. They are choking with hatred.

1222   Saint-Just turns round. Silence. He says:

'I despise the dust of which I am made and which speaks to you. I give it to you!'

1 – This is a quotation from Hugo, *Quatre-vingt-treize*.

And he holds out his hands to the gendarmes.

'Death! Death!' comes the howl from the entire unleashed Conven- 1223
tion. But not a single gendarme or usher dares arrest these two
fearsome men, and they go out free.

Violine says dreamily to Marcellin: 1224

'They are too great for us!'

'Yes, yes. You're probably right!' Marcellin agrees, pulling her by the
hand, as if he had become the sensible elder brother.

The clerk of court's office with the grim pigeon-holes full of dossiers. 1225
It is barely recognizable: the god of chaos reigns supreme. Absolute
confusion and panic. A man is turning round and round in circles,
first to the right, then to the left. He is balancing a pile of dossiers
two metres high. They are 'Next batch' dossiers, which he puts into
the 'Innocent' rack. He picks up a pile of 'Beheaded' ones and turns
his apoplectic face towards us; it is Tristan Fleuri, swaying under the
weight of his pile.

Another warder with a pile just as large is as confused as Fleuri; he 1226
runs to the right, then is sent back to the left.

Fleuri and this other warder, one summoned to the right, the other 1227
to the left, meet at full tilt. Catastrophe. The dossiers scatter and
bury several copyists.

Green Eye thunders. 1228

Fleuri quakes, plays dead, completely out of sight beneath his 1229
dossiers.

La Bussière eats Rouget de Lisle's dossier.]] 1230

Gendarmes come storming in and hand Green Eye a list: 1231

To be guillotined tomorrow morning: Robespierre, Couthon, Saint-Just, Henriot and all the Robespierrists. Prepare their dossiers.
Fouquier-Tinville

Green Eye looks up, bewildered, and says: 1232

'What a mess!'

Clerk of court's office. Door. Some soldiers burst in with sabres 1233
drawn.

1234   Scribes in complete panic. The gendarmes arrest them all, not forgetting

1235 [[Green Eye, who tries to scramble up his ghastly filing-rack and brings it toppling down on top of himself. Terrific uproar. He is pulled out from underneath it, fighting like a demon, so they stuff him into a sack which a gendarme ties up and throws out of the window.

1236 [[Exterior. Bonbec tower. Tumult. Soldiers with bayonets by the cannon. The sack in which Green Eye is tied falls from the top of the tower and is impaled on the bayonets.]]

1237   Fleuri. He peeps out from under the dossiers. Nobody notices him. He buries himself deeper; feet pass by in all directions; people trample over him without seeing him. The disarray is at its height.

Two hours later . . .

1238   Exterior of Les Carmes prison. Delirious joy. Barrels. Carousing. Dancing in the street. A blind old man with his organ plays tirelessly. The prisoners emerge from Les Carmes, freed. Joséphine, radiant. Her children smother her with kisses. One of the sinister tumbrils is being burnt and people are dancing round it.

1239 [[Fleuri, glowing with happiness, stops, shocked to see La Bussière, who is choking. People are trying to bring him round. Fleuri bends over him.

1240 [[La Bussière smiles wanly at Fleuri and says confidentially:

1241 [['I swallowed the *Marseillaise*!'

1242 [[Frenzied delight.]]

1243   Chappe telegraph. The news being signalled.

1244 [[Road. 'Thermidor' appears upon it in enormous letters. Dark sky. Tumbrils with Saint-Just, Robespierre. Couthon, guillotine, etc. Fear. Couthon's basket. Tigers. A volcano. Fire. Lava. The shadow of the blade on the executioner's face.]]

The fortress prison at Antibes

Tumult. Evening. Bonaparte's release from prison. The last formalities at the prison door. Moonlight. He comes out. He is about to move off. [[He sees an inert mass stretched out at his feet. He stoops down. **1245**

He raises the body. It is his mother; she is unconscious. She comes round. He embraces her. She cannot believe her happiness.]] **1246**

Salicetti on the run, plunging across a muddy swamp. He is bleeding. His pursuers drive him on with stones.* **1247**

Waiting

Restored to his rank, but purposely kept out of action, Bonaparte comes to Paris to remind the Minister of War of his existence.

Office of the Minister of War, Aubry. Bonaparte is kept standing while the ill-mannered and pretentious Aubry gives him an order. **1248**

'We appoint General Bonaparte to the position of General of the Western Army Infantry in the Vendée.'

'No! I refuse,' says Bonaparte categorically. Aubry leaps to his feet, taken aback. Hoche enters at this moment. Bonaparte salutes. Aubry, in a rage, tells Hoche in scornful tones that Bonaparte has refused his commission. Hoche looks searchingly at Bonaparte and says:

'Does it inconvenience you to go to war under my command in the Vendée?'

Risking his head, Bonaparte retorts:

'When two hundred thousand foreigners are violating our frontiers, it certainly does inconvenience me to go to war against Frenchmen!'

Aubry rises and looks him up and down. 'Be silent, young man!' He goes out in a fury. Hoche and Bonaparte look at one another in silence.

[[In an adjoining office Aubry tells Cambacérès of Bonaparte's refusal.]] **1249**

---

* *A very recently rediscovered print contains the telegraph (scene 1243) and a two-shot sequence in which Salicetti, cornered in a quarry and surrounded by sans-culottes, is literally trampled underfoot.*

1250   Hoche and Bonaparte exchange not one word; suddenly, Hoche extends his hand to Bonaparte, who shakes it. And he goes out.

1251 ⟦ Aubry rubs his hands in satisfaction, for Cambacérès is writing his signature, having already collected several other signatures.

Liberty – Equality

The Committee of Public Safety decrees that General Bonaparte shall be struck from the list of officers in active service, on account of his refusal to accept the post assigned to him.

Signed: *Cambacérès, Letourneur, Merlin, Berlier.*

Aubry goes out with Cambacérès.⟧

1252   The minister's office. Cambacérès, this future great man of the Empire, personally hands to Bonaparte the document he has just signed, measuring him with a look. Bonaparte reads; not a muscle on his face moves. He salutes smartly and goes out.

1253   A recess forming a tiny withdrawing-room in the antechamber. Joséphine is there with Hoche. He laughs, his mouth close to hers. Bonaparte passes slowly, without seeing them, his face inscrutable.

1254   Hoche and Joséphine. Hoche, his eyes involuntarily drawn to the unfortunate young general, calls Joséphine's attention to him. She looks at Bonaparte and questions Hoche with immense curiosity. The first spark.

⟦When there is not enough for two, there is certainly not enough for six!

1255 ⟦ Bonaparte's shabby room in the rue des Fossés-Montmartre. He is there with Talma, Junot, Marmont, Louis Bourrienne.

1256 ⟦ They haven't a sou between them. They empty their pockets of all they possess and spread out on the table knives, keys, knick-knacks and trinkets. Napoléon adds his watch; Marmont, with a sigh, his ring. They make some calculations; it won't go very far! Bonaparte hesitates, and then makes a decision. He picks up the few books he has left and throws them on to the table. He has nothing else left to keep. Junot takes the lot in the tablecloth, which he knots at the

134

corners. The poor young men are plunged in silence. Bonaparte paces up and down like a wild animal. Talma tries to calm him down. Bonaparte explodes:

'I am suffocating in this cage!'

Talma and his friends stare at each other. What is he talking about? His room? Talma asks him:

'What cage are you talking about?'

As if he could not possibly be referring to anything else, he replies, ingenuously: 1257

'Great heavens, France, of course!'

They look at him. He commands their admiration. He continues pacing like a wild beast. 1258

Bonaparte suddenly looks at a great map of the world on the wall, and says in a low voice: 1259

'I have one last resort.'

'And that is?' Junot looks at him questioningly.

Bonaparte replies with faraway eyes: 1260

'To found an empire.'

Junot; his eyes seem to say, 'But, for God's sake, where?' Bonaparte points and says, 'Here.'

On the map, the Orient, the Indies, Alexander's empire. 1261

Bonaparte, more thoughtful than ever, goes on: 1262

'Or there.'

He points to America and Canada.

Junot stares at Bonaparte, smiling incredulously, but Bonaparte's eyes are filled with such faith in himself and his destiny that Junot's smile freezes and he clasps Bonaparte's hand. 'Let us go!' he says. He takes up his sword. This time Bonaparte smiles, giving him a friendly cuff on the cheek. 1263

In his search for some way of making a living, he believed he had found a new path open to him.[1]

1 – 'During this period he was a wretched creature, mentally and physically. You'd

1264 [[A case full of books, which a hand is finishing packing. A plank is placed over it to form a lid; nails, a hammer; it is Bonaparte in a bookseller's premises, ground floor. He hammers his fingers. At last, it's fixed! Satisfied, he lifts the case from the ground; all the books fall out through the bottom. Angrily he picks up his shabby hat and leaves through the window. The manager arrives with a list, to talk to him. He searches for Bonaparte all over the place without success, even in the packing-case!]]

1265 **Reinstated to his rank, but given an obscure post in the army ordnance office, Bonaparte brings his plans for the Italian Campaign to Pontécoulant.**

Pontécoulant's office on the sixth floor of the Pavillon de Flore. Pontécoulant is pacing back and forth. He is in the middle of being shaved; lather on his face. Bonaparte, in his shabby general's uniform, is talking to him, his plans unfolded in his hand. Pontécoulant stops shaving, fascinated, then riveted, by the astuteness and genius of this young man. Barras, passing by, salutes Bonaparte with a fatherly air. Pontécoulant says to him: 'The plans of this young man are quite extraordinary.' He forgets that he has not finished his shave, and, with his chin covered with soap, he begins to write.[1]

1266 Schérer's general staff with the Army of Italy, pretentious and inept. Schérer reads and laughs till the tears run down his face at some plans which he shows to his officers, who ridicule them.

1267 The plans, signed by Bonaparte. Schérer's hand unrolls the plans and writes:

-----

meet him in the streets of Paris, wandering along with an awkward, uncertain gait, wearing a miserable round hat pulled down over his eyes, his badly powdered ill-kempt side-locks falling over the collar of that iron-grey frock coat which was to become so notorious. His hands were long, thin, blackened and he wore no gloves because, he said, they were an expense he could do without; his boots were badly made and ill-polished. He looked quite unhealthy, as his jaundiced complexion emphasized the morbid shadows cast by his features which were emaciated and angular. Thus he wandered, looking immensely sad . . . He never laughed. He thought he'd found a new direction, exporting books. But his first venture, shipping a crate of books to Basle, was a failure' (Arthur-Lévy, *Napoléon intime*, 1892).

1 – The next day, from the sixth floor where he took refuge from people in search of favours, he watched the arrival of the thinnest, frailest man he had ever seen in his life, a young man, said Pontécoulant, with a ghastly pale complexion, shoulders hunched, frail and sickly-looking (Arthur-Lévy, *Napoléon intime*, 1892).

**These plans are the work of a madman! Let the fool who drew
them up come and execute them.**

Schérer

General laughter. Complacent stupidity. Shadows of dancers on one   1268
of the walls of the office.

Bonaparte at his lodgings. He is in the middle of cooking. He shakes   1269
the stove with comic severity. A parcel has just been delivered to him;
he breaks the seal.

His roll of Italian plans with Schérer's note: 1270

**These plans are the work of a madman! Let the fool who drew
them up come and execute them.**

Schérer

His impassive face.   1271

He is about to burn them when he changes his mind; he goes to the   1272
window.

The rain is driving in through the broken window-pane. Bonaparte   1273
folds his plans to cover the frame.

[[The gluttonous.]]   1274*

Fairy-tale splendour, surpassing the imagination. The domain of
Mme Tallien. A swirl of gold, lights, voluptuousness.

The starving.

Window of Mme Tallien's town house, the interior of which we have   1275
just seen. Gaunt faces in the snow, looking in with eyes brimming
with envy, hatred or despair. Snow is falling.

A queue at the door of a baker's shop. A picture of the poverty of the   1276
time. Violine is there, and has been for some hours. Snow cloaks the
poor people's shoulders, which are bowed with hunger and cold. The
baker comes out with a soldier and says: 'There's none left!' And he
closes his shutters. A group of poor people are overcome with fury
. . . they invade the shop. The others move off, more bowed than
ever. Violine is among them.

* *This short sequence survives only in fragments.*

1277 [[Small street. A bill-poster is finishing off his work. Violine is aghast. She has just read:

CITIZENS

A STATE OF FAMINE REIGNS. TO SAVE CORN, THE PROPOSED AMENDMENT TO KILL ALL THE BIRDS OF FRANCE MUST BE ADOPTED.

Commander of the National Guard

Violine runs away, stumbling in the snow.

1278 [[The poster. A dead branch, with many birds on it, right next to the poster. The birds are facing towards the text, as if they were reading. They fly away.

For two months, under the cloak of anarchy, Paris had been filling with Chouans* and émigrés who, exploiting the people's misery . . .

1279 [[Le Peletier Section, at the convent of the Daughters of Saint Thomas, at the end of the rue Vivienne. Feverish activity. The *sectionnaires*** are being armed. Royalist orators from Saint-Jean d'Angély–Lafarge, Lacretelle the Younger, Pozzo di Borgo and Salicetti – are stirring up the crowd against the Convention.

1280 [[Pozzo makes an inflammatory speech. There are shouts of 'Long live the King!'

---

* *See note to scene 1298.*
** *In 1790 Paris was regrouped into forty-eight districts, called sections. The* sectionnaires *played an important part in the Revolution, organizing, for instance, the fall of the Girondins. The sections almost immediately adopted revolutionary-sounding titles – the Le Peletier section being named after one of the martyrs of the revolution. In 1795, the sections were to be replaced by twelve* arrondissements, *and run by municipal councils in place of the assemblies of the* sectionnaires. *The hostility of most of France against those who symbolized the Terror gave the royalists a chance of winning the forthcoming elections to the councils. But the members of the Convention decided that two-thirds of the members of the new councils were to be drawn from the Convention, thus dashing the hopes of the royalists. Supported by thirty out of the forty-eight sections, and by a part of the National Guard under the command of General Danican, the royalists attempted a coup d'état against the Convention on 13 Vendémiaire (4 October 1795). Danican's troops and the royalist insurrectionists were quickly dispersed by Bonaparte.*

A haggard, savage-looking man, bearing all the signs of wretchedness,   1281
who is demanding a gun through clenched teeth, is asked:

'What are you? Dantonist, Robespierrist, royalist?'

The man glares at his questioners and replies with awesome truth   1282
and grandeur:

'I am hungry!'

As if he were in a conspiracy of State, a man in a dress-coat gives a   1283
bundle to a shopkeeper who produces a chicken from under his
counter. The man hides the bird under his coat while the shopkeeper
counts: a bale of paper money for a chicken!]]

Joséphine's house, 8 rue Basse-Pierre, Chaillot. Daytime. Her   1284
boudoir. Barras, wearing a dressing-gown, is pacing up and down,
preoccupied. Joséphine reclines languidly on a divan, her bad-
tempered pug Fortuné at her side. Barras looks down into the street.

Some sentinels hail one another. Some *sectionnaires* come by and   1285
disarm the sentinels.

In the street, shutters are being closed everywhere. Fear.]]   1286

Joséphine's house. Barras says thoughtfully: 1287

'We must find someone!'

Joséphine, as she powders herself, says casually:

'Why don't you consider that droll young Buona . . . Buona . . . parte?'

Barras wheels round. His jealousy is apparent. It shows in his eyes.
He goes over to her and says brutally: 'No!' She laughs, putting her
powder-puff over his face. He laughs. He draws closer to her,
amorously. She resists. He says: 'Very well. I'll think about it.' She
gives way to him.

And on 12 Vendémiaire . . .*
The Convention. Indescribable chaos. Everybody is speaking at once.   1288

* *The Vendémiaire sequence has survived in a fragmented state; some of the shots that do
not appear in Kevin Brownlow's restoration have survived but in an unusable condition.
All that can be said with certainty is that the exteriors were dropped from the script.*

Carnot tries in vain to make himself heard. Fear hovers over the assembly.

1289 Outside, the soldiers are having difficulty keeping back the crowd who are bent on killing the deputies.

1290 The Convention. Bonaparte, his shaggy mane of hair dishevelled, enters a public gallery in the midst of the howling mob, and looks on impassively. He is lost in the vast crowd, and anyone seeing him so shabby and puny would certainly never believe that in a few hours' time he would save the Convention.

1291 The *sectionnaires* occupy the Pont-Neuf.

1292 Convention. Menou, who has been trying to exonerate himself, is arrested, amid threats. The wrangling continues.

1293 An officer, alarmed, comes on to the rostrum and begins to speak. The people listen to him.

1294 The *sectionnaires'* drums beating the charge upon the Place du Carrousel.

1295 Thousands of *sectionnaires*, the dregs of the suburbs, descend on the Tuileries. The inky blackness of this nocturnal revolt.

1296 Lanterns are shattered by gunshots.

1297 The great vessel of the Convention is out of control. Painting by Delacroix.

1298 Barras yells apoplectically:

'I need a general immediately to put down this royalist insurrection.'[1]

1299 The Directors. There is a shower of names: 'Brune. – No! Verdière. – No! Hoche! – not here.'

1300 Barras goes on:

'I propose the victor of Toulon, Bonaparte. [[What do you think, Carnot?']]

1301 Carnot. His thoughtful expression. A second's pause. He agrees.

1 – There were scores of emigrants, landowners and nobility among the dead; most of the prisoners, however, were Chouans (royalist rebels or, to be more precise, Breton royalist insurgents) from Charette (Bonaparte's first report on Vendémiaire).

Bonaparte absolutely impassive. Junot is amazed and can scarcely believe his ears, but Bonaparte does not make himself known. 1302

Fréron gets to his feet: 1303

'Does anyone know where he lives?'

'No! No! Nobody knows.' There is a frantic search, with ushers scurrying about and leafing through books. 1304

Junot is going to call out. Bonaparte stops him. Junot cannot understand it. Bonaparte goes out, enigmatic, taking Junot with him.[1] 1305

Exterior, Convention. Terrible crush. Bonaparte and Junot come out. Bonaparte is calm and deep in thought. Junot is watching him, biting his nails. 1306

Bonaparte's room. He comes in. He listens. 1307

Alarm bells, drums, guns. 1308

Bonaparte's room. He sits down and thinks. His forehead, his eyes, over what he is seeing. On the right a map of France pierced by stilettos which seem to stab at the cities of Paris, Lyons, Marseilles, Nantes, Bordeaux, Toulon, etc. Red patches appear and spread with names upon them: Tallien, Fouché, Robespierre, Couthon, Fréron, etc. These red patches finally merge to form one huge red stain upon which appears in enormous letters: 1309

THERMIDOR

On the left, in the space of forty seconds, the whole Revolution passes before his eyes in gigantic scenes, one on top of the other, twenty, thirty, forty at a time in every direction. His brow and eyes dominate all this; he sinks deep into his reverie. Junot does not dare speak to him. His reverie continues. The map of France, which is red with blood and like a pounding heart, continues to throb, and now serpents advance upon every frontier, representing the forty English ships blockading Brest, the 15,000 Austrians at the gates of Strasbourg.

The window-panes of Bonaparte's room burst into fragments. Only the plans for the Army of Italy, forming one of the panes, remain in place. 1310

1 – Bonaparte used to tell the story of how he was in the Assembly when he heard a voice shout out: 'If anyone knows General Bonaparte's address, please can they go and tell him he's expected at the Assembly Committee' (Lacour-Gayet).

1311 Junot listens in the direction of the staircase.

1312 On the dingy landing, Barras with his great sword, his composure gone, appears with a brilliant staff of officers. Junot opens the door. Barras enters.

1313 Bonaparte salutes him. Barras tells him of his decision and, checking his watch, says:

> **'I give you three minutes to come to a decision, General. Without an iron hand the Convention is lost.'**

And he goes on to the landing to join his staff, taking Junot out with him.

1314 Bonaparte alone. His eyes are ablaze. He goes to his lighted stove, takes out a small live coal with some tongs, hesitates and, summoning up all his willpower, places this smoking coal in the palm of his hand.

1315 The coal burns the flesh, which sears and smokes.

1316 His face impassive. His lips are compressed a trifle more tightly than usual.

1317 The smoke from the coal lessens.

1318 Bonaparte smiles. He throws the coal back. Barras enters in great anxiety.

1319 Bonaparte says to him:

> **'An iron hand, did you say?'**

Barras, astonished at the question, confirms the fact. *Bonaparte looks at him and says:

> **'*I accept!* I have no liking for those I shall be serving, but when the territory is threatened, the first duty is to rally to those who hold the reins of government.'**

1320 Barras grasps his hand. Seeing blood on it, he says in shocked surprise: 'What is the matter with your hand?' 'Nothing,' says Bonaparte, swathing his hand in his handkerchief. He raises his head. Junot can contain his joy no longer. Bonaparte says:

> **'I warn you, Barras, once my sword leaves its scabbard I shall not sheathe it again until order has been restored.'**

* *The meeting-place where the* coup d'état *of 13 Vendmiaire was hatched.*

142

He goes out without his hat.

Exterior, house. [[People are running in the streets with torches and 1321
lanterns. They are hiding. A poor woman sobs in the doorway. She
has six hungry wailing children. She is breast-feeding two of them;
the others will probably die. Dishevelled spectre of poverty. Barras
and his staff pass her by, taking no notice; they have other things to
think about! But Bonaparte stops, gives all he has on him, and forces
the grumbling Barras to do likewise;]] then they climb into the
carriage.[1]

The wretched woman's joy.]]   1322

Junot comes running downstairs to catch up with his general, who 1323
has left without his hat, as he often does. Junot climbs up beside the
coachman.

[[That evening Bonaparte entered History once and for all, never again to leave it.

Doors of the Convention. An even greater crowd than a short while 1324
ago. The carriages are completely hemmed in by the people and
extricated with great difficulty by the grenadiers and the Convention's
infantrymen. An arms magazine. Bonaparte enters with Barras and
gives orders.]]

The Convention. He enters. They look upon him as the Messiah. 1325
They crowd round him. 'Order!' he snaps. 'Everyone to their seat.'
Everyone returns to their places. From this moment he again becomes
what he was at Toulon, a totally different man: the leader. He
commands almost without movement or gesture. Tallien tries to
speak; Bonaparte gives him a look; Tallien falls silent.

Guns are brought in. 'Distribute them!' says Bonaparte, motioning 1326
to the deputies. The Convention members are astounded and begin
to realize the gravity of the situation.

Alarm of two or three members who do not dare touch the guns for 1327
fear they will go off by themselves.

Adjoining room. General Menou, imprisoned and under close watch. 1328

1 – The woman's name is Marianne Huvé. I could add another terrible detail: one
of her children lies dead before her, from starvation; but truth must be used
creatively and I am obliged to rise above events, mitigating or transposing them.

Bonaparte arrives and, without preamble, interrogates him, while couriers are continually setting off with orders which he issues as he goes along. Menou replies:

'We have only five thousand men at our disposal against forty thousand. As for our forty cannon at Les Sablons – the only ones we possess – they must be in the hands of the *sectionnaires* by now.'

Indicating Menou to the officers present, Barras says:

'Now, shoot him!'

Bonaparte turns round: 'No, let him go free.' 'But . . .' 'That is an order!' snaps Bonaparte. Menou is unbound, and he tries to throw himself at Bonaparte's feet.

1329 Room in which are gathered the officers of the five thousand men; an odd assortment, in shabby uniforms. Bonaparte runs his eagle eye over them: 'You, there!' he says to a tall major of the 21st Chasseurs dressed like a wild man, who steps forward for his orders.

'I like the look of you! You will take three hundred cavalrymen and bring me the forty Sablons cannon which must be in Paris by one o'clock in the morning.'

The major is disconcerted to receive so explicit an order and tries to make a proviso . . . 'Pardon me, General, but what if . . .' 'Do as I say!' says Bonaparte, cutting him short. The major is about to leave the room. Bonaparte brings him back on the threshold.

'Your name?'

The officer:

'Murat, General.'

He salutes and goes out.

1330 Bonaparte gives orders simply, without moving, to ten officers standing round him. He dominates them all. He is the hub of the wheel.

1331 Convention hall. The office employees are transforming it into a defensive camp. Supplies of cartridges are brought in. The Convention members, clustered together, look on. Bonaparte enters. Like schoolboys who have left their benches without permission, hampered by their guns, they hurry back to their places in the tiers of seats.

Silence. Bonaparte looks at them and crosses the hall. You could hear a pin drop. He goes out. The deputies breathe again. A mighty force has just passed through their midst. They are now more confident.

Night, moon, wicket-gate of the Louvre. Bonaparte is placing his cannon. He sets up a battery of forty at the Tuileries, four in the Place du Carrousel, two at the Pont-Royal, two in the rue de l'Échelle. 1332

Murat idly whittles with his knife at the pommel of his whip – he is carving Bonaparte's head. 1333

VENDÉMIAIRE

Church of Saint-Roch.* Daytime. The cannon are in position. The grenadiers are waiting for the *sectionnaires*. 1334

In a motley group of 'patriots of 1789', dressed in eccentric garments, waits Tristan Fleuri, stiff as a post with emotion. He has to stretch up his neck almost to breaking-point in order to see anything from under his helmet, it is so enormous. Suddenly his legs begin to tremble. 'What's up with you?' asks his comrade, a grenadier, who turns out to be the giant Moustache. 'Can't you see him, then?' 'Who?' 'Him!' Bonaparte passes, sunk in gloom at the prospect of fighting against fellow Frenchmen. 1335

Bonaparte halts, looks at Fleuri. Fleuri is overwhelmed and hangs his head. Nothing can be seen but his helmet. Bonaparte shrugs his shoulders and continues on his way. Tristan sways as if he were about to swoon. Moustache supports him. Fleuri, delirious with joy, says: 1336

'You saw how he looked at me? He knows what's what!'

The others laugh up their sleeves at his simple-mindedness.

Bonaparte surveys the *sectionnaires*, weighing them up; then he commands his bombardiers: 1337

'No shot is to be used! You will fire blanks.'

He turns to the infantry:

'Shoulder arms.'

The infantry obey.

* *The meeting-place where the* coup d'état *of 13 Vendémiaire was hatched.*

1338 ⟦ Silence. A parley is to take place.

1339 ⟦ Front rank of the 'patriots of 1789'. Tristan Fleuri, who has decided to wear his helmet back to front in order to see more clearly, is rooted to the spot as he sees

1340 ⟦ young Marcellin in the front rank of the *sectionnaires*, full of curiosity, worming his way through with his drum.

1341 ⟦ Tristan Fleuri in despair. He dares not explain his reasons to those around him. Tears come to his eyes.⟧

*1342 Balcony of the Hôtel de Noailles. A gun-barrel in a hole cut through the wood of the window-frame; behind the window, an émigré, undoubtedly a royalist, in the garb of the *ancien régime*, is taking aim. Someone speaks to him. He turns round. We recognize him: Pozzo di Borgo!

1343 The gun-barrel. He aims at Bonaparte and fires.

1344 Bonaparte's horse is killed under him. 'Fire!' Bonaparte commands the cannon.

1345 A blank charge is fired.

1346 The *sectionnaires* retreat; although there are obviously no fatalities, they unmask their batteries. 'Fire!' shouts their general, Danican. A salvo.

1347 Infantrymen, grenadiers and patriots fall.

1348 'Fire!' Bonaparte commands his infantry, having mounted another horse.

1349 Fleuri. His gun is trembling. At the end of his gun-barrel, in the smoke, he sees

1350 his small son Marcellin playing the drum with a very martial air.

1351 Fleuri cannot fire, but he sees

1352 Bonaparte watching, still as a rock.

1353 Then, in wild desperation, dripping with sweat, Fleuri closes his eyes

* *The scenes at the Hôtel de Noailles were certainly not shot as written; as they survive in the print, they are incomplete. In all probability Moustache, Marcellin and a lot of Fleuri were cut from the shooting script.*

and fires at random, his gun raised at forty-five degrees.*

He wounds Pozzo di Borgo, who has been following the battle feverishly from the window at the Hôtel de Noailles.   *1354*

The fray begins.   *1355*

Bonaparte grimly directs the fighting.   *1356*

The *sectionnaires* lose ground and take refuge in the church of Saint-Roch. They have cannon placed on the steps.   *1357*

The battle is renewed.   *1358*

Marcellin fights like a little lion.   *1359*

Tristan Fleuri in a skirmish. He makes to fire his gun: it does not go off. He is obliged to floor his enemy with a punch on the nose. He looks at his gun. In a fury, he throws it to the ground. He tries to draw his sabre: no use; it must be rusted in. Ironically, the gun goes off on its own on the ground between his legs. Fleuri tugs at his sabre with such frenzy that he pulls off the handle, leaving the rusted blade in the sheath. The others laugh. At this moment he receives such a blow on the head from a musket-butt that his helmet is forced down over his eyes and he cannot get it off again. Since he can no longer see clearly he lashes out at random and begins to fight with Moustache, who tries to subdue him.   *1360*

Battle. Fleuri is suffocating, wriggling like the damned and begging to be got out. An attempt is made to free him from his iron mask. Eight men pull, four at his feet, four at his head.   *1361*

His fingers splay out wide. At last the helmet gives. The men tumble backwards. Fleuri is purple in the face. He thanks the men.   *1362*

A final infantry salvo.   *1363*

Bonaparte triumphs. The *sectionnaires* inside the church demand a parley.   *1364*

Bonaparte orders the cease-fire.   *1365*

The spokesman stands on the church steps with his eyes bound, and says: 'We surrender.'   *1366*

* In the print, Fleuri is standing on the steps of the Hôtel de Noailles, either as a guard or after having taken refuge from the skirmishing. His gun goes off by accident, wounding Pozzo.

1367   Bonaparte. He gives an order.

1368   The *sectionnaires* throw down their arms as they file past Bonaparte's troops.

1369   Young Marcellin jauntily throws down his drum and passes on.

1370   Tristan Fleuri sees him; beside himself, he jumps

1371   on Marcellin and sets about giving him a sound spanking. But a colossal lady cook, on the side of the *sectionnaires*, comes to the defence of the 'little hero', and Tristan and the cook embark upon a epic tussle, amid laughter. She pulls out tufts of his hair; he pulls out the hairs sprouting from her chin. Bonaparte has come up to them, as sombre as ever. In the middle of fighting, Fleuri sees Bonaparte. He stares; he comes to a standstill; he stammers as he tries to come to attention; but the cook takes advantage to pitch in to him with some heavy blows. The cook triumphantly turns round to the royalists and says, pointing to Bonaparte and his officers:

'This whole bunch of epaulette-wearers is making fun of us. As long as they eat and grow fat they couldn't care less whether the poor people die of starvation.'

1372   Bonaparte interrupts, impassively:

'Good woman, take a look at me. Who is the fatter of the two of us?'

This sharp retort makes everyone burst out laughing, particularly Tristan, who is guffawing fit to split his face. Bonaparte whips round and looks at him. Under his gaze, which bores into his skull, Tristan loses his nerve and suddenly takes to his heels. Laughter louder than ever. Bonaparte has disappeared.

1373   Carriage surrounded by people trying to ill-treat the coachman and the man inside.

1374   Bonaparte goes over to it. He prevents them from being killed, for a noose had already been put round the coachman's neck. He recognizes Salicetti! In the carriage: Pozzo! He hesitates, and rescues them. Salicetti weeps.

1375   Murat, looking fearsome, his clothes torn, almost naked, his arms covered with blood, rides up at a furious gallop, laughing. He says:

'It is all over, General!'

'Thank you, Murat,' says Bonaparte sombrely, wiping away the blood oozing from one of his hands.

Moustache before Bonaparte. He looks at him. He coughs to attract his attention. He succeeds. Bonaparte turns around. Moustache says to him in an undertone: 1376

'The Convention is saved. Why are you so downcast, General?'

Bonaparte gives him a long look and points to

sectionnaires lying dead on the ground. Moustache looks round and his eyes come back to Bonaparte, who says in a low, sad voice: 1377

'Because the people have to be saved in spite of themselves!'

Street. Crowd acclaiming Bonaparte who sits, taciturn, astride his horse. A torrent of joy pouring forth. There is a heavy crush. 1378

Interior, boudoir. In the room are Joséphine, several women and several men. The window gives way under pressure from outside. She asks: 1379

'What's that noise, Monsieur Fouché?'

Fouché replies, with his proverbial sagacity:

'It is Bonaparte re-entering History, madame.'

Joséphine crosses rapidly to the window and looks out. Joséphine. Her eyes grow misty with sensual feeling.

Convention. A surge of wild curiosity. Suddenly all return to their places and sit down, their guns at their sides. Silence. Then the door at the far end of the hall opens and Bonaparte appears. All rise with one accord. Bonaparte stands motionless in the doorway. 1380

Barras rises and says: 1381

'I propose that the saviour of the Convention be nominated for the rank of General-in-chief of the Army of the Interior.'

All shout their agreement in great waves of cheering. 1382

Bonaparte, impassive. 1383

A deputy who, at the time of the attack upon the Convention, had shown particular cowardliness, comes simpering up to the young leader and says: 1384

'Through my voice the Revolution thanks you and . . .'

Bonaparte retorts, scathingly:

'From this morning on, *I* am the Revolution.'

The Hero of the Hour[1]

1385   A puppet-seller in the street. There is a crowd round him. He is selling little Bonapartes. Roaring success. Violine buys one and hugs it to her heart.

1386   Street near Bonaparte's house, thick with people.

1387   Bonaparte's landing, thick with Convention members and soldiers.

1388   Bonaparte's room, full to bursting. Bonaparte's brother Louis, Junot, Marmont and Sébastiani are trying, short of using violence, to control the importunate crowd, and they form a barrier by a table at which we see (back view)

1389   Bonaparte. He is jostled; he is on the point of being submerged; he gets to his feet and stares round at everybody.

1390   Everyone leaves the room, with the exception of his aides-de-camp.

1391   In the street the crowd yells: 'Long live Bonaparte! Long live General Vendémiaire!' Total strangers embrace, everyone dances.

1392   [[The blind man, in his usual place, grinds the same old tune. He no longer has his little monkey.]]

1393   Bonaparte's room. They are listening. Bonaparte, impassive as ever, picks up his hat, puts it on Sébastiani's head, claps his coat over his shoulders, takes Sébastiani's, and pushes Sébastiani to the window, saying: 'You salute in my place.' Sébastiani opens the window and salutes the crowd.

1394   The crowd applauds, ablaze with enthusiasm. The anarchy is over, at last! One can breathe freely again.

1395   Room. Bonaparte in disguise goes out with Junot.

1396   Landing. He elbows his way through the inquisitive throng who are waiting for him to come out but do not recognize him.

1 – He was the hero of the hour. They called him 'Vendémiaire' (Lacour-Gayet).

Door of the house. Junot and Bonaparte plunge into the crowd   1397
without being noticed. They too look upwards.

Like a clockwork toy, Sébastiani appears at the window, salutes and   1398
withdraws.

In the street. Junot delighted, Bonaparte impassive. He questions a   1399
frenzied bourgeois: 'What's going on?' 'Where have *you* been hiding?'
the man thunders, adding:

**'I've got two peasants here that don't know General Bonaparte
has saved France.'**

The crowd all but set on them. They slip away. Junot is shaking with
laughter.

[[Zoological Gardens. One of Bonaparte's favourite walks. Placidly,   1400
like two bourgeois, Bonaparte and Junot visit the aquarium.]]

In the street below the window the crowd continues its adoring praise   1401
of Sébastiani.

[[Zoological Gardens. A keeper explains to Bonaparte: 'You must not   1402
confuse the whale with . . .' Bonaparte listens conscientiously. A
newsboy goes running past.

[[The headline of his newspaper reads: 1403

BONAPARTE SAVIOUR OF THE REVOLUTION

The news-seller speaks to Bonaparte: 'Paper, citizen?' 'No, no. Go
to the devil!' says Bonaparte irritably.]]

Bonaparte's street. The ovation swells.   1404

[[Zoological Gardens. Bonaparte meditatively approaches an eagle and   1405
sits down to take a close look at it. He is thoughtful. The keeper goes
on: 'You must not confuse an eagle with . . .' 'Hush!' whispers Junot,
giving him some money to make him go away. The surprised keeper
goes out.]]

Bonaparte's staircase. The banister gives way; there is a crush of   1406
deputations carrying banners on which is written:

**TO THE SAVIOUR OF THE REPUBLIC,
LONG LIVE GENERAL VENDÉMIAIRE!**

[[Eagle's cage. The eagle and Bonaparte, in profile. They look at one   1407 another. Can it be the eagle from Brienne? The eagle comes closer to Bonaparte and Bonaparte caresses it as he used to at school. Almost imperceptibly, Bonaparte smiles.

1408 ⟦ Laetitia. Clustered round her are all her children, their eyes glued to a letter, which she unfolds, trembling a little.

My dear Mama,
You will have learned from the public news-sheets everything that concerns me. I have been nominated by decree General of the Army of the Interior. We have triumphed, and the past is forgotten.

The sunlight gilds all their faces as they radiate sheer joy.

1409 ⟦ Laetitia. She lifts up her eyes and says:

'Let us hope that it lasts! . . .'⟧

THE VICTIMS

1410 Roll-call of the victims of the terror – same tableau as before. The same despair, the same tragedy in the faces.

1411 The same Fleuri wearing his same warder's uniform. He calls out names, but whereas before his voice was choked, now it is terrifying.

1412 Condemned prisoners being dragged along.

1413 Fleuri. His expression is very fierce. One might almost think there has been a mistake and that this is a repeat of a previous scene.

1414 Some condemned prisoners. Now we see hundreds of guests at the 'Victims' Ball', who are vastly amused to see this re-enactment. It is the great hall of Les Carmes, its walls doubly steeped in the blood of the September Massacres and the Terror; but now the walls are festooned with garlands of flowers. Striking and original decorations. Velvets, gauzes, flowers. They find no entertainment more to their taste than to recall those scenes of horror which constituted the daily routine in the prisons for two years.

1415 The condemned themselves begin to laugh.

1416 Fleuri. His list. It is not names of condemned prisoners that he is calling out now, but:

> '50 bottles of Ay wine,
> 60 of Falerno,
> and 80 of Muscat.'

He continues the list, we see that the ghastly spot where the bloody roll-call was once compiled has been transformed into a butlery for the serving of wines and the washing of wine-glasses.

In this feverish reaction of life against death, a thirst for joy seized the whole of France. Six hundred and forty-four balls took place in the space of a few days over the tombs of the victims of the Terror.

Serving-boys and bottles fly about with improbable industry.   1417

To be admitted to the Victims' Ball it was necessary to have been imprisoned, or to prove the death of a father, a brother or a husband.

On a buffet, mountains of sandwiches, pâtés, cakes. An intensely   1418
colourful array. Nouveaux riches. Unbelievable luxury. Fantastic
elegance. Manners both brazen and refined.[1]

1 – Everywhere there were incredible festivities. According to police reports the
discreet back rooms in theatres became veritable dens of debauchery and vice;
there is a record of 644 public balls. This new society is racked with feverish
excitement: life reacting against death. The newly rich set the pace; ruined aristocrats
go where the money is and mingle with the parvenus . . . Mme Tallien at her thatched

153

1419   A cloakroom. A young girl, her back towards us, is taking the guests' coats. She turns round. It is Violine. Near her, Marcellin is tied by the foot to a column, so that he cannot wander away.

General Vendémiaire.

1420   Violine. She has been smiling as she puts away the garments; suddenly she turns pale. She has to sit down. Fortunately her companion is not overcome on seeing a brilliant general, for it is Bonaparte in dazzling splendour, who is holding out his cloak. Bonaparte is barely recognizable: he is more attractive than anyone could have thought possible. All his clothes are new, his hat, his cravat and his belt are all gilded, his spurs sparkle like two stars . . . He passes on. Violine follows him with her eyes, completely bowled over, and once he is out of sight she pulls one feather from the enormous plume in the hat which he has left, and tucks it in her bosom. Her brother Marcellin says: 'I'll tell the gentleman.' 'Be quiet, will you!' 'I will, I will. I'll tell him!'

1421   Bonaparte makes his entrance into the ballroom. Sensation.

1422   Curiosity. He is the object of minute scrutiny.

Bonaparte's sudden fame after Vendémiaire was eclipsed by the charm of the three most celebrated beauties of the day . . .

1423   The usher announces:

'Madame Tallien.'

1424   Aged twenty-five, very beautiful, scantily clad, almost licentious, her velvety black hair is short and dressed in tight curls all over her head; this is called the 'Titus' coiffure. She is radiant, exuberant with health and happiness and queen of the easy life. Venus of the Capitol, perfectly harmonious.

1425   A wave of admiration. A court is formed. The *ancien régime* is always to the fore where feminine charm is concerned.

1426   Bonaparte looks at her impassively.

---

cottage residence in Chaillot throws the great Tombstone Ball. Everything to say about this kingdom of Thérézie has already been said – an element of sadism underlies the pleasure: the Victims' Ball, at which one of the most favoured costumes is the hangman's, is sufficient to enlighten us in this regard. There is dancing everywhere – at Carmes where the blood of 116 priests is still spattered on the walls, at the Saint-Sulpice cemetery gates where a poster announces the Redcaps' Ball (Louis Madelin).

The usher announces:

'Madame Récamier.'

She is seventeen years old, with the beauty, grace and simplicity of a 1428 Raphael Virgin. Not a single jewel. The more one looks at her, the more beautiful she seems.

Fresh surge of admiration. Another court forms, if anything still 1429 larger than the one which is buzzing like a swarm round Mme Tallien. All the old gentlemen are there.

Bonaparte looks at her impassively. 1430

JOSÉPHINE

The usher announces: 1431

'Madame Joséphine de Beauharnais Tascher de la Pagerie.'

Thirty years old, this woman displays a grace unique to herself. Her 1432 body is unhampered by corset, bodice, or any other impediment. She moves with nonchalant grace, highlighted with a natural ease in careless poses which lends her an exotic languor. Her matte complexion with its transparent ivory shimmer glows softly beneath the velvety gleam of large, deep-blue eyes with long lashes curving gently upward. Her hair, which has a kind of glinting sheen, escapes in tiny ringlets from a filet of gold, and the unruly curls add an indefinable charm to a face of excessive but unfailingly attractive mobility. Her toilette completes the impression she gives of filmy lightness; her gown is of Indian muslin and its wide, floating skirts ripple mistily about her figure. The corsage, draped in deep folds across her bosom, is caught at the shoulders by two black enamelled lions' heads. The short sleeves are gathered above bare arms of great beauty, which are clasped at the wrist with two narrow gold bracelets. Between them these three women have bewitched Paris and have seen the most illustrious fall in homage at their feet, those beautiful feet on which they wore only light buskins, with emeralds on their toes.

A third wave of admiration, for Joséphine. 1433

Bonaparte. This time a tremor runs through him. Glimpse of the 1434 scene with the boot at Mlle Lenormant's door. He is drawn to her as a moth to a brilliant light.

1435   He starts to move towards Joséphine's group of admirers.

1436   Joséphine's group. Compliments, admiration from numerous admirers. Barras, revealing all too plainly his liaison with Joséphine, is among the most ardent. Bonaparte mingles with the group. He is close to her, completely fascinated.

*1437 ⟦ Joséphine notices two gilded swans with a long garland of roses suspended from their beaks. She takes one of them, and with a laugh carries it swiftly round the group, encircling her multitude of admirers with a chain of flowers which not one of them dares break. Laughter. She is divine! We are her prisoners!

1438 ⟦ Joséphine. She stops laughing to look at Bonaparte, a prisoner in the group.

1439 ⟦ He is annoyed and breaks the chain of flowers, bursting away from the group. Hearing the protests of Joséphine's admirers, he turns round, looks them up and down, and abruptly strides away. Deeply offended, at first Joséphine does not know what to do; but then she decides to laugh.

1440 ⟦ Joséphine joins Mme Tallien and Mme Récamier.⟧

1441   Their three heads. With great interest they follow

1442   Bonaparte, who does not see them. He is surrounded by a throng of acolytes and does not know how to escape their compliments.

1443   Joséphine looks enchanting as she says, dreamily:

> **'He is really charming, this young Buona-parté.'**

Mme Tallien and Mme Récamier nod knowingly to one another.

1444 ⟦ Moving swiftly, Joséphine puts herself in his path, though seeming not to have done so intentionally. Bonaparte reaches her, sees her, makes it clear he is in a hurry to leave.⟧ She looks at him curiously. He raises his eyes and looks at her. A golden silence. General Hoche comes up with a smile, shakes Bonaparte by the hands, and, exercising the rights he believes he has over Joséphine, he invites her to accompany him to the buffet. She declines, giving him a vexed look. He tries to discover the reason for this behaviour, and looks at Bonaparte again.

---

* *This scene was changed: it is now Joséphine and Mmes Tallien and Récamier who are tied up with garlands of roses.*

Hoche. 1445

Joséphine. 1446

Bonaparte. 1447

Hoche is quick to understand feminine caprice. His despondency is 1448
plain to see. Bonaparte is on the point of moving off, but she motions
him to stay. It is Hoche who must leave. [[Mme Tallien comes up
behind Joséphine. While Joséphine is playing with her redoubtable
fan, which until now has been serving in place of her heart, Mme
Tallien puts her hand over her eyes, smiling, and then moves off with
her group of admirers.]]

Bonaparte looks deep into Joséphine's eyes. This disturbs her, and 1449
she tries to shield herself with her fan. To make conversation she
says:

**'It was here, Monsieur Buona-parté, that I was summoned to
the scaffold!'**

'– Yes!'

Hoche steps resolutely forward and recalls the scene when he held 1450
Joséphine close in his arms to comfort her.

Icy displeasure. Joséphine glares indignantly at Hoche. Bonaparte 1451
smiles.

[[Tristan Fleuri is pouring champagne. He shakes like a leaf when he 1452*
has to fill the general's glass. He is so busy looking at Bonaparte that
he forgets to keep an eye on the glass and

[[the champagne flows into Bonaparte's boot. 1453

[[Bonaparte starts back in a fury. Joséphine laughs. 1454

[[Tristan's despair.]] 1455

Mme Tallien dancing. She is perhaps the most beautiful of them all 1456
at this moment.

Onlookers. Enthusiastic applause and laughter. 1457

[[Bonaparte notices a crowd of poor people at the windows, looking in 1458

---

* *Tristan's scene with the champagne bottle was transformed: he courts a woman to whom*
he tipsily offers champagne; in return he gets a kiss, at which point her wig falls off, revealing
. . . a man!

inquisitively from outside.

1459 ⟦ Throwing his purse to a maître d'hôtel, he says:

'Set up a buffet outside for those poor people.'

'Oh!' objects Mme Tallien, pouting. Several *nouveaux riches* follow suit, but Bonaparte glances up and draws her attention to

1460 ⟦ the pediment of the door, on which the word 'EQUALITY' stands out clearly in huge letters, while 'LIBERTY' and 'FRATERNITY' are lost beneath festoons of flowers.

1461 ⟦ Mme Tallien confesses: 'You are right.' To Joséphine she says: 'He is perfectly charming, your Bonaparte!'

1462 ⟦ Serving boys and footmen, led by Fleuri, set up a buffet outside Les Carmes. The delight of the crowd. 'Long live Bonaparte!' Barrels are rolled up.

1463 ⟦ Dandies dance in a ring round the 'democratic' table. Poor people are dancing inside at the Victims' Ball. Some of the rich begin to dance outside with the poor.⟧

1464 In a small withdrawing-room near the cloakroom Hoche and Bonaparte are playing chess. Joséphine is standing behind Hoche and watching Bonaparte.

Centre: Hoche, Joséphine, Napoléon; far right, Mme Tallien

Violine sees her and is troubled.   *1465*

Joséphine.   1466

Bonaparte. Their eyes meet.   1467

Violine. She understands.   *1468*

In the looking-glass Hoche catches sight of the glances being   1469
exchanged between Bonaparte and Joséphine.

Chess-game and Bonaparte. He says to Hoche, moving his hand   1470
towards a piece:

> **'Take care! I am about to take your queen.'**

Hoche looks into the mirror, rises abruptly and says: 1471

> **'I've lost! You're decidedly a better general than I.'**

And he walks away, very dignified. Bonaparte is about to get to his
feet. Joséphine smiles and holds him back. She plies her fan as a
sailor his oar; her eyes flash, and she burns her way into Bonaparte's
troubled soul. He makes an effort to rise, ready to leave, but he falls
back, utterly vanquished.

Violine at the door of the cloakroom, with tears in her eyes, suddenly   *1472*
runs away.

[[The buffet outside. Carnival. The dandies and the *merveilleuses*, led   1473
by Mme Tallien, are making a tour of it. Confusion and fusion.
Equality. 'This is magnificent!' proclaims Tristan Fleuri, standing
on a barrel and wiping away tears of joy.

[[Joséphine and Bonaparte come to the long window of the room and   1474
look at

[[the festivities outside. The wine is flowing where once blood flowed.   1475

[[The ubiquitous old organ-grinder is made to sit down and eat. Before   1476
he starts he feeds his dog. For the first time ever he is seen to smile.

> **'Long live Bonaparte!'**

everybody shouts.

[[Joséphine and Bonaparte at the window, standing very close to one   1477
another.

1478 [[Tallien, Mme Tallien and others, concealed by some hangings, whisper and laugh as they watch Bonaparte falling in love with the fascinating Joséphine.[1]

1479 [[He draws closer to her. She turns suddenly and looks at him; her face has taken on a mocking expression. She bursts into peals of laughter and darts away. She can afford to now, for she feels that he is caught.]]

1480 She meets Barras, who offers her his arm. She leans upon it with coquettish ostentation.

1481 Bonaparte. Euphoria around him, behind him, above him. He remains standing where he is, like a guilty schoolboy. He does not dare look up after her, and flicks obsessively at some non-existent dust on the lapel of his coat. A woman minces up to him, all aflutter at the prospect of addressing the general, and says in an affected voice:

'What kind of weapons do you fear most, General?'*

Bonaparte looks at her and, picking up the fan which Joséphine has left on a piece of furniture near the window, shows it to her and says:

'Fans, madame!'

Astonishment.

Having ordered all arms to be seized from private citizens, Napoléon receives an unexpected request.

1482 Bonaparte at his staff headquarters, rue des Capucines. Already the style is severe and sober. Nothing is superfluous. He is followed by his brother Louis, aged seventeen, Murat, twenty-eight, Junot, twenty-four, Muiron, twenty, Marmont, nineteen, and Lemarrois, seventeen. Bonaparte is listening with great interest to a very young man.

1483 Eugène de Beauharnais, aged fourteen, his face bathed in tears,

---

1 – With his ardent love for this woman of Creole blood, Bonaparte amused many of those who had known her from her previous escapades as a good sort, of easy virtue, irresponsible, amoral, yet, for all that, very captivating (Louis Madelin).
* *In the film this exchange occurs between Bonaparte and Joséphine, after the chess game and just before Barras comes to lead her away.*

clutching a sword to him, begs:

> **'I beg your permission to keep the sword belonging to my father, Comte Alexandre de Beauharnais.'**

The child's intense emotion, his pleasant face, the warmth and ingenuousness of his plea, touch the general. He gives him a friendly tap on the cheek, then looks at him closely, a long, penetrating look: Joséphine's son! The child is anxious. Bonaparte consoles him, saying paternally: 'Yes.' The child is delighted and can barely restrain himself from embracing Bonaparte. He kisses his hands.   1484

Next day, to thank the general.

Antechamber of the staff office. A large number of senior officers in attendance. Joséphine is there with her son Eugène; she looks divine beneath her dark veils. An official tries to send her away again, since it is quite clearly impossible that the general will be able to grant her even a second with all these people to see, when Bonaparte appears unexpectedly in the doorway. He stands for a moment in surprise, then crosses to Joséphine, kisses her hand and shows her into his office.   1485

Bonaparte's office. He gives her a seat. His awkward delight. Some secretaries come in, deliver papers, go out, come back in again. Bonaparte, annoyed, locks the door.   1486

Bonaparte approaches Joséphine. Extremely child-like, spontaneous, tender, audacious and timid, he talks, laughs, tries to kiss Joséphine's hands, while she reacts with great modesty. Her dog Fortuné, which she is carrying in her arms, obliges Bonaparte to keep his distance by baring its teeth.   1487*

Eugène looks up admiringly at this kind, young general, who has his arm round his shoulders as a father might.   1488

Antechamber. Earlier there were ten people waiting. Now there are twenty, thirty, generals, important people with dossiers, all still waiting. They look at the time. They show their surprise. They chat. Still more arrive. It is becoming stifling in the antechamber. Junot knocks. There is no reply. He gently tries to open the door: it is locked!   1489

---

* This sequence was extended: with great humour, Gance emphasizes Napoléon's shyness and awkwardness with this cool woman of the world.

1490   Bonaparte's room, 1 rue d'Antin. Bonaparte is down on one knee, making a declaration of love. Corsican ardour. Sincerity. Romanticism. It is all there. He is making passionate vows of love to his friend Talma, who is giving him a lesson in love-making, correcting his intonation and gesture. Bonaparte stands up. Talma looks at him and says, with a good-humoured smile:

'How you love her!'

1491   Bonaparte. His eyes answer 'Yes!', belying the calmness of his face.

1492   'To work!' says Bonaparte. He takes up his globe, while Talma settles himself to read a tragedy, lying back in an armchair with his feet up on the back of a chair.

1493   Bonaparte with his globe. Some books on the table. He tries to work, but:

1494   The globe. The distance from New York to Paris is the distance from Joséphine's ear to her mouth, from Melbourne to Moscow is the distance from her chin to her eyes – for Joséphine's smiling, ethereal face covers the globe. Bonaparte's hand turns the globe and Joséphine's head turns with it, her wonderful hair covering America and Asia.

1495   Bonaparte. His elation.

1496   He turns the globe back until Europe is facing him; and, suddenly, he presses his lips to Paris.

1497   Talma is shocked at this apparent madness. 'What is the matter with you?'

'Are you kissing Paris?'

1498   Bonaparte replies like a Musset lover:

'Paris? It's Joséphine's mouth!'

1499   And, indeed, Joséphine's marvellous face is filling Europe, so that Paris is her mouth. And now Bonaparte, with growing elation, kisses the entire globe, eyes, ears, hair. His love embraces the entire earth. Mingled strength and passion. To conquer the world must be no more than a pleasant game, when one is basking in a smile such as this.

He came every day to the Hôtel Chantereine.

Blue night sky. Balcony. She is talking to him. Below, Bonaparte's 1500
shadow can be seen.

Violine, her face ravaged by tears. Her heart is breaking in the 1501
shadows. She watches, urged on by fatal curiosity. She steals softly
along the wall, crying, crying . . .

A tiny spring welling among the mosses. 1502

She moves away, her back towards us, looking very small. 1503

A dead leaf blown in the wind. 1504

The grand vestibule of the Hôtel Chantereine. Hortense is playing 1505
at diabolo. As she plays she is having a serious discussion with her
brother Eugène.

Hortense asks Eugène: 1506

'Eugène, do you really think that Mama is going to get married?'

Eugène rocks on his chair and answers 'Yes!' as if there were no
question about it. Hortense sighs.

'Do you like him, then, this Buona-parté?'

Eugène replies: 'Yes, a great deal! Do you, Hortense?' She says: 'So-
so!'

Door of the vestibule. It bursts noisily open and Bonaparte, alert, 1507
eager, gay, a huge bouquet of flowers in his arms, asks: 'Where is
your mother?'

The children have risen to their feet and welcome him: 'Mother is 1508
coming.'

'Sit down, monsieur,' says Hortense, affecting a cool tone, which 1509
makes Bonaparte laugh. He lifts her high into the air, spins her round
in the sunlight and kisses her. She blushes and is overcome with
confusion. Eugène laughs. Bonaparte brings the two children together
and in a low voice makes a mysterious proposition of some kind,
taking a handkerchief out of his pocket. They both laugh.

Boudoir. Joséphine is finishing her toilette. Barras, completely at 1510
home and at ease, is sitting astride a chair and talking to her.

Joséphine, Hortense, Napoléon

1511 Joséphine looks complacently at Barras in her mirror, and makes her reply into the mirror as she powders herself:

⟦'You wish me to marry in order to be rid of me. Very well. I accept!'⟧

Barras gives a smile of gratitude.

1512 She suddenly turns round and, placing her hands on his shoulders, she says to him with feline insistency:

⟦'But then you will appoint that little Bonaparte to the command of the Army of Italy?'⟧

Barras drums on the back of his chair and looks at her. They smile at one another. 'You are very kind, my dear Barras,' she says.

1513 Bonaparte, his eyes blindfolded, is groping his way about.

1514 Vestibule. He is playing blind man's buff with the children; he bumps into the furniture and captures a coat on the coat stand.

1515 The children, gasping with laughter.

1516 Bonaparte runs. Chairs topple over. The flowers fall and scatter on the ground.

1517 Boudoir. Joséphine, her toilette complete. 'Heavens, what is that noise!' She is startled and goes out of the room. Barras follows her.

Door of the boudoir leading in to the vestibule. Joséphine appears 1518
and looks out. She starts back a little and says to Barras: 'Take
advantage of this to leave.' Barras hesitates; he looks at Bonaparte,
whose eyes are blindfolded. Quietly he slips away. Joséphine smiles
and then moves forward without a word.

Bonaparte, who has been groping about, seizes her. 'Hush!' she 1519
motions to the children, who smother their laughter.

Bonaparte and Joséphine. Bonaparte's hands touch Joséphine's eyes, 1520
her hair. He takes her hand and kisses it fervently, for he has
recognized her. Joséphine breaks out into peals of laughter and begins
to take off the blindfold. Bonaparte stops her and says despondently:

**'In love, my dear Joséphine, one should not see more clearly
than this!'**

And he clasps her gently to him. She winces, realizing that Bonaparte
is not deceived by her coquetry.

Joséphine's small bare feet, clad in buskins, crush – oh! without 1521
intending to – the flowers he has brought.

That evening.

Fitting-room. Twenty open cardboard boxes, gowns, hats every- 1522*
where. Suddenly, a commotion. Someone is brought in.

Flight of steps. Shadows of people carrying the unconscious form of 1523
Violine up the steps. A servant says: 'This way.'

Fitting-room. Violine lying stretched out. 1524

A doctor feels the young girl's pulse and points to a small half-empty 1525
bottle which she is holding in her tightly clenched hand.

General anxiety. 1526

Violine opens her eyes and sees 1527

The hazy, inverted image – for she is lying down and they are behind 1528
her – of Barras and Joséphine standing very close beside one another.

Violine closes her eyes again; tears well up from beneath her eyelids. 1529

The doctor smiles and says: 'She is saved.' 1530

* *Scenes 1522 to 1530 and 1537, 1538, 1540 and 1587 have only recently been found,
and are not yet included in the projection print.*

[[Beneath its brilliant exterior, France had never been so poor, and the five members of the Directorate, improbable as this may seem, were reduced to borrowing notepaper from the concierge of the Luxembourg.

1531 [[A vast salon inside the palace, left shabby and unfurnished. A wilderness. More salons in as sad a state. Broken window-panes swathed in cobwebs. In the foreground, a rickety table and five straw chairs. Round the table are Barras, Carnot, Rewbell, Letourneur and La Revellière. They are frozen. The concierge, hobbling and grumbling, glares at these gaudily dressed directors; after a moment's hesitation he hands over a box of notepaper, then he goes out, shrugging his shoulders, while Barras warmly supports a candidature, which Carnot approves. He obtains the assent of the three others and writes:

The Directorate unanimously appoints Napoléon Bonaparte in place of General Schérer as commander-in-chief of the Army of Italy.

8 Ventôse, Year IV

1532 [[Hands passing the pen and signing one after the other: Rewbell, Letourneur, La Revellière, Carnot and last of all Barras.]]

1533 Bonaparte's room. A blackboard. Bonaparte, a piece of chalk in his hand. Figures, complex equations. He solves a cube root in a few seconds, using the Pic de la Mirandole method. Joséphine is superimposed over all these calculations, on his books, on the ceiling, everywhere.

1534 Landing. Junot runs upstairs, not four steps at a time, but eight at a time. The banisters have never been shaken with such enthusiasm.

1535 Bonaparte's room. Bonaparte turns round. Junot almost chokes as he gasps out:

'It has happened! They've appointed you general-in-command of the Army of Italy!'

Bonaparte is unmoved. He finishes his cube root. Junot cannot get over it. Then he goes to his window, takes down the plans for the Army of Italy from the pane they have been covering. He reads Schérer's note, half washed away by the rain:

> These plans are the work of a madman! Let the fool who drew
> them up come and execute them.
>
> *General Schérer*

Bonaparte. Inspired passion wells up within him. He is like a volcano 1536
before the eruption. The silence which precedes fifteen years of
thunder. He is caught up in a maelstrom of light, while the words

AT LAST!

appear in enormous letters which come hurtling towards us.

Joséphine before her triptych mirrors. What pretty shoulders! They 1537
can be seen only in the mirrors (for she is hidden by a screen) but
how much the better for that. Violine smiles and trembles all at once.
Joséphine says to Fleuri, who is nervously fingering his hat:

**'I am taking your daughter into my service. She'll be happy,
and, since you are so set upon it, you'll be able to leave for the
army without any worry.'**

Violine blushes, stammers, kisses Joséphine's hand. Joséphine finds
her charming and caresses her; then she gives her a comb to hold up
her hair, which is falling down. Joséphine undresses to try on a gown.

Vestibule of the Hôtel Chantereine. Bonaparte, hatless, strides swiftly 1538
across, followed soon after by Junot, who is left gasping by this
breakneck haste. The children and then the bewildered servants
come running in after them.

Joséphine's boudoir. Bonaparte bursts in. She is frightened. 1539

Violine stands petrified. She does not have time to speak or to feel. 1540

Bonaparte speaks, allowing no argument: 1541

**'We must get married, madame. Quick, a notary, the banns
. . . the certificates!'**

Joséphine's stupefaction as she looks over the top of the screen, thus 1542
revealing in the mirror a back unequalled even by that of the Borghese
Venus. 'But! . . .' she ventures to say.[1]

Bonaparte gives her the reason, which for him overrides all other 1543
considerations:

1 – Great lover that he is, what will she make of him as a husband? Now he is offering
her his hand, begging her acceptance. After all, what has she left to lose? She is
hard pressed by circumstance; it is like gambling at cards. He is young and ambitious.
And he is general-in-command.

'I have given myself three months to conquer Italy.'

1544   Joséphine is vanquished, for he has commanded.

1545   She has wrapped herself in a shawl and hurries to right and left.

1546   The servants, the children, the coachman are running about. Orders, counter-orders. Panic. Bonaparte gives concise orders to Junot. Violine goes out; she too is caught up in the whirlwind.

On 9 March 1796, at ten o'clock in the evening, in the presence of Monsieur Leclercq, registrar of the Second Arrondissement . . .

1547   In attendance are the two witnesses, Barras and Tallien, and Joséphine's honest, trustworthy Calmelet, standing modestly to one side. With her indefinable Creole languor, her sweet smile, her amber skin, her chestnut hair knotted in Greek style, and dressed in one of her loose, flowing tunics which accentuate the lithe grace of her movements, Joséphine is musing, her chin in her hand, as she warms her dainty arched feet at the dying fire. A little anxiously Joséphine looks at the time. Bonaparte is late. What if he should not come!

⟦Two hours later.⟧

1548   Same place. Barras is showing his impatience. Joséphine is tapping her feet. The registrar has gone to sleep. Calmelet goes out, looking worried.

1549 ⟦ Violine's tiny room. Tristan Fleuri is finishing piling up birdcages and flowerpots, but she is in a hurry. 'Go now, Papa . . . I have work to do!' He laughs. 'All right, all right . . . I'm going!' She pushes him out, giving him a kiss. He walks away cheerfully. She bolts the door and then she fetches out some large, white veils from a drawer; she sets about sewing with great care and skill.⟧

1550   Bonaparte's room. He is in his shirt-sleeves. Unbelievable chaos. Bonaparte is lying flat on his stomach on top of plans and maps, surrounded by mountains of books and notebooks. He is writing with his right hand while he manipulates dividers with his left and dictates to his aide-de-camp Lemarois.* His door suddenly flies open and Calmelet, taken aback on seeing him in such a state, remains standing in the doorway. Bonaparte has not heard him.

---

* *Lemarois was dropped from the scene.*

Calmelet exclaims urgently: 1551

'What about your marriage, monsieur?'

Bonaparte. His shocked realization: 'Quickly, my dear, good Calme-   1552
let. You have saved my life! . . .' And Bonaparte, running the risk of
breaking his neck, drags the worthy Calmelet down the stairs at top
speed, pulling on his coat and boots as he goes.

Outside, in his haste he runs under a ladder. He stops in horror and   *1553*
goes back again, with Calmelet looking on in astonishment, to try to
cancel out the ill omen. Calmelet hastily does the same and bumps
into the ladder, knocking it over.

Like a whirlwind, Bonaparte bursts into the room where they have   1554
been waiting for him, followed by his aide-de-camp Lemarois and
by Calmelet. 'Now, Monsieur le Maire, marry us quickly!' The
registrar, waking with a start, thinks the place is on fire. Bonaparte
kisses Joséphine's hands. She is sulky, but his ardour is such that she
finally smiles. The registrar gets to his feet and begins in a doleful
voice: 'In the presence of . . .'

Bonaparte interrupts him.   1555

'Faster, monsieur!'

1556   The frightened registrar continues, more quickly.

1557   Bonaparte.

                    'Skip all that, monsieur.'

        The registrar does so and stammers:

                    'In the name of the law, will you take . . .'

                            'Yes.'

1558   says Bonaparte, cutting him short.

1559   Quickly, quickly. He signs, urging everything on. Tallien, Barras and
        Joséphine laugh. It is all done in such a military manner.

1560 ⟦ They descend the staircase, followed by their witnesses. Nobody
        else. They exchange handshakes in the porch before taking their
        leave.⟧

1561   Joséphine, aside to Tallien and Barras:

                    'He frightens me, your Buonaparté.'

        The two friends smile and reassure her.

1562 ⟦ Hôtel Chantereine, night. All the big windows are lit up from inside.
        One by one they are plunged into darkness, and one, which previously
        showed no light, glows into life, as does a tiny light in one of the small
        windows of the servants' quarters at the top of the house.⟧

                    ### The marriage of Violine

1563   She is very pale; an inexpressible emotion has her in its grip. She
        finishes arranging the bridal gown which she has made out of filmy
        veils. It transforms her into a little sylph.

1564   Her heart is beating fast. She arranges her hair like Joséphine's.

1565   Joséphine's bed recess. The bed is edged with a garland of flowers
        caught up at each end in the beak of a gilded bronze swan; the bed
        reveals itself in a large wall-mirror with a mahogany frame inlaid with
        fillets of gold. The draperies are of clear yellow silk trimmed with
        gold, looped up over curtains of violet silk trimmed with black. It is
        a Pompeii (Goncourt).

1566   Joséphine, infinitely soft and sensual, *en déshabillé*.

Violine now moves her bed and reveals what it has been hiding.   1567

An altar, which she has tastefully arranged on the shelf above her   1568
bed. This altar, which might at first have been thought to be to the
Virgin, has nothing religious about it; we see, instead, one of
Bonaparte's spurs, a glove belonging to him, the one dropped at
Toulon, the feather taken from his hat in the cloakroom at the
Victims' Ball, and, stuck to the wall and forming a background, an
Épinal print – *The Conqueror of Toulon* [[– and she has written round
this shrine:

To Napoléon Bonaparte.]]

Violine listens. She is quite alone. She looks at her little collection.   1569
It is the first of many altars to be erected by the people in their homes
in homage to the new Alexander. She lights two candles, which she
sets up one on each side of her altar, then she murmurs a prayer with
heartfelt fervour.

Violine prays and turns towards the wall, which we cannot see, and   1570
she gazes at it with an expression of touching mysticism. Her attitude,
her words, her silences, her sighs, her stifled laughter, her tears, her
fervour, her emotion – all confirm us in the impression that, in the
shadow next to her, someone she loves hears her avowal of love. Her
hair, silvery in the moonlight; a love scene in which only the woman
can as yet be seen.

The object of such tender transports: it is the shadow of Bonaparte   1571
on the wall! Can he have entered suddenly and taken her by surprise?

Violine speaks to him with tears and smiles in her eyes, her hands   1572
clasped together.

The shadow moves a little, as large as Violine herself.   1573

Violine moves closer and closer to the shadow. Such inner turmoil,   1574
such passion; a little lost soul fluttering against this shadow. Suddenly
we see that it is the doll, the 'five-sous Bonaparte', the 'hero of the
hour' sold in the streets, which is placed in such a way that its shadow
falls, life-size, on to the wall.

Violine totally absorbed in her illusion moves closer still; now she   1575
touches the wall, she closes her eyes and slowly kisses the cherished
shadow, sobbing.

Alcove. Joséphine and Bonaparte exchange a kiss.   1576

1577   Violine's wall. Violine's kiss. The image of love.

1578 ⟦ Laetitia with her three daughters. Sunshine. Harmony. She is finishing reading a letter and says to the children:

'Married!'

She murmurs:

'Let us hope it lasts!!'

Smiles. Youth, hope all around her.⟧

And on the night of 21 Ventôse, Year IV . . .'

1579   A carriage draws up under the peristyle of the Hôtel Chantereine. Mounted staff officers are waiting by the carriage doors; Bonaparte's brother Louis, and five aides-de-camp: Marmont, Lemarois, Murat, Muiron and Duroc.

. . . with only a paltry forty thousand francs to divide among his Italian Army . . .

1580   Interior of the carriage. Bags of gold, books, documents, plans. Almost buried and leaving just a tiny space empty for the general. Junot and the war administrator Chauvet are working.

Shooting the journey to Italy

. . . Bonaparte set out, forty-eight hours after his marriage, to conquer the world.

Flight of steps. The door opens. Joséphine, Bonaparte appear, followed by Barras in full dress.* 1581

Bonaparte and Joséphine. 'His face so pallid beneath his dishevelled hair, so sunken that he seemed at death's door, wretched, almost pitiful, expressionless, lips compressed, eyes veiled' (Madelin). He looks up at Joséphine, dazzling in her beauty, almost maternal. Bonaparte's eyes light up, and, though motionless, he manages to convey his hopeless love for her, in all its disturbing depth and intensity. Such genius blazes in his eyes, accentuated by his tragic immobility, that, in a movement of what might almost be compassion, she slowly bends down to his mute lips. 1582

The staff officers straighten up. He descends the steps. 1583

Joséphine and Bonaparte. He has just moved away from her. She stretches out her beautiful arms towards him in farewell and, turning slightly to the ever-mocking Barras, who makes one last small fatherly wave of the hand to the future conqueror of Italy, she says dreamily: 1584

'He is a truly charming young man.']]

At an almighty crack of the whip, the horses leap away. 1585

Joséphine's eyes follow the departing carriage. She waves her handkerchief as Barras turns his attention to her. His glances full of meaning. She does not respond. He seems to be saying: 'Aren't you going to ask me in for a little?' She says: 'No!' He kisses her hand and leaves her. She remains where she is, pensive.]] 1586

A window-pane. Violine turns away and hides her grief in the shadows. 1587

Joséphine's boudoir. She comes back in. To distract herself she begins to play the harp. After a few opening chords, she collapses in sobs. Violine softly opens the door a little way, and when she sees Joséphine so overcome and shaken with sobbing, she quickly dries her own eyes and goes to her mistress, full of compassion. Joséphine looks up at Violine and says: 1588

'I am jealous, Violine.'

* Barras was dropped from these scenes.

Violine's shock. 'Can it be me? No, that's impossible. Well, then?' She asks:

'But of whom, madame?'

1589   Joséphine, her face bathed in tears:

'Of France!'

1590   Violine smiles tearfully.

1591   ⟦ Interior of the carriage. Bonaparte orders it to stop and gets down, alone, to the surprise of his companions.

1592   ⟦ Exterior of the Convention. Moonlight. Bonaparte passes. The sentry presents arms.

1593   ⟦ Guardroom. Some Convention soldiers are laughing, drinking and playing at diabolo.

1594   ⟦ Bonaparte slips furtively past without being seen.

1595   ⟦ Bonaparte arrives at one of the great doors of the amphitheatre. He pauses. He opens the door and, reverently, takes a step forward.⟧

1596   Convention hall. Moonlight floods the famous arena; nothing stirs. Very small, very far away, Bonaparte stands alone in the great doorway.

A FAREWELL TO THE REVOLUTION

Mysteriously drawn towards that forge of the Revolution, there to meditate upon the future . . .

1597   Bonaparte at the door. Noble thoughts. The heavy door swings shut behind him. Surprise, concern even, as he tries to open it; impossible! His concern increases. He overcomes it and walks forward to the Convention desk; the whole place is deserted.

1598   He gazes musingly at the famous tiers.

1599   The empty hall. Silence. Is it an illusion? Can these be disembodied souls trying to take up again the places which they once occupied on earth: fleeting, vague, translucent forms come and go, rise and sit.

1600   Bonaparte. He is filled with awed amazement at this miracle.

1601   No! No! It is no illusion. The hall is peopled with phantoms. Ten, a hundred, a thousand, which become clearer and clearer, though still transparent. On all sides, the tiers fill up, and the galleries too become crowded with shadows, looking pleased and attentive.

Bonaparte, fearing this hallucination, tries to get out, but the gigantic spectral figure of Danton rises out of the closed door, seeming to emerge from the very wood. The ghost of Danton, twice life size, advances and, taking Bonaparte by the hand, leads him to the desk, overlooking the Assembly. Silence. And Danton says to Bonaparte: 1602

'Listen, Bonaparte, the French Revolution is about to speak to you!'

A section of the tiers. Now we can recognize the giant shades of the great leaders of the Convention, in the places they occupied when alive. Danton, Héraut de Séchelles, Marat, Hébert, Vergniaud, Brissot, Couthon, Saint-Just, Robespierre, Camille Desmoulins, Barbaroux, Fabre d'Églantine, all are there, serene, happy. Death has extinguished their passion and consolidated their ideas; and this cohesion, this visible brotherliness of the great spirits, who spent their lifetime at each other's throats, is supremely moving. 1603

Bonaparte. An inexpressible emotion grips him. Reverently he takes off his hat. 1604

Unanimity. All the great spirits of the Revolution rise as a sign of respect for the young leader. 1605

Robespierre makes a sign. 1606

They all sit down again. 1607

Robespierre remains standing and asks:[1] 1608

'We have realized that the Revolution cannot prosper without a strong authority. Will you be that leader?'

Bonaparte replies with a nod: 'Yes!' 1609

Saint-Just rises and says: 1610

'If the Revolution does not spread beyond our frontiers, it will die at home. Will you lead it into Europe?'

1 – 'If the Revolution does not spread, it will die like a fire starved of fuel. Napoléon's wars? Were they of my choosing? as he said himself. Was it not always in the nature of things, inevitably, that we were put in the position of having to fight to be the victors rather than the vanquished?'

1611 Bonaparte. His increased energy. He nods: 'Yes!'

1612 Marat rises. His face is benevolent as he asks:

'What are your plans, Bonaparte?'

1613 Bonaparte replies:

'The liberation of oppressed peoples, the fusion of great European interests, the suppression of frontiers, and . . .'

1614 Silence. He hesitates.

1615 Tense expectation.

1616 Bonaparte says:

'The universal Republic.'[1]

1617 Wild, unanimous enthusiasm.

1618 Galleries. Thousands of ghostly figures applaud with their transparent hands. In the foreground the figures of famous men can be seen: Voltaire, Jean-Jacques Rousseau, Diderot, Montesquieu, Beaumarchais, the Encyclopaedists, all those who, in one way or another, have played a part in the drama, of which this is the final act. Peace is restored; they are attentive once more.

1619 Bonaparte:

'Europe will soon become a single people, and any man, wherever he travels, will always find himself in a common fatherland.'[2]

1 – Bonaparte was, by his own admission, obsessed by the idea of 'a Europe regenerated'. We must, he said, save the people in spite of themselves (Elie Faure). To sweep away all the old-established institutions abroad and at home was an attempt to realize the dream of a universal Republic presided over by the French, and it was another idea that sprang from the Revolution. Its origins can be traced back to the orators and pamphleteers of the eighteenth century of which Napoléon was the son and heir (Jacques Bainville, _Histoire de France_).

2 – 'I wanted to set in motion a fusion of the great European powers, just as I had done with factions in France. I was not worried that people might grumble at first because I knew that in time they would rally to my side. Europe would thus soon have become one nation and anyone travelling through it would always be in this one same fatherland. This _will_ happen, sooner or later, through force of circumstance. The impetus is already there, and I think that even after I've gone, and the system I've created is no more, there is no real chance for stability other than a coming together, a confederation of nations . . . War is an anachronism. One day victories will be won without cannon or bayonet. He who would disturb the peace of Europe would be for civil war' (Napoléon, quoted by Elie Faure).

The tiers. The great revolutionaries, in close, affectionate ranks, 1620
voice exultant approval.

Bonaparte. 1621

**'To achieve this sacred end many wars will be necessary, but
I proclaim it here for posterity: one day, victories will be won
without cannon and without bayonets.'**

Thunder of applause. The hall, relatively dim in the moonlight, grows 1622
gradually brighter.

All the great revolutionaries rush towards him, surround and con- 1623
gratulate him. Danton moves them aside, and once more taking
Bonaparte by the hand, he says:

**'If you should one day forget that you are the direct heir of
the Revolution, we shall turn our wrath against you.'**

Bonaparte shows that he has understood the important lesson that
the past has just given him. Danton embraces him.[1]

An imposing spirit, a foreigner, standing apart, dressed in the style *1624
of a seventeenth-century Englishman, says to him:

'Do not succumb to the temptations of power.'

'Who are you?' 1625

says Bonaparte.

'Cromwell,' 1626

replies the ghost, shaking him by the hand.

Exultation. A surge of joy. 1627

---

1 – 'Such a faith in Democracy, yet hatred of anarchy, it is that carries Napoleon
through all his great work . . . To bridle-in that great devouring, self-devouring
French Revolution; to *tame* it, so that its intrinsic purpose can be made good, that it
may become *organic*, and be able to live among other organisms and *formed* things,
not as a wasting destruction alone: is not this still what he partly aimed at, as the true
purport of his life; nay what he actually managed to do? Through Wagrams,
Austerlitzes; triumph after triumph – he triumphed so far' (Thomas Carlyle, *On
Heroes, Hero-Worship, and the Heroic in History*, 1841).
* *Gance originally intended to add a whole series of great revolutionaries from other nations;
the Cromwell sequence would have been shown in England, then replaced by a similar sequence
involving Bolívar for the film's Bolivian release, and so on. George Washington was intended
for the American release.*

1628   A lone man, with an austere, foreign-looking face, says to Bonaparte:

'Follow my example.'

1629   Who are you? The ghost replies:

'Washington!'

1630   Marat, Danton, Couthon, Vergniaud, Valazé, Barbaroux, Saint-Just, Robespierre, all – eager, immense, epic – sing: *'Amour sacré de la patrie . . .'* as formerly at the Cordeliers'. Now it is the dead singing.

1631   The ghostly figure of the wonderful woman in the red Phrygian cap sings: *'Liberté, liberté chérie . . . '*

1632   The ghost of a sans-culotte continues: *'Combats avec tes défenseurs.'*

1633   The ghost of an old man repeats: *'Combats avec tes défenseurs . . .'*

1634   The hall continues the sacred hymn. Solemn communion. The voices gradually fade, while the great spirits, more and more translucent, grow blurred and dim.

1635   Danton, scarcely visible now, declaims: *'Aux armes! Citoyens . . .'*

1636   The ghosts have all but vanished and the *Marseillaise* is barely audible; the faintest mumur can be heard: *'Marchons, marchons . . . '* The ghosts have disappeared. Silence. There is nothing left but the moonlight, and far off, very small, standing at the Convention desk, the heir of the French Revolution.

1637   Bonaparte is now bathed in moonlight. Tears, the first and perhaps the last, are running down his ecstatic face.*

1638   The carriage. Horsemen ride up to the doors, keep pace at a gallop, take letters and ride off again in various directions.

1639   Interior of the carriage. The countryside flashes past. Bonaparte buried under plans, books, documents, bags of all shapes and sizes. Near him Junot and Chauvet.

* *Instead of tears, Bonaparte's head is bathed in steadily increasing light.*

In his left hand a portrait of Joséphine, which he looks at frequently. 1640

He hands out notes through the door to some officers: at the same 1641
time, he writes a letter.

'Each moment draws me away from you, beloved, and with
each moment I find less strength to endure this separation.'

He looks up and hands out another note through the carriage door. 1642

Provisions.

The horseman rides off.

Bonaparte feverishly carries on with his letter: 1643

'I send you a thousand kisses, but give none to me for they sear
my blood . . .'

He looks up, for another officer has ridden up on the left, and he 1644
scrawls a note for him, saying:

The Directorate.

The horseman rides away.

Bonaparte turns back to his beloved letter and to the portrait, which 1645
he kisses.

Another officer appears on the right; he scribbles an order for him: 1646

Field hospitals.

The officer gallops away.

Bonaparte continues his letter after gazing some more at his cherished 1647
portrait.

THE BEGGARS OF GLORY*

1648 Legs and feet on the march along a sunlit road. Feet mostly bare. Some soldiers have only one shoe, others have bound their feet with oakum.

1649 Some are dragging along pigs or ducks, others chickens in crates on wheels, with only their heads sticking out.

1650 Bonaparte's soldiers on the march towards Italy. Any commentary would be superfluous. They are still the soldiers of Year II, bellies empty, heads full of song, the creatures of legend. The sun streams down.

1651 Men have been harnessed to the supply wagons, which bear the words 'ARMY OF ITALY' on their canvas awnings. Their shoulders are bleeding.

1652 The men are singing the *Chant du Départ* (*The Song of Departure*), that second *Marseillaise*.

'La victoire en chantant . . .'

1653 Fleuri, Moustache appear, preceded by Marcellin, who is playing his drum. Fleuri is tired out and cannot keep in step. He is also carrying far too many packs, piled up like an obelisk on his back, and he keeps treading on his trousers.

1654 Moustache turns towards Fleuri and says consolingly, giving him a pinch of snuff:

* *The scenes in which Joséphine and Violine are together in front of the altar of 'The Hero of the Hour' (1656 to 1663) open this sequence here. The rest of the scenes in 'The Beggars of Glory' were either adapted for the Triptych Section (p. 185) or appear, slightly changed, in the single-screen ending put together by Gance for general release in 1928. Instead, after the scenes 1656 to 1663, we have a series of scenes, missing from the published script, leading up to 'The Entry into Italy', in both versions of the film:*

  Bonaparte finds the carriage too slow for him; he continues his journey on horseback. The generals awaiting him with the Army of Italy at Albenga, Masséna, Sérurier, La Harpe, Augereau, etc., are highly resentful; they regard Bonaparte as an upstart, and they decide to demonstrate their feelings. When he arrives, they turn their backs on him. Bonaparte loosens his belt and throws his sword on the table. The noise causes the generals to whirl round in surprise. Bonaparte forces them to remove their hats simply by staring at them. He then puts his on, and sits down to discuss his plans for the forthcoming campaign. The generals are apoplectic when he announces that the Army of Italy will take the offensive. They are even more dismayed when he announces a review of the army in just two hours. A sequence follows showing the appalling state of the soldiers, in which we have the last appearance of Fleuri in the triple-screen version: he gets into a ridiculous fight with another soldier over his opinion of Bonaparte, and ends up by losing his trousers.

180

'One last effort, my friend; not more than fifteen hundred kilometres!!!'

Fleuri takes a pinch, pulls himself together and, sneezing away, steps out energetically with his left foot, but he loses the rhythm. He is the only one not marching in step.

Pretty girls harvesting grapes watch these 'proud barefoot beggars' and their hearts go with them. | 1655

Violine's room, dawn. She is at her altar; the bed has been pulled out. She is praying for him. She has the 'hero of the hour' doll in the centre of the altar. | 1656*

The door of her room opens. Joséphine, who is looking for something, is about to come in and stops short in surprise in the doorway as she sees | 1657

Violine, back view, praying. | 1658

Joséphine begins to understand Violine's religion of love. She softens and enters noiselessly. | 1659

Joséphine gently stoops down to Violine, and when her head is close to Violine's, she calls her. Violine turns her head, sees Joséphine and panics, trying to hide her altar, but Joséphine makes her stay on her knees, smiles at her, kisses her and, kneeling before the altar, she too prays. | 1660

* *See note to scene 1647.*

181

1661 Violine. Infinitely appealing in the simplicity of her emotions: tears in her eyes.

1662 The altar. The 'hero of the hour'.

1663 The two heads, side by side, in reverent wonder.

1664 Road. Galloping dispatch riders. Murat at the head. They come up with the soldiers we have just seen, who are still marching along.

1665 The soldiers stand aside. Make way! Make way! He is coming! Who? Him, Him! And their eyes begin straining to try to see Him better when He passes by.

1666 Now the men are so white with dust that their faces look no different from their clothes; they are marble figures on the march.

1667 Along comes Fleuri. From behind he appears to have no trousers on, but from the front he passes muster, though one can see he is wearing only a piece of cloth held together by threads at the back.

*1668 The three friends surprised and excited by the announcement that the general will be passing through. Fleuri's breath is quite taken away. 'We'll see him! He will recognize me!' Quickly they try to remove the dust clinging to their tired faces. They polish their buttons. Fleuri, ignoring such obvious means of trying to please, cleans his nails feverishly – with a sabre! 'Attention!' shouts an officer. A single movement, and the men become statues.

1669 On the march. In such a cloud of dust that the carriage can barely be seen, with mounted outriders before and behind, Bonaparte comes storming past and is gone. The three friends, in the settling dust, can hardly believe it. They are completely speechless. The officer gives the command: 'Forward, march!' . . . They set off once more, and the trees, the houses and the labourers who have come running on to the road appear Lilliputian beside the laughing giants passing by. They are already being transfigured by Legend.

1670 One, two; one, two; one, two

'La Liberté guide nos pas . . .'

* The scene of Fleuri preparing to meet Bonaparte is transferred to the review sequence in the single-screen version of the ending. As Bonaparte rides, up, Fleuri takes two paces forward and says: 'General – I was at Brienne.' Bonaparte stares at him for a brief moment, then shouts: 'One pace forward . . . march!' The troops absorb Fleuri into line once again and Bonaparte rides off. Poor Fleuri collapses with disappointment.

Suddenly they begin to exclaim, for they see 1671

a giant shadow on the road, gliding along before them: it is the shadow 1672
of the eagle following Bonaparte into the sun.

3 DECEMBER 1925

[*The published script ended here. 'Abel Gance's great innovation, the Triptychs, will be the subject of a special publication,' announced the Plon edition. But it did not appear until a French magazine, L'Écran, devoted an entire issue to Gance in April/May 1958.*

'The Entry into Italy', as the next section is called, was the only sequence intended for the Triptych Section, and the only sequence to include panoramic shots, extending, like Cinerama, across three screens. Napoléon *ends on a multicoloured, multi-screen cataclysm of images, so powerful that they defeat even Abel Gance's powers of description.*

After Gance completed this Triptych, he edited the double-storm sequence at the end of the Corsican section for the triple screen. Later, in 1928, for the opening of the first 'alternative' cinema in Paris – Studio 28 – he put together a third Triptych – 'The Victims' Ball' – and two short triple-screen sequences – 'Marine' and 'Galops' – using material taken from the Corsican scenes. With these, he showed his documentary about the making of the film, Autour de Napoléon.]

Triptych Section

THE ENTRY INTO ITALY

First contact with the Army of Italy

1 Triptych shot. Unbroken panorama. General shot of the Albenga camp. The entire ragged army is lying on the ground. The men have gone so long without food that they have barely enough strength left to attend to camp duties. Bonaparte appears. He leaps into the saddle and rides to the middle of the camp. He takes in the whole of his army with a wide, sweeping gaze, then he gives the command:

'Attention!'

Continuation of the shot. The order is rapped out with such magnetic authority that the whole army is on its feet in an instant. A central aisle is formed. Bonaparte gallops up and down in each direction and his eagle gaze gradually electrifies this crowd, which already seems to sense his future power. He leaves the field followed by his staff. The soldiers watch them move off, on the verge of cheering in their dawning enthusiasm. A sudden, extraordinary, almost miraculous wave of infatuation spreads from soul to soul. The leader has arrived. Iris fade.

One hour later.

2 Panorama triptych. Open iris on the central screen. Hold for two metres, then suddenly unmask the lateral screens by opening their synchronized irises. The entire Army of Italy appears, drawn up impeccably for review by the new commander, a sea of men with bayonets and hearts asparkle. The eye, suddenly taking in three

times more space, breathes more freely. A euphoric atmosphere is established; the images begin to sing and the rhythm will gradually become predominant.

Contrast between the disorder of the tattered uniforms and the impeccable order of the serried ranks, testifying to the young leader's authority over his men. The camera pulls back sharply in half-second bursts and reveals in the space of five seconds one or two thousand grenadiers. There are guns of all sizes, shapes and ages, there are even some ancient blunderbusses to be seen. The camera pulls back another hundred metres in half-second bursts and reveals a thousand cavalry lined up. In the foreground: Murat, a half-naked demigod.

Another triptych showing a different view. The General Staff appears. 3 Junot whirls along the front of the troops, shouting: 'Attention! . . .' Thirty thousand men have just presented arms again and become statues representing France – suffering, destitute, but magnificent.

Central screen. Medium close-up. The drums begin to roll. 4

Panoramic triptych. Bonaparte appears on horseback in the central 5 aisle, followed by his staff. Masséna, Augereau, La Harpe, Victor, Cervoni, Sérurier, Lemarois, Marmont. Swiftly they traverse the ranks, for now everything must keep pace with the leader's swift train of thought.

In a few hours Bonaparte was to see around him the sudden blossoming of an extraordinary, almost miraculous infatuation . . . the leader had arrived.

Continuation of the triptych shot. In the distance Bonaparte continues his inspection. Some flags which formed the foreground are gradually caught by the wind and begin to flap, blocking the view, creating a fade.

'Break ranks.'

6   Framed by black on the lateral screens, close-up of Bonaparte on the central screen. He is issuing the order just seen. Then the camera pulls back a little to reveal Bonaparte full length, surrounded by hundreds of men cheering him. The fervent enthusiasm increases still more. Flags and arms are being brandished, and hats on the ends of the guns. Bonaparte takes off his hat and salutes his army.

7   Central screen framed by black. High angle of the camp. The formations have almost broken up. The men are dispersing, eager and jubilant.

8   Panoramic triptych. High angle of the camp. Forest of guns and flags. Cheering. Great wave-like movement towards the cameras. On horseback, Murat crosses the whole width of the triptych. Epic delirium. Iris fade.

For the first time the army slept confidently.

9   Central screen framed by black. Rapid fade in. General shot of the camp by night, shot in its entirety by the brachyscopic lens.* In the distance, forming a crest on the rocks, rows of tents where the leaders are sleeping. The men sleep on the ground in the open air. They have never slept so well as on this night. In the foreground the flags are draped across stacks of arms. Epic reverie in the serene light of the moon. Blue tint. Fade very slowly.

10 Triptych. Fade in slowly on the right screen. The extreme edge of the camp beside the phosphorescent sea. Bonaparte on horseback comes into shot. He gazes at the sea and the tents. Then the central screen lights up; then, a while later, the left screen, revealing an endless vista of tents. And Bonaparte pensively contemplates his army. Iris fade.

On the morning of 11 April 1796, this ragged crowd would awake with the spirit of the Grand Army.

---

* *A wide-angle 14mm. lens developed for this production.*

Panoramic triptych. Fade in on general shot of the men, still asleep 11
before reveille, which will soon be sounding.

Central screen framed by black. High angle, the tents. In the 12
foreground Bonaparte moves forward on an escarpment of rock. He
looks at the camp. We sense that he is about to speak.

Central screen. Close shot of Bonaparte, rear view, watching the 13
sleeping camp. Now the army's dreams materialize before him. In
fluid superimposition a battle scene unfolds, an infantry charge. Then
the dream battle fades. Bonaparte gives a sign and the drummers,
who are in the foreground, stand up. They adjust their equipment,
set their drums rolling and sound reveille. Round about them, the
men get up so rapidly that they do not have the time to notice the
transition between sleeping and waking and will almost believe that
they are continuing their dream.

Panoramic triptych. General shot of the waking camp. All the men 14
are already astir. The triptych pans up to reveal the tents lined up on
the crest, from which the officers are emerging; higher up, the jagged
rocks; higher still, an old ruined tower where the sentinels are posted;
at the very top, Bonaparte at the edge of the rock, his imperious
silhouette etched against the dazzling sky. There, lost between heaven
and earth, dominating this host of men, he already seems to dominate
the world. His silhouette now takes on an unaccustomed outline. It
seems to polarize all the morning light, and the muffled echoes of the
Marseillaise linger on.

Central screen. Close shot of Bonaparte taking all this in with an 15
expansive, circular gaze. He gradually absorbs into himself all the
electricity vibrating in the atmosphere. The silence in which he
encloses himself is heavy with storms, like the silence that precedes
the most brilliant meteors. He says:

'Soldiers!'

Continuation of the shot. His whole body shakes with tension. Will
and authority multiplied tenfold.

Panoramic triptych. General shot of the camp. Every face is lifted 16
towards the rock, as if a thunderbolt had just struck, for there are
gleams of lightning in his eyes and echoes of thunder in that voice.

Panoramic triptych. High-angle shot down on to the whole of the 17
camp, as Bonaparte sees it. The waves of the immense ragged army

spread as far as the horizon. Men push eagerly forward to see and hear him. Rubbing their eyes, they gaze at him as he stands, looking so very slight upon the rock. This is the reed speaking to the forest, and the forest ceases its rustling.

18 Synchronous triptych. The same image repeated on the three screens (invert the image to make it symmetrical). Tents as far as the eye can see and the motionless crowd, immobilized by the irresistible summons.

19 Close shot of Bonaparte on the central screen. He shouts:

'Soldiers! . . . You are naked, ill fed! . . .'

Continuation of the scene. He looks down at them and talks as it were to each of them, man to man, with a force of persuasion that sweeps aside every objection. Already every man is under his sway.

20 Panoramic triptych of the spellbound host. The men's faces light up.

21 Close shot of Bonaparte. He says:

'The government owes you much, but it can give you nothing.'

22 Panoramic triptych of the crowd. A great thrill of sympathy runs through it, since these are the words they have long been hoping for.

Dieudonné, Kruger and Gance – preparing to shoot the Montezemolo sequence

Close shot of Bonaparte, a little larger. He says: 23

'The patience and courage you display amidst these rocks are admirable, but they will not win you glory . . .'

Triptych of the tents. Complete and absolute attention. 24

Triptych of the crowd in the middle of the camp, galvanized in the 25 light which floods it ever more brightly, like a more intense vibration of this epic ardour.

Close shot of Bonaparte, still larger. He says: 26

'I will lead you into the most fertile plains of the world . . .'

Continuation of the scene. His outstretched arm points towards the future frontiers of France on the distant horizon, and traces the boundaries of his empire in the sky.

Panoramic triptych of the crowd. Enthusiasm spreads from man to 27 man, breaking in huge concentric waves.

Triptych of the tents. 28

Close-up of Bonaparte. The light increases round him like a pre- 29 mature sunrise over Austerlitz. He says:

'Rich provinces and great towns will be in your power.'

Panoramic triptych. The great storm of collective enthusiasm is 30 unleashed. Great waves of ardent jubilation run through this crowd of wretched men. They already feel themselves capable of vanquishing the world. The crowd moves towards Bonaparte, in order to hear him better, and this movement compresses it, makes it denser, consolidates its will, harnesses its energy.

Close-up of Bonaparte. He says: 31

'There you will find honour, glory and riches . . .'

Panoramic triptych of the crowd which continues to draw closer and 32 condense. It now forms a compact block, a mass which will sweep Europe when it is unleashed. This is the very heart and soul of the future Grand Army.

Three different shots of the crowd, ranged side by side on the 33 triptych. Unanimity in the expression of feelings.

34 Close-up of Bonaparte, face only. (Tight close-up.) He exhorts with voice and gesture; but he is more than a captain: he is also a psychologist. He says:

'Soldiers of Italy! . . . will you lack courage and constancy? . . .'

35 Carry the momentum of his peroration by broadening it with a succession of different shots: tight close-up, close-up, close shot, full length shot, general shot, then back to him standing on the rock at the edge of the cliff. Beginning with Bonaparte's eyes, we pass through a rhythmic succession of brief images which progressively enlarge the field of vision until it encompasses the whole of the army.

Bonaparte is now no more than a luminous speck in the distance.

Panoramic triptych of the crowd in a paroxysm of enthusiasm.   36

Synchronous triptych of the tents. Same action.   37/38

Triptych shot of the tents on the ridge of the rocks. Same action,   39
more intense.

Panoramic triptych. Reverse shot of the camp as Bonaparte sees it.   40
Same action, at its height.

Bonaparte, now mounted, seen from below (the army's view). He   41
rides along the edge of the precipice and the camera pans to follow
him. He comes to a halt, a minute figure, standing out sharply
against the backdrop of the looming Alps, on the edge of the cliff.
Accompanying images on the lateral screens: clouds filtering dazzling
beams of light.

Panoramic triptych of the army. The men's eyes never leave him.   42
They are still cheering.

Bonaparte on horseback, poised between heaven and earth. He turns   43
and gazes towards the endless horizons. Graduated white iris-mask.
Accompanying clouds on the lateral screens.

**And now, turned to face Italy, the tempter shows them the
promised land . . . It is he who will lead them into it.**

Continuation of the shot. He tears himself away from his vision as
one awakening from an amazing dream. He urges his mount. The

camera pans after him.

Before me, the Italian plains, the rivers glittering like gold yataghans, the immense and fertile plains of Piedmont.

(Napoléon's *Mémoires*)

44 Central screen. Close-up of Bonaparte, from behind, turned towards Italy.

45 Panoramic triptych of the Italian plains seen from the summit of the Alps. A golden haze floats over all, a mist of enchantment which renders the promised land more secret, more modest, tempting the tempter even more. 'Three hundred metres below, the nestling villages, the Po; the Tamaro, that white girdle of snow and ice of a prodigious height on the horizon, enclosing this rich basin of the promised land, these gigantic barriers which seem the boundaries of another world, which nature has been pleased to render so formidable' (Napoléon's *Mémoires*).

46 Continuation of the close-up of Bonaparte from behind. He turns round in deep emotion, murmuring: 'Italy! . . . Italy! . . .' He ponders at length the consequences of the promise which he is about to make, gauges all its responsibilities, but his star is smiling upon him and he becomes strong in his resolve. In the curt, incisive voice which will reverberate for centuries in men's memories, he declaims:

'Soldiers! . . . I give you my promise . . .'

47 Close-up of Bonaparte, who seems to grow in stature against the sky. The sun rises until it is directly above him; he stands out, black, against the gigantic globe, which is as yet pale.

48 Panoramic triptych of the army as far as the eye can see. The spark has kindled in their hearts. A shout bursts from every breast. A beam of sunlight runs caressingly over the men like a benediction. Electrified, they run to surround their leader on the edge of the precipice. It is there that the spirit of the Grand Army is born.

49 Bonaparte on the edge of the precipice. He looks at all of them at once. He does not speak, but his silence breaks in great waves of mute exaltation. A sort of collective telepathy is established and Bonaparte's will takes over the will of his men and absorbs it to saturation point. His spirit speaks to all of them at once; and it speaks to his dream armies and to the gentle, transparent phantom of

Joséphine, which returns to obsess him. And it speaks to the eagle, which has just settled on the rock. And it speaks to his Valkyrian, chafing steed. And it speaks to the fire and it speaks to the sea. And it speaks to the planets and to his star. And now Bonaparte's head seems to be in the sun itself. And this conversation with glory becomes vertiginous, like the gulf of light which opens at his feet.

The sun floods the army with the radiant conviction of the young   50
leader. Extension of this grandiose fervour and enthusiasm by multiple shots and, as it were, by waves, whose length gradually increases with distance.

Close-up of Bonaparte, his head in the sun. He smiles beatifically.   51
Allow the sun to fill the whole screen. Iris fade to white.

Two hours later, by a miracle of speed, the Grand Army was on the march.

Central screen. Fade in on head of column marching towards camera,   52
which pulls back. There we see all the most epic of France's soldiers, and, lost in this ocean of men, we shall recognize Blaise Alboise, Moustache and Tristan Fleuri. Behind them, as far as the eye can see, the ragged army. A surging wave of humanity which will flow unendingly. Suddenly, the lateral screens light up. This time the picture will be a true triptych. The image on the right will be shown, reversed, on the left, as if seen in a mirror, and the movements of the two images will be rigorously synchronized. These lateral views will be of a winding road snaking down among giant boulders. Two absolutely identical armies will be descending at the same pace towards the bottom of the central screen, forming a flowing, curving pattern which harmonizes amazingly with the central image in a play of strictly symmetrical photogenic masses. In the centre, the head of the column will carry on marching, while infantry, cavalry, artillery, and baggage train file past on either side.

In the space of a few days, an astounded Europe was to see the rise of a star which would change the face of the world.

(Madelin)

Central image. Bonaparte surrounded by his General Staff contem-   53
plates the army marching past. On the lateral screens the grandiose march-past continues. The army passes through some vineyards. Pretty girls who have been harvesting the grapes watch these 'proud

barefoot beggars' and their hearts go with them. In the centre, Bonaparte dictates his orders to his aides-de-camp, wheels his mount round and sets off again at a gallop. Same procession on the lateral screens: infantry, then cavalry, then artillery.

54 Central screen. The heavy wagons pass by. It is a long while since the last ox was eaten, so men have been harnessed to the supply wagons, which bear on their awnings the inscription 'ARMY OF ITALY', or 'LIBERTY OR DEATH', or 'LONG LIVE THE REPUBLIC'. The poor broken bodies toil beneath this crushing burden. Their shoulders are bleeding under the coarse ropes. Their faces are pitiable in their painful obstinacy, which, none the less, will eventually triumph. On the lateral screens two human masses continue to unfurl. Iris fade.

Forty-eight hours later, at Montenotte, Bonaparte, laughing, opened the gates of Italy.

55 Panoramic triptych over the village of Montenotte, high angle shot. The guns have already prepared the ground for the task. The soldiers of the Republic rush pell-mell through the disembowelled houses with their caved-in roofs. And the Austrians are gripped with fear in the face of this incredible army of madmen, practically unarmed, charging down upon them with fierce, wild laughter. A hundred of these barefoot soldiers fall; the others carry on; nothing will be able to check their onward rush. It is a veritable avalanche.

56 Triptych revealing the battle in all its aspects. Central screen. Close-up of Bonaparte, impassive, attentive to every phase of the combat. On the right: one, two, three, five, ten aspects of the battle, mixed, superimposed, intermingled. On the left: a cavalry charge, followed by the camera tracking alongside at top speed. Unforgettable image. All those laughing demons, sabres drawn, riding as one with their horses, leaping on towards death, singing. Several of these centaurs fall, but the charge continues, growing more and more fantastic, like some legendary charge . . . Murat at the head lashes himself with his crop; the Austrians are seized with horror, like the Moors before the Cid Campéador. It is no longer war: it is the Iliad.

57 Panoramic triptych. A kind of apocalyptic vision. General shot of Montenotte blazing like a brand. The flags stream against the ruddy sky. In the foreground, to the side, Bonaparte follows the fluctuations of the battle. He issues some orders. Bombs fall about him and burst. He remains impassive, inscrutable, impenetrable, but we realize from

his blazing eyes that the enemy is routed and that the tricolour is sure of victory once more. The battle continues to unfold on each side, framing the central figure. The close-up fades. Continuation of the complete panorama. The Austrian flags which flew from the rooftops are torn down and the French flags take their place. They stream in the raging wind of the Revolution and flicker like flames. Iris fade.

(The scenes which follow will gradually gain in intensity. Each scene must burn out the memory of the one before. The film will blaze out a path of fire. The rhythm must be sovereign master. All these tableaux will move with a passionate momentum. Create for each scene, be it only one second long, an incomparable ambiance of nobility and richness of soul.)

And through the open door swept the strongest and richest torrent of human power that history had ever seen unleashed.

(Albert Sorel)

Triptych, fantastic rhythm. In the centre: head of marching column. 58
A terrifying torrent. Young women fling themselves into this wave of humanity which sweeps them along. Throughout the army, this France on the march, women's smiles now mingle with the haggard, bruised faces; songs of rejoicing mingle with the war cries. No bread; only love.

On the right-hand screen, followed by his General Staff, Bonaparte gallops towards the camera, which pulls back. The lens is turned at an angle to reveal the columns massed along the verge of the road, cheering Bonaparte as he passes.

Same shot reversed on the left screen, giving extraordinary breadth to the field of action, and showing Bonaparte twice over, thus augmenting and intensifying his will by giving it substance, showing in concrete form the legendary gift of ubiquity whereby he seemed to be everywhere at once. Fantastic ride. Attained here is a peak of lyricism and rhythm in the image.

Now, in the centre, the women marching at the head of the column with the future *grognards*, the 'grumblers' of the Old Guard; pretty French girls from home and beautiful Italians picked up along the way. All these heroes' lovers strike up a marching song: *Auprès de ma blonde*. And the song spreads like a flame to light up every heart, and every heart in its turn lights up each face. The song passes from man to man, takes over the whole column. It is no longer an army on the march: it is a song of France swooping across the world. It is a solemn, manly chorus which rises up into the air of a morning brilliant with hazy light.

On each side, Bonaparte, with veritable centaurs in his wake, passes like a comet. The troops stand aside on the edge of the road. Their eyes strain to see better, to imprint him ineradicably on their memory. The women gaze at him with such naive, profound, sincere admiration that one immediately feels that he could command the unhesitating sacrifice of their lives. Like a trail of gunpowder, his passage kindles their enthusiasm, and there is a continuous crackle of cheering. The entire Revolution gallops after him. The epic spirit is born here.

Protract this scene in the rhythm of *Auprès de ma blonde*.

On learning of this dazzling, tempestuous entry into Italy, the people of Paris open the flood-gates of their enthusiasm.

Iris fade.

59 Central screen framed by black. Shot of Barras on the rostrum of the Convention, announcing to the people of Paris the first victories of the Army of Italy.

60 Triptych of the crowd at the Convention, multiplied *ad infinitum* by the uniting and fusing of the three general shots. Ten thousand mouths roar with enthusiasm.

On 16 April 1796, having outstripped the entire army and General Staff, he stands on the heights of Montezemolo at an altitude of 2,700 feet.

(Schuermans)

61 Fade in on panoramic triptych of mountains as far as the eye can see. Sweeping, majestic prospects of alpine peaks. The solitary silhouette of Bonaparte stands out on the central screen, between heaven and earth.

His eagle eye inscribes in the Italian sky all his desires and victories.

62 Panoramic triptych of the plain stretching away at his feet. His dream armies flood past in fluid superimposition, while his legendary shadow falls over the entire width of the triptych. He stops for a while in the middle of the central screen to watch a charge of centaurs sweeping

198

across the plain, then he continues on to the right. Now the haunting face of Joséphine lights up on the right screen, only to flit over on to the left screen. The battles continue to unfold in fluid superimposition; then, to right and to left, the map of Italy and Joséphine's face alternate in rapid succession in a relentless chase, seductive rivals within Bonaparte's soul. His shadow now appears on the central screen, in the middle of a transparent globe of the earth rotating round him.

Then the close-up of Bonaparte fills the central screen, while 63 Joséphine appears simultaneously on the two lateral screens. Here we see his obsessive, passionate love for her made objective and tangible.

Then everything fades out; nothing remains but Bonaparte in the 64 centre of a transparent globe of which he is the axis.

Continuation of the panorama of peaks, with Bonaparte's silhouette 65 standing out in strong relief on the central screen. On the lateral screens the images fade and clouds appear; dream clouds, symphonic clouds. To the right, in superimposition, ranks of tents as far as the eye can see rising tier upon tier into the sky. To the left the mounted ghost of the young leader gallops among romantic cirrus clouds.

While the 'beggars of glory', their stomachs empty but their heads filled with song, march out of History and into Legend . . .

Central screen. The globe rotates about the head of Joséphine, which 66 fades as the transparent figure of Bonaparte appears. On the lateral screens, the soldiers march past and seem to cross the earth, whose central motor is the shadowy figure of Bonaparte. They are still the soldiers of Year II, bellies empty, heads full of song, the creators of legend. They are majestic in their wretchedness, full of the grandeur of antiquity. They are sculpted by the sun, so white with dust that their faces are almost the same colour as their clothes; they are like walking statues of marble. They sing the *Chant du Départ* (*The Song of Departure*), the second *Marseillaise*; and the rhythm of the images matches exactly the rhythm of their marching feet. The portable camera will be on the march for this whole sequence, marking time in the same rhythm: one, two; one, two; '*La victoire en chantant . . .*'; one, two; one, two; '*nous ouvre la barrière . . .*' On the central screen the globe revolves, while the shadowy figure of Bonaparte, the face of Joséphine and the map of Italy, appear one after the other, then mix, then merge. On the lateral screens, the heavy supply-wagons follow up the infantry. Their awnings billow as if a sense of rivalry were forcing them to emulate the flags, and the glorious inscriptions 'ARMY OF ITALY', 'LIBERTY OR DEATH', tremble in the wind as it whistles them an epic melody. The rhythm becomes increasingly marked: one, two . . .; one, two . . .; '*La liberté guide nos pas*'; one, two . . .; '*et du nord au midi*'. This is truly the Revolution on the march, the French Revolution traversing the whole world.

Napoléon's spirit, soaring on a fantastic dream, plays with the clouds at destroying and building worlds.

(The broad panoramas will now give way to separate action on each of the three screens, making possible extraordinary juxtapositions of images. Every symbol becomes palpable. The cinema enters a new era; from being melodic, it becomes symphonic. The orchestration of the images on three screens will render tangible the symphonic rhythm of the overture to this *Iliad*: the *Marseillaise* of the image.)

List of Final Footage*

Left screen	*Central screen*	*Right screen*
Clouds	Bonaparte, on the heights of Montezemolo, standing at the edge of a precipice, watches the march-past of his army; lost in a fantastic reverie, he allows himself to be lulled by the rhythm of the war-symphony. For him, action becomes poetry. He plunges into it with abandon, and the wild images of might and heroic deeds ride neck and neck, vying for pride of place. 2 metres. 104 frames.	Clouds
Premonition. The shadowy figure of Bonaparte, standing motionless, lost in the clouds. 1 metre. 52 frames.	Close-up of Bonaparte. Ubiquity. 1 metre. 52 frames.	Shadowy equestrian figure of Bonaparte gallops through the clouds. 1 metre. 52 frames.
Storm clouds. 10 frames. Flames. 10 frames. Breaking waves. 10 frames. Air, fire and water obey him.	Close-up of Bonaparte, eyes only, lightning in his gaze. 30 frames.	Storm clouds. 10 frames. Flames. 10 frames. Breaking waves. 10 frames. Air, fire and water obey him.
	The whirlpool of figures on the maps becomes vertiginous. 11 frames.	

* *The triptychs are projected onto a triple-width screen, and three projectors running simultaneously are needed to show them. This final footage is a shot-by-shot breakdown of the climax of the film.*

Left screen	Central screen	Right screen
Foreground: drummers marching. The camera pulls back to reveal the Army of Dust on the march towards Italy. Rhythm = 1, 2. 2 metres. 104 frames.	Sea swell. 4 frames. Bonaparte's eyes. 12 frames. Sun on the mountains. 10 frames. Shadowy figure of Bonaparte transparent over a battle. 10 frames. Whirl of letters. 10 frames. Bonaparte's eyes. 7 frames. Whirl of letter on maps. 40 frames.	Foreground: drummers marching. The camera pulls back to reveal the Army of Dust on the march towards Italy. Rhythm = 1, 2. 2 metres. 104 frames.

Title across the full width of the Triptych:

And in the sky, a strange conductor beats out the rhythm of the army.

Left screen	Central screen	Right screen
Clouds.	Head of column on the march. At the front come the drums. Suddenly, they all cry out, looking at . . .	Clouds.
Clouds.	. . . a giant shadow gliding along the road in front of them. It is the shadow of the eagle following Bonaparte into the sun.	Clouds.
Clouds.	The troop stops, turns and watches the eagle's flight in the sky.	Clouds.

The eagle spreads, giant-size, across the full width of the triptych. The beating of its wings keeps time with the rhythm of the *Chant du Départ*. 1, 2.

Left screen	Central screen	Right screen
Close-up of the Brienne eagle. 20 frames.	Map of Italy, with superimposition of battles. 20 frames.	Close-up of Bonaparte at Brienne. Suffering and genius. 20 frames.
Close-up of Joséphine, smiling, roguish and sensual. 20 frames.	Map of England, with superimposition of rapidly multiplying figures and of twinkling stars. 20 frames.	Close-up of Bonaparte at Toulon, with superimposition of flames. 20 frames.

Left screen	Central screen	Right screen
Left screen Lurid glows and shadows of 10 August. 20 frames.	*Central screen* Map of Toulon, with superimposition of figures and battles. 20 frames.	*Right screen* Close-up of Laetitia. 20 frames.
Flames. 18 frames.	Close-up of Bonaparte. Eyes of flame. 18 frames.	Flames. 18 frames.
Sea swell. 30 frames.	Flames. 13 frames. The shadows of Danton, Marat, Robespierre and Saint-Just following the marching Revolution. 17 frames.	Sea swell. 30 frames.
Maps on which figures swirl in fantastic gyrations. 30 frames.	Gradually Bonaparte's soul is revealed. Flame and ocean form the leitmotif. Whirlpool of foaming water: the maelstrom. 18 frames. Transparent shadow of Bonaparte over a battle. 12 frames.	Maps on which figures swirl in fantastic gyrations. 30 frames.
The sun in the clouds. 30 frames.	Maelstrom. 18 frames. Bonaparte looking about with eyes flashing and sparkling with laughter. 12 frames.	The sun in the clouds. 30 frames.
Joséphine shines out from the centre of the globe. Smiling seduction. 52 frames.	Whirl of figures over charts, ballistic equations predominating. 17 frames. Waves. 13 frames. Maelstrom. 22 frames.	Map of Italy across which spreads Joséphine's smile, while the pensive shadow of Bonaparte appears over Corsica. 1 metre. 52 frames.

Left screen	Central screen	Right screen
Infantry charges in transparent superimposition over an apocalyptic landscape. 30 frames.	Sun in the clouds. 15 frames. Sun in the clouds. 15 frames.	Infantry charges in transparent superimposition over an apocalyptic landscape. 30 frames.
Clouds. 15 frames.	Close-up of the eagle. 15 frames.	Clouds. 15 frames.
Infantry charges in fluid superimposition. 30 frames.	Flames. 15 frames. Waves. 15 frames.	Infantry charges in fluid superimposition. 30 frames.
Mounting storm clouds.	Good omen. Exaltation becomes increasingly religious. The men set off once more beneath the great shadow with its beating wings.	Mounting storm clouds.
Clouds (*id.*)	The shadow of the eagle on the road, seen in a high angle shot from behind the head of the column with the men in the front ranks partially in shot.	Clouds (*id.*)

The eagle spread across the three screens. Its wings beat in time with the steps of the marching men, and the song rising from their mouths, and the beating of their hearts: *La Ré-pu-bli-que – nous appel-le* . . .

The drums beat out the rhythm.	The drums beat out the rhythm.	The drums beat out the rhythm.

Blue   *W.*

(The same image, repeated three times, strangely magnifying its force of expression, amplifying the rhythm.)

The eagle across the three screens. The winged conductor beats time. *Un Fran-çais – doit vi-vre – pour – elle* . . .

Clouds racing wildly.	The head of the marching column, high angle from behind the first ranks. The shadow of the eagle becomes transparent and superimposes itself over the men.	Clouds racing wildly.

From this scene on, blue tint on the left film and red tint on the right film, so that the triptych screen is one gigantic tricolour flag with the Revolution marching across it. The *Chant du Départ* and the *Marseillaise* blend in with the orchestra, the musical counterpoint echoing the visual counterpoint.

Blue	*White*	*Red*
Shoulders, sacks, on the march, the camera itself is marching in step with them, so that all the audience too marches on to glory.	Same image.	Same image.
The sun in the clouds. 37 frames.	Force, euphoria, apogee. He is no longer looking earthward, but up into the heavens.	The sun in the clouds. 37 frames.

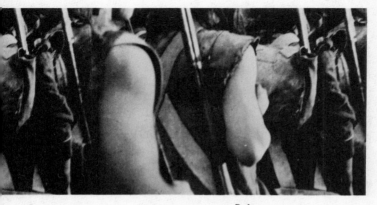

Red

Blue	White	Red
Close-up of the eagle.	Maelstrom.	Close-up of the eagle.
19 frames.	34 frames.	19 frames.
Flames.		Flames.
15 frames.		15 frames.
Whirl of figures.	Bonaparte's eyes.	Whirl of figures.
16 frames.	30 frames.	16 frames.
Waves.		Waves.
14 frames.		14 frames.
Maelstrom.	Whirl of figures.	Maelstrom.
17 frames.	17 frames.	17 frames.
Clouds.	Maelstrom.	Clouds.
16 frames.	30 frames.	16 frames.
Whirl of figures.		Whirl of figures.
14 frames.		14 frames.
Eyes.	Whirl of figures.	Eyes.
13 frames.	33 frames.	13 frames.
Flames.		Flames.
9 frames.		9 frames.
Waves.		Waves.
11 frames.		11 frames.
Eyes.	Maelstrom.	Eyes.
7 frames.	12 frames.	7 frames.
Figures.	Eyes.	Figures.
11 frames.	12 frames.	11 frames.
Maelstrom.		Maelstrom.
6 frames.		6 frames.
Eagle.	Maelstrom.	Eagle.
12 frames.	30 frames.	12 frames.
Figures.		Figures.
7 frames.		7 frames.
Clouds.		Clouds.
11 frames.		11 frames.
Eyes.	Figures.	Eyes.
7 frames.	12 frames.	7 frames.
Maelstrom.	Eyes.	Maelstrom.
10 frames.	12 frames.	10 frames.
Figures.		Figures.
7 frames.		7 frames.
Flames.	Maelstrom.	Flames.
8 frames.	28 frames.	8 frames.
Waves.		Waves.
6 frames.		6 frames.
Sun.		Sun.
8 frames.		8 frames.
Figures.		Figures.
6 frames.		6 frames.

The maelstrom fills all three screens and goes into a spin; the whole Revolution, swept on at delirious speed towards the heart of Europe, is now one huge tricolour flag, quivering with all that has been inscribed upon it, and it takes on the appearance of an apocalyptic, tricolour torrent, inundating, enflaming and transfiguring, all at one and the same time.

Appendix

The Enrolments of 1792

After the publication of the script, several magazines published selections from the shooting script, giving us a valuable insight on how it was developed during the making of the film. The following sequence, which does not appear in the final film, is given as an example.

In April 1792 France, totally unequipped and disorganized, declared war on Hungary and Bohemia. Within weeks Austria had joined in, routing the French in Belgium. By the beginning of the summer France was in great danger. On 11 July the Assembly issued the proclamation known as 'The Nation is in Danger!'. The response was unanimous and enrolment booths were set up all over France to sign up the 'Defenders of the Nation'.

The following sequence would have appeared between the 'Marseillaise' sequence and the scenes of 10 August 1792.

248b   Exterior. Open [iris] onto: a sans-culotte billposter pasting up a large poster in the shape of a flag. We read:

FRENCHMEN!

Our land is invaded – 30,000 flashing bayonets are turned against us. 180,000 combat troops under Cobourg have captured the frontier 40 leagues from Paris. The royalists are plotting. The whole of the Vendée groans under arms. France is suffocating in the clutches of the foreign war while the vast fires of civil strife consume her.

THE NATION IS IN DANGER!

Citizens, to arms!

The camera rapidly approaches the last two sentences which fill the screen. Then the camera abuptly replaces the poster and looks at its readers. Unusual faces, filled with heroic exaltation. There are 10, 20, 100, 1,000 faces, all moved by the same feelings; they dissolve little by little into a single immense head which synthesizes them all. It is the face of France in 1792; its expression leaves the frame of History to enter that of the Epic. Flash-fade in red.

Open fast in red.

THE NATION IS IN DANGER!
3 July 1792

Close fast in red.

The dominant characteristic of these scenes, from shot 249 to shot 350: to surpass the lyricism of the movement of Rude's *Marseillaise*. Go from the overall picture into the detailed drawing. Fan the flame of enthusiasm in every spectator. Let historical truth die when it is too abstract and pluck from my soul the images that these abstractions create.

249   The Pont-Neuf. Firing of the alarm cannon on the Pont-Neuf. Thousands of people rush up to the cannon. A municipal officer on horseback, his tricolour sash worn crosswise, escorted by cavalry, proclaims the tragic decree and howls:

'THE NATION IN DANGER!'

(References: Victor Hugo, *Quatre-vingt trois*.
Madelin, *The French Revolution*)

250a   Drummers on the march. 1 metre.

250b   Trumpeters on the march. 50 cm. Close-up.

250c   Cannon on the Pont-Neuf. A flash. 20 cm.

251a   A crossroads. Different municipal officer. Same action as 249. 1 m 50.

251b   Drummers on the march. 80 cm.

251c   Trumpeters on the march. 40 cm. CU.

252a   Pont-Neuf cannon. A flash. 20 cm.

252b   Another crossroads. Another officer. Always the same terrible announcement. 1 metre.

252c   Drummers on the march. 60 cm.

253a   Trumpeters on the march. 30 cm. CU.

253b   Pont-Neuf cannon. 20 cm.

253c   Another crossroads. Another municipal officer. 80 cm.

254a   Drummers on the march. 40 cm.

254b   Trumpeters on the march. 20 cm. CU.

254c   Pont-Neuf cannon.

255a   Another crossroads. 50 cm.

255b   Drummers on the march. 30 cm.

255c   Trumpeters on the march. 20 cm. CU.

256   Pont-Neuf cannon. 20 cm.

257   Reduce the rhythm down to 2 frames, accentuating the crowd at each announcement. Enlarge the cannon each time so that at the end of the rhythm it becomes a great mouth spewing hell. Rapid red fade.

258   The Pont-Neuf. Rapid fade-in. A change has happened. In fact they are in the final stages of setting up a vast voluntary enrolment booth. The platform is draped in the tricolour, and the table is made out of a plank set on drums. The exaltation is unbelievable. Everyone wants to sign up at once.

259a   Enrolment booth. An old man of 75 signs up. His hand shakes with age.

259b   Drum roll from the soldiers on duty.

260   A cart or the roof of a stage-coach.

261a   Another enrolment booth. A child of 12 signs up. His hand shakes with youth.

261b   Drum roll from the soldiers on duty.

262   Interior of a church. The representatives of the people

receive the enrolments. The stained glass windows are aflame with light.

(Reference: Louis Blanc)

263a   The church. An invalid, with an amputated right arm, signs with his left hand.

263b   Drum roll from the soldiers in the church.

264   A rose garden in flower. (We are in July.) Enrolment in the open air in the rose garden.

265   Mid shot. A pretty young woman signs up.

266a   Close-up. Rose petals falling on the register.

266b   Drum roll.

267   Place de Grève, on the pillory itself. Enrolment.

268   A tavern. Little Marcellin wants to sign up.

269a   A tavern. The representatives find him so small that they burst out laughing and refuse. The mortified child gets off the rostrum amidst the laughter.

269b   The drums roll.

270   Marcellin sobs.

271   Full shot. The standard bearer of Charlet looks on as though he were seeing all the enrolments at once.

272   Close-up. His face doesn't move, but two tears trickle down the creases in his thin cheeks.

273a   Full shot. The breeze opens the wings of his flag.

273b   A crowd sings 'To arms . . .' Crane shot.

273c   The drums roll. Crane shot.

274a   Exterior, Ramponneau. A crowd tries to go into the Ramponneau inn. Fleuri's water-cart is seen coming along the pavement in the distance.

274ba   Guns are distributed.

275a   Exterior, Ramponneau. Tristan Fleuri, immobile. He watches what's going on. What's going on [pleases him] too.

His smile is radiant, he blinks. It is as though stars were falling into his eyes.

275b   There are no more guns, sabres: are distributed.

276a   Exterior, Ramponneau. He leaves his water-cart and joins the crowd trying to push its way into the Ramponneau inn.

276b   There are no more sabres: axes, pikes and javelins are distributed.

277a   Interior, Ramponneau. In front of the vast fireplace the voluntary enrolments continue.

277b   There are no more axes, pikes or javelins: clubs are distributed.

278   Interior, Ramponneau. Mid-shot. Standing on a chest, his huge body lit by the flames from the hearth, Danton speaks. The flames, just behind him, frame him from head to foot and will give us the impression that he is actually standing in the fire. A huge bust of Franklin inscribed with the name of the celebrated physician is beside him. Danton thunders.

'What must we have in order to conquer the enemies of the nation?'

279   Interior, Ramponneau. Danton chants as if the flames in the hearth were speaking:

'Daring, and yet more daring; nothing but daring!'

280   Interior, Ramponneau. The flames surround Danton's face.

281   Interior, Ramponneau. The bells of the city ring out. Danton says: 'Those bells aren't ringing the alarm – they're ringing the charge against the enemies of the Nation!'
                                                    (Reference: Dayot)

282   Interior, Ramponneau. Camera R. At the end of the room. The mobile camera seems to be looking for someone. It finds him and stops in a mid-shot, in front of a young man sitting away from the rest, in a dark corner of the room. His chin resting on his hands, he watches. His soul is open, his face inpenetrable. It is Bonaparte, in the same tattered outfit.

283   Interior, Ramponneau. Danton speaks.

284   Interior, Ramponneau. Six close-ups of the crowd. Faces

drunk with words. Tristan Fleuri, squashed by the crowd, is almost suffocated as he pitches in the groundswell of enthusiasm.

285 Interior, Ramponneau. Mid-shot. Tristan Fleuri is squeezed out towards a table where he will be almost alone in a corner of the inn. Near him, a woman and her child are loading guns. Fleuri makes a last move backwards onto a chair. On the table there is the wherewithal to write. Fleuri stuffs his fingers into his ears for a second, then he hurriedly starts writing, as if to escape the electrifying contagion of the enrolments.

My little Violine,
Having received no news of you, I assume that you have arrived safely at Beaucaire. Write to me at once. Paris is seething with activity. One can no longer call one's soul one's own. I am having great difficulty in resisting the impulse to sign up . . .

286 Interior, Ramponneau. Then Tristan lifts his head, ensnared by the volcanic speech.

287 Interior, Ramponneau. Danton, calling on the bust of Franklin to bear witness, cries:

'Is that not so, Franklin?'

288 Interior, Ramponneau. A flicker from the hearth lights the face of the statue of the physician. CU.

289 Interior, Ramponneau. The crowd applauds.

290 Interior, Ramponneau. Tristan can't resist it any more. He is on the point of tearing up his letter and rushing over to the recruiting sergeants. A duel with his conscience. Violine passes very quickly in front of him. And yet, no. 'I must work for her!' He gets out his handkerchief and . . .

291 Interior, Ramponneau . . . he ties his foot to the leg of the table. Then he stuffs paper in his ears and tries to go on with his letter. Rapid fade.

Everywhere. At the same time. As if the same wind had blown across the whole of France . . .

292 Enrolment booths in the provinces. Simultaneously. In rhythm. Enrolment booths in the provinces. Local characteristics and costumes, native soil of the Pyrenees, Provence, Berry, Brittany, Gascony – drums and bugles. Enrolments on a barge, in a barn, in a stage-coach, in a field of wheat. Very short typical scenes.

293 Marat's bathroom. In the foreground, the famous bath-tub which stands out like an enormous black clog. In profile, Marat looking out of the open window. His funereal acolytes stand respectfully behind him. Marat looks:

294 Exterior, Ramponneau. The swelling crowd, applauding Danton as it tries to push its way into the inn.

295 Marat's bathroom. CU. Marat turns to his companions and says:

'Heroism has turned into quite an epidemic!'

He shrugs his shoulders.

296 Marat's bathroom. General shot. A heavy silence falls in the unhealthy room. Slow fade.

297 Interior, Ramponneau. Fast opening: Danton finishes his speech and points to the enrolment table, saying in exalted delirium:

'Do away with ink, citizens, you should be signing the engagement to save the Republic in your own blood!'

Continuation of the close-up of Danton.

298 Interior, Ramponneau. Close-up of Fleuri, his eyes riveted on Danton.

299 Interior, Ramponneau. Danton turns to a witness:

'Is that not so, Carnot?'

300 Interior, Ramponneau. Mid-shot of Carnot, who is presiding at the enrolment table and who shows approval.

301 Interior, Ramponneau. Thunder of applause in the room.

302 Interior, Ramponneau. Danton sits down again.

303   Interior, Ramponneau. A signatory. He is an untidy giant, with splendid eyes and a childlike smile. He wears the trousers, jacket and emblems of a constitutional guard of Louis XVI.

'Aren't you a soldier already?'

304   Interior, Ramponneau . . . the recruitment officer says to him, inviting him to get down off the platform.

305   Interior, Ramponneau. The giant dips a pen into a vein in his wrist,* he lifts his eyes and says:

'Of the King, yes, but not of the Republic!'

306   Interior, Ramponneau. Without batting an eyelid he asks where to sign; they hand him the register.

307   Interior, Ramponneau. Bottom of a page of the register. He writes his name in bloody characters . . .

MURAT

. . . while a little blood from his left wrist trickles onto the register.

308   Interior, Ramponneau.**

309   Interior, Ramponneau. This time Fleuri, a mere drop of water in the ocean of collective madness, can resist no longer. He too is going to sign up; he stands up, his decision taken. He has completely forgotten that he had tied his foot to the table leg and, along with the table, he falls into the crowd, who laugh at his predicament. His face is copiously spattered with the spilt ink.

310   Interior, Ramponneau. People burst out laughing all around him. They deride him. They boo him.

311   Interior, Ramponneau. Fleuri escapes, abashed.

312   Exterior, Ramponneau. Fleuri reaches his water-cart, but

---

Gance later shot this scene for his sound-track version, Napoléon Bonaparte. *Much taken with it, he wrote the scene yet again – in his scenario* Christopher Columbus *– giving it to the highly romantic Diego de Arana, when he signs on for the great journey.*
**Original illegible.*

he can't pull it out because yet another booth is standing there, beside which Madame Sans-gêne, in person, standing on an upturned wash-tub, makes a speech of such lyricism that those who have miraculously escaped the enrolments inside Ramponneau are carried away by this latest enthusiastic assault and come to sign the famous registers.

313   The street. Madame Sans-gêne. Sergeant Lefèvre collects signatures while his wife pours out torrents of eloquence, intercut with killing glances. CU.

314   The street. Fleuri feels lost. He is just about to sign up when his face lights up with an idea. There is one way he can be saved: cooling his enthusiasm; and, getting behind his water-cart, he turns on the hose. Under the shower, as he thought, his exaltation disappears; he thinks he is free at last. He turns off the water and starts to leave, but he hadn't allowed for . . .

THE SOLDIERS OF YEAR II

315   The street. The National Guard is leaving to join the army, in the spirit of the painting by Cogniet. Enthusiasm gives way to a sort of collective dementia. Strangers kiss. The most legendary soldiers that France has ever possessed are all there.

316   The street. General shot. Four close-ups. Rhythm, marching.

317   The street. The most austere Jacobins are caught in this maelstrom of passion and join up.

318   The street. Dripping wet, Fleuri watches. His eyes can no longer take it all in. His heart overflows. He is intoxicated.

319a   The street. Close-up of Fleuri. His legs begin to march in time with the soldiers, he marks time harder and harder, in the middle of an enormous puddle of water which splashes up at each step.

319b   The street. Drums.

320a   Close-ups. The soldiers' song.

320b   Alarm cannon.

321 The street. Fleuri in ecstasy, caught by the demon of war; he sees:

322 the drums. Crane shot. The camera on a crane moves up to the drums which become enormous. Very fast.

323 The Marseillaises. Crane shot. The camera moves up to their faces which become huge mouths. Very fast.

324 The cannon, crane shot, which becomes a whirlpool of fire. Very fast.

325 The drums and the trumpets, 4, 6, 8, 16, 50, 100, 1,000 in 5 seconds.

326 Madame Sans-gêne's smile. The camera moves up to her. We only see her magnificent eyes. Very fast.

327 The street. The ineffable smile of a conquered Fleuri. 'I abandon myself to thee, O bloodthirsty Odin!' He paces himself and leaps as though he were jumping over the camera.

328 The street. Enrolment table. People fall back, because, dropping like a bomb, pushing the people about to sign up aside, a radiant Fleuri, his face blackened with ink, says to Madame Sans-gêne: 'Here I am!' and, despite the dripping water, Madame Sans-gêne, after weighing up the soul of this adorable great child for a second, pulls him towards her and kisses him.

329 The street. Lefèvre gives an uneasy glance and growls.

330 The street. Fleuri signs. He would certainly be less happy at the gates of heaven.

331 The street. The laughter of the crowd.

332 The street. Tristan descends from the platform like a drunken king. They give him a pike and two javelins. Then nobody bothers with him any more. In any case his life is no longer his own. He has just delivered it to France. He stands there, embarrassed, examining the prehistoric arms he has just been given; then he moves off towards his water-cart.

333 The street. Tristan reaches his water-cart. His little Marcellin is crouched there, still crying at having been refused.

Tristan thumps him on the shoulder and says, as if he were being strangled by 50 Legions of Honour:

'Console yourself, little one, I'm part of it!'

334   The street. Shot of the two heads. Marcellin lifts his tear-stained face to his father. A smile starts to spread as he catches sight of the ink-stained face, then the thought of being left alone mists his eyes and he begins to cry again. So Tristan picks him up and rocks him like a baby, whilst the visions that have conquered him drift through his mind.

335   Crane shot – 3 superimpositions. Drums, Marseillaises, Mme Sans-gêne, cannons, bells, his daughter Violine, Charlet's flag, Danton, drums; all of this liquid, melting, continuous, diaphanous, pitching and tossing, as if from one dream to another.

336   The street. Fleuri's face. A serene melancholy whence goodness spreads its rays. He rocks his child.

337   The street. General shot. And as he sits there a little circle of children, aged between 2 and 4, materializes around him, comically dressed as sans-culottes with little wooden sabres. And these children, who cannot yet speak, begin to sing:

'Madame Veto had promised . . .'

338   The street. Fleuri laughs more and more happily as the children circle round him. He continues to rock his little one. Very slow fade.

339   Open 5, 4, 3, 2, 1 V. Onto a general shot. Interior, Ramponneau inn. Camille Desmoulins has replaced Danton. Same movement; same enthusiasm. Bonaparte in the same spot as before, his chin on his hand. Groundswell all around him. He watches. He listens. He analyses. His eyes plunge into the present to bring back the future.

340   Interior, Ramponneau. Suddenly the crowd in the room, attracted by something going on outside, moves as one person to the doors and windows, in a rush of intense curiosity. Bonaparte stands up to look as well.

341   In the street. A regiment of the National Guard is passing, and the young commander of the regiment, on horseback,

appears to be the centre of attention.

342 From the crowd in the foreground, a unanimous shout of unbelievable enthusiasm:

'Long live Marceau!'

343 Close-up, Camera A. And it is indeed Marceau, Lieutenant-colonel of the National Guard at 23! His face like a girl's and his frailty add to the impression that his youth makes on the crowd. He smiles, he salutes. A sunlit flag frames his pure brow.

344a Interior, Ramponneau. Bonaparte among the crowd. He watches him, like a young Caesar looking at a statue of Alexander. His eyes focus on . . .

344b The street . . . the insignia of the lieutenant-colonel.

345a Interior, Ramponneau. Bonaparte's face. His eyes come back to his own tattered outfit, to the sleeve of which he pins . . .

345b Interior, Ramponneau . . . his narrow Lieutenant's stripe.

346 Interior, Ramponneau. Bonaparte. He appears deeply distressed.

347 Interior, Ramponneau. General shot. The crowd go back to their places and Desmoulins continues.

348 Interior, Ramponneau. Bonaparte stays at the window watching . . .

349 In the street . . . the little colonel of the National Guard, who disappears from view, escorted by the enthusiastic crowd.

350 Interior, Ramponneau. Bonaparte. His will grows; and grows. CU 1, 2, 3, 4. Gauze. Fade to black. Hold in black for ten seconds.